D1860164

Religion and Politics in Mizoram

Religion and Politics in Mizoram

Dr. Anup Shekhar Chakraborty

KALPAZ

©Author

All rights reserved. No part of this work may be reproduced, stored, adapted, or transmitted in any form or by any means, electronic, mechanical, photocopying, micro-filming recording or otherwise, or translated in any language, without the prior written permission of the copyright owner and the publisher. The book is sold subject to the condition that it shall not, by way of trade or otherwise, be lent, resold, hired out, or otherwise circulated without the prior publisher's written consent in any form of binding or cover other than that in which it is published.

The views and opinions expressed in this book are author(s) own and the facts reported by them have been verified to the extent possible, and the publishers are not in any way liable for the same.

First Published, 2020

Published by

Kalpaz Publications
C-30, Satyawati Nagar,
Delhi – 110052
Ph.: 011-47034999, 9811692060
www.kalpazpublications.com
E-mail: kalpaz@hotmail.com

Printed at: G. Print Process, Delhi

Cataloging in Publication Data—DK
Courtesy: D.K. Agencies (P) Ltd. <docinfo@dkagencies.com>

Chakraborty, Anup Shekhar, 1980- **author.**
Religion and Politics in Mizoram / Dr. Anup Shekhar Chakraborty.
pages cm
Includes bibliographical references.
ISBN 9789353240561 (PB)

1. Kuki Chin (South Asian people)—India—Mizoram—Religion.
2. Christianity and politics—India—Mizoram. I. Title.

LCC BR115.P7C43 2019 | DDC 261.70954166 23

Contents

Preface

The book is an outcome of an intense unease that I confronted while listening to debates, discussions and conversations on Secularism in India over the years. Discussions and writings on the topic would neatly pitch Hindus and Muslims in polar camps and conjure a deep sense of self pity for the colossal people across South Asia. The discussion in Chapter 1 of this book presents *A General Discussion on Indian Secularism and revisits old debates and re-raises old questions*. The chapter thus unearths the silence that one notices in the context of experiences from the proselytized tribal communities of Northeast of India.

Chapter 2 titled *Proselytisation and the Zo Hnahthlak*; Chapter 3 titled *Politics of Zo Christianity, Representational Leadership and 'Being Secular' in Mizoram*; Chapter 4 titled *'Belonging', 'Claims of Belonging' and the 'Tolerance' debates in an Ideal Zo Christian State*; and Chapter 5 titled *'Mizo Women, the Nexus of Patriarchy and 'Being Secular''* attempt to present narrations that run contrary to the imported ideas of relations between religion and politics as evolved in the west. This book is an attempt to share practices that have been engineered among communities in South Asia to untangle the webbed relations between religion and politics; and in doing so construe the 'formal' and the 'informal' ways in which religion and politics contradict, and complement and circumvent each other in the everyday. The idea of secularism and being secular in South Asia indeed opens interesting arenas of debates and contentions. India in special remains a spectacle in the operation of secular politics amidst a cacophony of religiosity and religiously informed 'believers'.

Drawing largely from my earlier writings on Mizoram I would re-raise old questions which have haunted generations and communities elsewhere and pin them to the Zo context: what does being 'secular' or being 'non-secular' or 'asecular'[1] mean among the *Zo hnahthlak*? Does the notion of secular get cornered by the profound expression of Zo-Christian religiosity?

The line wedging the 'Believers' from those clubbed as 'Non-Believers' is neatly marked by those following the ways of Zo-Christianity, anyone deviating from that neat line is condemned as being a 'Non-Believer'. My discussions in *The Indian Journal of Secularism* (2017)[2] arrives us to the understanding that the *Nexus of Patriarchy* plays the self-proclaimed role of cleansers of the Zo society and thus monitor the Zo community into a faith (Zo Christian) abiding, culture conscious, 'peoplehood'. Also that the leadership attunes itself to the directions and dictates of the Church and the *Nexus of Patriarchy*, for instance, the leadership grounds its popularity and legitimizes its authority (political, institutional, situational) by aligning itself to the volatile mood swings of the church and its agencies, thereby reaffirming the humorous popular aphorism: *'Mizoram-ah chuan Sawrkar a lalber a, Kohhran a thuber'* ('In Mizoram the Government is the highest authority, and the Church has the final say').

The content of what I call the 'Customized-Localized Gospel' was decoded into a language that was receptive to the 'savage tribes'. 'Being a Zo/Mizo' and 'Being a Christain' began to be seen in unison among the *Zo hnahthlak*. The conversion from 'head-hunters to Soul hunters' within a span of five decades earned the Mizo/Zo/Kuki/Chin people of South Asia the title of '*Pathian ring tu te*' ('*believers*'). The constricting predominance of the Christian ethics in Mizoram can be understood by the fact that 'the government and the bureaucracy have not been able to touch the masses as the Church. Religion is thus elevated to a higher plane and centrality is tagged to it. Therefore, in order to gain the required connectedness to the 'people' especially the elites try to go with the tide and without any spirituality they enter the Church activities in order to gain popularity and mass appeal. So in short, they dictate terms in their interest through the church.'[3]

The discussions in the chapters of this volume by interweaving political histories of political parties, the evolve of their leaderships, and their interactions with the Indian state and its constitutional provisions including the internal tensions of plural constitutional provisions with that of tribal ways of life and rules of the Customary Laws coming in uneasy conversations with Christianity and the secular ideas helps one to construe the uncomfortable issue of 'being secular' in a state that declares itself to be the 'most peaceful Christian State in India'.

My ethnographic presence coupled with my growing up days in the Mizoram enabled me to follow closely and chart these complications in the mundane everyday of religion and politics. With the intent to fill the larger jigsaw of secularism and religion and politics vis-à-vis Christianity in South Asia, I weave these interesting conversations and engagements between the '*this wordly*' and the '*that wordly*' from the Mizoram in the Northeast of India into the chapters of this book. The five chapters absorb and elaborate the discussions from my past writings on Mizoram and Christianity to bring home ideas of Zo Christianity, 'being Secular', Tolerance debates and the ideas of *mihringna* (being human) and the positionality of women among the *Zo hnahthlak*.

Notes and References

1. Charles Taylor. (2007). *A Secular Age*. Cambridge, Mass.,: Harvard University Press; Craig Calhoun. (2008). 'A Secular Age'. *European Journal of Sociology*. Cambridge Journals Online. 49 (03): 455–461; Barry A. Kosmin and Ariela Keysar. (ed.). (2007). *Secularism & Secularity: Contemporary International Perspectives*. Hartford, CT: Institute for the Study of Secularism in Society and Culture (ISSSC); Max Weber. (2001). *The Protestant Ethic and the Spirit of Capitalism*. London, Routledge Classics.
2. Anup Shekhar Chakraborty. (2017). 'Constrictions, Circumvents, and Collations: Politics of Zo Christianity, Representational Leadership and 'Being Secular' in Mizoram.' *Indian Journal of Secularism (IJS)*, Vol. 21, No. 3, Oct-Dec. pp. 38-83.
3. Pi Vanramchhuangi ('Ruatfelanu'), Director HRLN Mizoram, Social Activist, *Personal Interview*, Chaltlang, Aizawl: 28th& 29th January 2008.

Acknowledgements

I acknowledge the institutional support of ***Netaji Institute for Asian Studies***, Kolkata for this study. A word of appreciation to the Honorary Director of my institute Professor Suranjan Das (Vice Chancellor Jadavpur University) for always encouraging and showing the way when the road ahead seems dark and instilling faith in the power of reading and writing. I convey my 'thank you' to Professor Sarvani Gooptu for always showing me the 'silver lines in the clouds' each time I felt lost. I extend my 'thank you' to Dr. Vivek Mishra, Mr. Sandip Halder and the support Staff for making the office workplace feel like 'home'. To Vivek Mishra in special for improving my vocabulary in English and for friendship, the teamwork is really fulfilling. The academic freedom and the easy access to books stacked up the library at my institute enabled me to reframe and connect multiple ideas and sources and create this larger canvass to narrate the complexities in the operation and experience of religion and politics among the *Zo hnahthlak* in Mizoram, India.

I thank Professor Sumantra Bose (International and Comparative Politics, London School of Economics) and Professor Apurba Mukhopadhyay (former Professor, Political Science, Burdwan University, and Netaji Institute for Asian Studies) and friends from Mizoram who have spared their time to read and give valuable comments and suggestions on the drafts of the chapters.

Special thanks to my teacher Dr. Bonita Aleaz (former Professor, Political Science, University of Calcutta) for teaching me the 'A's and B's of Christianity and politics, I remain ever grateful.

I acknowledge the various conversations in the field and learnings that I have had over the years of my engagements in studying people and politics in Mizoram. It is these conversations and learnings that I have attempted to complicate while elaborating on state-society, politics and people in Mizoram, in the discussions in the various chapters of this book.

Anup Shekhar Chakraborty

Introduction

Sam. 22:28 *'Ram chu Lalpa ta a ni: Hnam tin chunga rorel tu a ni si a'*
(Psalm 22:28 *'for dominion belongs to the* LORD *and he rules over the nations'*)

To a large multitude of people[1] across South Asia the location of Mizoram in the cartography of India remains puzzling. At best people can loosely locate it as 'somewhere in Assam'. To the politically informed population Mizoram faintly rings the bells of 'Laldenga and the insurgency in the Christian dominated area, the erstwhile primitive head hunters', 'the Looshais' and the success of India's democratic mechanisms at taming 'Them' as reflected through the dual processes of: (1) the signing of the Peace Accord (1986)[2] and (2) the implementation of 'Cosmetic Federalism'.[3] To the other less-informed majority it remains a geo-political puzzle, mapping its geographic location and its habitants becomes a quest in itself.[4]

The very term 'Mizo', 'Mizoram' just like the term 'North-East' evokes in the minds of the mainland Indians an 'alien culture', Chinkys, backward tribals, Christian tribals, 'Open sex societies', underdeveloped area, forests, junglees[5] (Wild, Uncivilised), tribes with weird food habits infamously known as the 'dog-eaters' and so on. Beyond these stereotypical images of the people of the North-East and especially the Mizo, mainland Indians are perpetually perplexed by the external features of the people of the region and club them into a neatly compartmentalised category of 'Chinkys', or Chinese, totally bypassing their identity as Indians and pushing them at the realms of the 'final Other'.[6] The underlying realities of 'Politics in Mizoram,' more specifically the construction of identities, its contestations and the associated 'Politics of Silencing' which exhibits its expressions in the from exclusions and inclusions- justified in the name of 'State-Building', hardly echoes beyond the *Zo tlang ram.* The outside world beyond the Zo Hills are hardly aware of the underlying politics of identity, culture, space, 'continued colonisation' and 'internal colonisation,' patriarchal hegemony, religious persecutions and also of state-led 'victimisation of the marginalised-women and others'.

The North-East in general has been experiencing the need for re-drawing the boundaries into North Eastern territorial zones and spaces[7] i.e. re-marking the geo-politics based on the logic of traditional game land[8] that the people had lost due to the British and other external forces.[9] The people of North-East India, specially the tribal people, differ from the plains people of India in respect of culture, customary behaviour, faith and race. What Ananda Bhagabati calls the distinctive "geo-ethnic character"[10] of the Northeast is helpful in clarifying the multicultural nature and the cultural differences between the people. The region's population is conveniently classed as "tribals" (referring to those in the thinly-populated hill areas) and the "non-tribals" (referring to the people in fertile plains and plateau), however, this misconstrues the larger complexities and over-lappings of 'hills-plains divide' and waves of Sansktitization and animism interface as operative in the region, given that tribal communities also live the plains and so do the non-tribals in the hills. The anxiety that looms a large over tribal people of the North-East as elsewhere has been 'how to preserve their culture and pristine identity(ies)'.[11]

The encapsulation of the everyday in the region is strongly marked by hybridity is a marked reality and transcends to the surreal. So much that hybridity has become the 'norm' and that we all become hybrid at the end. These braided entanglements with Identities, Religion and Politics as operative in ground zero in Mizoram shows the embededness of these markers on each other in the evolution of identity formation in the social, political, economic and the emotional scale; and also conveys how, why, and when the hegemonic power or 'those in control' organise; and define the parameters of 'the political community', and thereby telling us who is *included* and who is not, who is partly assimilated and who is eschewed, overwhelmed and silenced into invisibility.[12] The line wedging the 'Believers' from those clubbed as 'Non-Believers' is neatly marked by those following the ways of Zo-Christianity, anyone deviating from that neat line is condemned as being a 'Non-Believer'.[13] The Cartographic zoning for instance injected a sense of marked difference among Zo tribes in the region. The Welsh Presbyterian actively worked among the Northern tribes while the London Baptist Missionary Society worked among the Southern tribes. It is very interesting to note that the cartographic zoning also affected the projection and degree of belief in Christianity for instance Northerners began to stereotype Southerners as 'less believers'; and Southerners stereotyped the northern Christians as 'less believers' while retaining and claiming the position of 'strong believers' for their respective tribes. The denominational divide also worked very interesting complexities among the Zo Christians. For instance, from the Colonial times the Roman Catholics were considered to be non-Christian in belief system because of the relegated position of Mary; and interestingly the localized Christianity as practiced among the Zo does not proscribe divinity to women.[14]

The desire to create an *Ideal Zo Christian state*[15] has been strongly portrayed and at times has led to the voyeuristic intervention of the church and its agencies in both the private and public arena. The Post-Colonial 'Zo world' has witnessed the dual operation of Proselytization and Colonialism and the introduction of marked structural and functional changes in the Zo/Mizo society.[16] The loss of indigenous Zo way of life and the fear of being usurped by alien cultures compelled the Mizos/ Zos to live under the spectre of the Pan Optics[17] through the watchful eyes of the State, the Church and its agencies. This can be understood in the context of what Foucault refers to as *'Pastoral Power'*.[18] The kind of power the Church exercises over the individual that is intrinsically linked with assurance of salvation of next world. This salvation is linked to 'the notion of individualism' as individual salvation; and in the modern times, the salvation in the next life has been commuted to a salvation in this life signified by markers like 'health, wellbeing, security' etc., casually referred to as *'Changkangna'* (progressive/developed) in Mizo (Duhlian).

It is interesting to note that *'Being a Zo'* and *'Being a Christian'*[19] are the two issues around which religious identity politics in Mizoram is developed. The first issue has problems of parameters of definitions and it remains contested. While the second issue has elements of experiential-ness embedded to it as evident from the casual everyday use of language *'Khristian nilo in an hrethiam lovang'* ('Non-Christians will not be able to understand') to brush side those who do not belong to the Church as not being able to understand the Bible and its teachings. Both these issues are projected in the state-building process of an *'Ideal Zo Christian State'*.

Christianity manifests itself very differently in different places conditioned by specific social realities. The Christian experience among each of the Zo tribes intune with the experience of Christianity elsewhere throughout South Asia shows points of convergences and maneuverings of those receiving the 'new religion' and way of life. Clannish, intra-tribal, inter-tribal, animistic/traditional practices coupled with cartographic zoning of the Zo people have largely affected the moorings to the same. Christianity amidst the ostensible homogeneity among the *Zo hnahthlak* is veritably fragmented. Heterogeneity with a projected homogeneity is one of the marked paradoxes of Christianity among the *Zo hnahthlak*.

The discussions in this book arrives us to the understanding that the *Nexus of Patriarchy* plays the self-proclaimed role of cleansers and sanitizers of the Zo society and thus monitor the Zo community into a faith (Zo Christian) abiding, culture conscious, 'peoplehood' (*mihringna*). Also the discussions in this book clearly shows how the leadership attunes itself to the directions and dictates of the Church and the *Nexus of Patriarchy*. For instance, the leadership grounds its popularity and legitimizes its authority (political, institutional, situational) by aligning itself to the volatile mood swings of the church and its agencies, thereby reaffirming the humorous popular aphorism: *'Mizoram-ah chuan Sawrkar a lalber a, Kohhran a thuber'* ('In Mizoram the Government is the highest authority, and the Church has the final say').

The constricting predominance of the Christian ethics in Mizoram can be understood by the fact that 'the government and the bureaucracy have not been able to touch the masses as the Church. Therefore, inorder to gain the required connectedness to the 'people' the elites try to go with the tide and without any spirituality they enter the Church activities in order to gain popularity and mass appeal. So in short, they dictate terms in their interest through the church.'[20]

The extend of the Churches intrusion into the everyday of life and politics in Mizoram can be illustrated by the case of the uproar against the appointment of former Kerala BJP leader Kummanam Rajasekharan being sworn in as the governor of Mizoram. The Churches and the various political groups such as the *People's Representation for Identity and Status of Mizoram* (PRISM) organised state-wide protest movements to oust the new Governor. The Church conglomerate of 13 major Churches named *Mizoram Kohran Hruaitute Committee* (MKHC), served notices seeking all political parties and civil society organisations to oppose Rajasekharan, who was seen as an 'anti-secular governor,' given his past ideological connections and his posting as Governor of Mizoram was seen with suspicion that would affect Christianity in the state.[21] The PRISM circulated letters to mobilize the public to come forward to oppose and oust the new Governor. PRISM alleged that Rajasekharan was anti-secularism and a threat to Indian Constitution and Zo Christianity and Zo culture. Rajasekharan's membership to the RSS, Vishva Hindu Parishad (VHP) and Hindu Aikya Vedi were interpreted as sufficient evidence to his anti-Christian missionaries and Christians activities. He was the general convener of *Nilakkal Action Council* and was directly instrumental in the *Nilakkal Hindu-Christian conflict of 1983* mentioned the letter. PRISM suspected the timing of the appointment of Kummanam as the Governor by the BJP as a political tactic with an eye to the 2018 year end elections in Mizoram.[22] The new Governor of Mizoram

Kummanam Rajasekharan in response through social media maintained that his role 'henceforth will be apolitical.'

Such narratives were furthered by the Bangalore-based Global Council of Indian Christians (GCIC). The GCIC alleged that foreign funding was stopped by the central Government to check the growth of Christianity in the region. The Foreign Contribution Regulation Act (FCRA) 1976 has been stringently put to operation by the BJP at the centre and this has affected over 20,000 NGOs 20,000 and their licence cancelled. The GCIC alleged that Christian NGO receiving aid from America, Europe, Scandinavian etc., have been selectively targeted by the FCRA regime and pushed to severe financial crunch.

PRISM Media

CAB 2016, Media Release, Press Release

PRISM IN R DAY BOYCOTT (NDA atangin MNF inhnukdawk se, BJP atangin Mizo chu bang vek rawh se)

Aizawl 26th January, 2019: PRISM Party chuan India Republic Day boycott in kan office-ah flag dum kan zar a. Citizenship Amendment Bill avang hian MNF Party chu NDA leh NEDA atanga inhnukdawk tura phutin Mizorama BJP hruaitu leh member te bang vek turin kan phut.
Citizenship Amendment Bill hi Bangladesh ramri hawnna- kan ram, kan hnam leh kan sakhaw tana himlo anih avangin Lok Sabha-a an pharh hlimah India Hmarchhak State-a kan thawhpui te nen kan duhloh leh dodal thu India sorkarah thlen nghalin lian taka dodalna lantir anih theihnan sorkar kan ngenin kan theih ang angin hma kan la a. NESO te, Zirlai Pawl te leh NGO Coordination Committee in dodalna an kalpui leh midangin dodalna leh duhlohna an lantir zawng zawng kan thlawp vek a. Nasa zawka hma lak a la ngai kan ti hial a. NGO Coordination Committee hmalakna tha kan tih leh kan thlawpna lantirnan leh he Bill kan duhloh leh dodal zia lantirnan vawiina India Republic Day lawmna hi kan boycott a, kan party mi leh sa tumah Republic Day lawmnaah kan tel lo a. Kan office-ah flag dum kan zar bawk a ni.
He Bill dodal anih theih nana hma la lian thei leh nghawng nei liana hma la thei ber chu sorkar a ni a. All Party Meeting kova lian taka hma la turin sorkar kan ngen a, tun thlengin hma an la la lo hi a pawi kan ti a. He Bill hi kan duhloin kan dodal ani tih lantirna lian leh nghawng nei lian turin MNF Party hi NDA leh NEDA atanga a inhnuhdawh thuai a tul kan ti a. BJP Party-a awm Mizo zawng zawng te an party atanga an ban a tul kan ti bawk a ni.
PRISM chuan Kristianna hi a tha bik a ni tih lantir a, kan Pathian chawimawi tur te; kan chhehvel hnamte aia ropui zawk kan nih lantir tur te; Zohnahthlak (Zofa) te inpumkhatna atana kan unaute hipkhawm tur tein – Mizorama ram ralmuang, dik leh fel taka ro inrel, hna nei lo awm lohna, mi hrisel leh hlim chenna, ram hausa, hnam dangten tlawh an chak ram dinpui atan mi tin kan sawm che u a ni.
Tun hi duhthlanna hun a ni e.

No. PRISM/VI/2018-19/98 Date: 26.01.2019

Source: PRISM Website. https://www.myprism.in/ (Retrieved on 30.01.2019).
PRISM Press Release calling for Boycott of Republic Day celebrations 2019 in Mizoram

The anxieties and intolerance of the Churches and Zo Christianity to any other forms of religiosity or culturally alien elements or expressions can be construed from the fisted ethnic rumblings to issues such as Celebrations of Yoga Day 2017, 2018 and the Good Governance Day 2018 or the recent Republic Day Boycott 2019 (see, PRISM Notice on CAB 2016 issued on 26th January 2019).

Source: Photo circulated on WhatsApp January 2019.
The Boycott of Republic Day celebrations 2019 in Mizoram called by the major civil society organizations including the PRISM.

Being declared a Christian State, 'Sundays' holds a special meaning in the everyday life of Zo Christians. The names of the week days singularly point towards the importance attached to the day set for community prayers in the Church and a day set aside for *Isuah* (Jesus). Friday is called *Zirtawp Ni* that is the day studies (in schools) end; Saturday is called *Inrin Ni* that is the day for preparing oneself for Praying and Sunday is called *Chawl Ni* that is the day set aside for rest and God, a holy day, a day for introducing *Isuah* to little children through Sunday schools bible classes. New meanings were injected into the social understanding of Sunday within the Zo Christian Cosmology and the Zo people became very ardent observers of the Biblical Sabbath codes. Alongside these codes of Christianity celebrations such as Easters, Easter Mondays, Good Friday and Christmas evolved as important days for the believers.

Any Governmental program or visits on these days by political leadership from elsewhere across India is interpreted as undermining the sensibilities of the Zo Christians. For instance, Prime Minister Pt. J.L. Nehru's visit to Mizoram that fell on a Sunday was interpreted as 'anti-Christian' (see, Chapter 2). The Modi Government's decision to mark former Prime Minister A. B. Vajpayee's birthday 25th December as Good Governance Day has been construed as attempts to make Christmas insignificant by New Delhi/ the Hindus. Likewise, the institutional entry of Yoga into classrooms and government offices is being interpreted as attempts to underscore Christian ways of life. The resistance to yoga comes from the understanding that Yoga is intrinsically ingrained in Hindu ways of life. The conglomeration of Mizoram's church leaders *Mizoram Kohhran Hruaitu Committee* (Mizoram Church Leader's Committee) or MKHC has appealed to all Zo/Mizo Christians not to observe the International Day of Yoga. New Delhi and the BJP led government has been accused of circumventing the provisions of the National Education Policy, 2016: Chapter-4, Policy Frame Work; 4.4(2) Clause 12 (1) (c) of RTE Act (Free and Compulsory Education); and 4.12 (Self Development through Comprehensive Education) in matters of minority institutions and enforcing Yoga in schools a practice that is alien to minorities such as the Mizos. The MKHC protested against the designation of December 25 (Christmas) as Good Governance Day and the calling of a meeting of various Judges of the Supreme Court and High Court on Good Friday, which in the year 2015 fell on April 4.[23] Political parties like Mizo National Front (MNF) and the PRISM also joined the chorus opposing the practice of Yoga in schools and in the police department. The *Nexus of Patriarchy* and its agencies such as the YMA, KTP have been very critical of the presence of the Brahma Kumaris in Mizoram. The anti-Yoga, ani-Hindu stands have been extended to the Brahma Kumari centres at Aizawl and Kolasib as well.

Another public irritant for the religiously inclined *Zo hnahthlak* has been the *Transgender Persons (Protection of Rights) Bill* (2016). The Supreme Court of India in *National Legal Services Authority vs. Union of India* on 15th April 2014 passed a progressive judgement recognizing the Fundamental and Civil Rights of the Transgendered person.[24] The court ruled that transgender people should be treated as a third category of gender or as a socially and economically "backward" class entitled to proportional access and representation in education and jobs. This has unleashed and raised uncomfortable questions on homosexuality and Christianity in Mizoram. The Churches and the *Nexus of Patriarchy* in their zeal to build an *Ideal Zo Christian State* engage vociferously with regimentation and control of sexualities especially of the *Tuai* (Gay) and *Patil* (Lesbians).

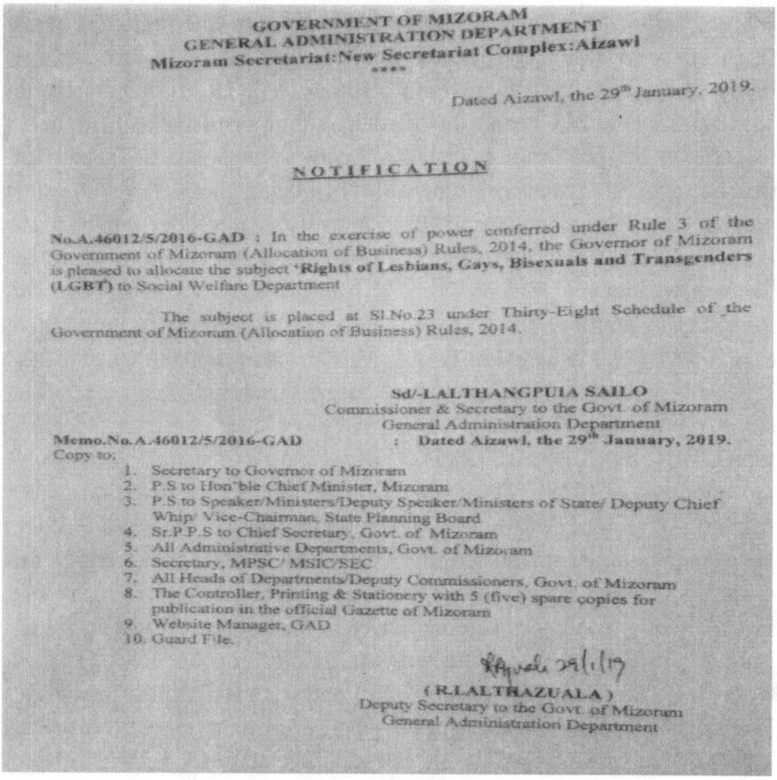

GOVERNMENT OF MIZORAM
GENERAL ADMINISTRATION DEPARTMENT
Mizoram Secretariat:New Secretariat Complex:Aizawl
****

Dated Aizawl, the 29th January, 2019.

NOTIFICATION

No.A.46012/5/2016-GAD : In the exercise of power conferred under Rule 3 of the Government of Mizoram (Allocation of Business) Rules, 2014, the Governor of Mizoram is pleased to allocate the subject '**Rights of Lesbians, Gays, Bisexuals and Transgenders (LGBT)** to Social Welfare Department

The subject is placed at Sl.No.23 under Thirty-Eight Schedule of the Government of Mizoram (Allocation of Business) Rules, 2014.

Sd/-LALTHANGPUIA SAILO
Commissioner & Secretary to the Govt. of Mizoram
General Administration Department

Memo.No.A.46012/5/2016-GAD : **Dated Aizawl, the 29th January, 2019.**
Copy to:

1. Secretary to Governor of Mizoram
2. P.S to Hon'ble Chief Minister, Mizoram
3. P.S to Speaker/Ministers/Deputy Speaker/Ministers of State/ Deputy Chief Whip/ Vice-Chairman, State Planning Board
4. Sr.P.P.S to Chief Secretary, Govt. of Mizoram
5. All Administrative Departments, Govt. of Mizoram
6. Secretary, MPSC/ MSIC/SEC
7. All Heads of Departments/Deputy Commissioners, Govt. of Mizoram
8. The Controller, Printing & Stationery with 5 (five) spare copies for publication in the official Gazette of Mizoram
9. Website Manager, GAD
10. Guard File.

29/1/19
(R.LALTHAZUALA)
Deputy Secretary to the Govt. of Mizoram
General Administration Department

Source: Shared through WhatsApp January 2019.

The post 2018 Election mood of Mizoram has become more revivalist in into nation and the Political Party in power that is the MNF has inclined towards the Chruch and its Nexus to put into function the operation of an *Ideal Zo Christian State*. The Oath taking ceremony of the new government in power post 2018 elections can be an instance to drive forward the enmeshing of politics and religion. The lines between religion and politics was blurred when that the new Mizoram Chief Minister, Pu Zoramthanga of MNF was sworn in to his office with Christian rituals. The swearing in of the new MNF government included signing of Bibilical hymns and reading of the "Gospel" followed by the National Anthem of India.

The *Nexus of Patriarchy* has clarified that it has no role to play in elections as it remains a political and doesn't influence voting in any manner and that it is the aims to infuse 'Secular spirit' while remaining staunchly Christian. However, in Mizoram like in most parts of predominantly Christian terrain of Northeast of India, the Churches play roles deeper than just the ecclesiastical and influence voting behaviour and regulate the destiny of political parties and candidates. Voters are said to be largely influenced by the view of the Church before going for voting. Representatives of various Churches said that they work mainly for the welfare of the people without any political motive. They also said that people are independent to choose any political party of their choice to lead the state. Religion, Politics and 'being Secular' thus converge into a complicated web to conjure a strange concoction of what I call: 'being Zo Christian in an *Ideal Zo Christian State* in a Secular India'.

It is this 'problematic of entanglements, accommodations and circumvents' of Religion and Politics that this book titled *Religion and Politics in Mizoram* attempts to understand through the study of the religion, state, society/people and politics in Mizoram.

Notes & References

1. This group of Indians can be broadly categorised into 3 distinct groups: (a) Those who directly served in the Indian Army or Administrative circles. (b) Those whose relatives had served in the Indian Army or Administrative circles in the northeast. (c) Those who were working as migrant labourers with the BRTF, BSF and others, which includes a significant population of Santhal tribes from Jharkhand/Bihar belt (ASC).
2. Jyotindra Das Gupta. (1998). 'Community, Authenticity and Autonomy: Insurgence and Institutional Development in India's North East' *in* Amrita Basu & Atul Kohli. (ed.). (1998). *Community conflicts and the State in India.* New Delhi/New York: Oxford University Press. pp. 183-214.
3. Sanjib Baruah. (2005). *Durable Disorder- Understanding the Politics of Northeast India.* New Delhi: Oxford University Press.
4. Lalhmingthanga former Finance Minister of Union Territory of Mizoram has mentioned similar experiences in his Foreword to A.C Ray's (1982) *Mizoram Dynamics of Change*. Calcutta: Pearl Publishers/ICSSR
5. In the "Life of the Lindsays" mention is made of a tribe living in the depths of the jungle, called "Cookies". At that date, they were evidently looked upon as wild men of the woods, reference being made to one who was captured but afterwards succeeded in escaping to the woods much in the same manner as a strange species of wild animal would be spoken of. *See*, Chapter-1 The Kuki-Lushai Tribes-Physical Characteristics *in* C.A. Soppitt. (1976). *A Short Account of the Kuki-Lushai tribes on the North-East Frontier (Districts Cachar, Sylhet, Naga Hills etc. and the North Cachar Hills) with An Outline Grammar of the Rangkhol-Lushai Language & A Comparison of Lushai with other Dialects.* Calcutta: Firma KLM Private Ltd for Tribal Research Institute, Aizawl, Mizoram. The debates at the academic circles in post-independence era marked by the tussle among scholars like Ghurye, Elwin, Srinivas and others and the policies

adopted by the independent Indian leaders from Delhi also reflected the reminiscent of such mental blocs.

6. Films in parts do represent reality. For instance, Shamit Amin. dir. *Chak De India.* (2007). India: Yash Raj Films International Ltd. Amin's Shahrukh Khan starrer film based on sports (Hockey) has two characters from the North-East (Manipur and Mizoram) who are meted out a 'foreigner' treatment and referred to as 'Chowmein' (Chinese, chinky) by their bully team-mates. The internal conflict of the characters from the North-East on the issue of being recognised as authentic citizens of their own country is well summed up by a dialogue of the characters from the region: 'there is no pride(happiness) in being treated as foreigners in our own country' (direct translation: Mine).
7. Anup Shekhar Chakraborty: (2008c).'Manufacturing of Spaces: The 'Others' in Zo/Mizo Politics'*South Asian Journal of Socio-Political Studies (SAJOSPS).* Vol.9 No.1, July-December, pp.39-43; (2008b).'Mustering Empowerment experiences from Mizoram: A Leap from 'Private' to 'Public' Living Spaces', *Global South SEPHIS e-magazine*. Vol.4 No.4, July; (2008a). 'Emergence of Women from 'Private' to 'Public': A Narrative of Power Politics from Mizoram' *Journal of International Women's Studies (JIWS)*, Bridgewater. Vol. No. 9, 3 May. pp. 27- 45; (2009b). 'Where are 'Our women'? Locating Women through the History of Proselytization in Mizoram', *Dharma Deepkia- South Asian Journal of Missiological Research- issue on Mission In Contexts Of Violence And Uncertainty*. Issue 30, Vol.13 No. 2 July-December; (2009a).'Regulating Citizenship: Politics of 'Check-In' and 'Check-Out'', *Refugee Watch Online (A Co-Publication of Refugee Watch)*, 18 February; (2012). 'Construing And Gleaning The Vexing Notion Of The 'Outsider' In Mizoram: Pre-Statehood To Post-Statehood Times', *QUEST- The Journal of UGC Academic Staff College, Nainital, Kumaun University*. Volume 6, Issue. 2. pp. 297-304.
8. Anup Shekhar Chakraborty. *Ibid.*; (2013a). 'Elementary Aspects of 'Otherness' in Mizoram: An Enquiry into the Nature and Processes of Social Inclusion and Exclusion in a North East Indian State'.*Occasional Paper VII*, Department of Sociology, University of North Bengal. Shivmandir, Siliguri: The University of North Bengal Press.
9. The British were not the sole actors in unleashing the wave of subjugation and domination in the North East Frontier region. The French, the Scots, the natives from other parts of the Raj as well as the native states such as the Bengali, the predominantly mercantile community like the Baniya/Marwari etc., in different degrees and at different times acted as external forces (ASC).
10. Ananda C. Bhagabati. (1982) 'Emergent Tribal Identity in North-East India,' in B. Chaudhuri (ed.). *Tribal Development in India: Problems and Prospects*. Delhi: Inter-India Publications, p.218.
11. Anup Shekhar Chakraborty. (2015a). *Politics of Autonomy & Ethnic Cocooning in Mizoram*, New Delhi: Authorspress.
12. Anup Shekhar Chakraborty. (2013a). *Op.cit.*
13. Anup Shekhar Chakraborty. (2015b). *Hegemony To Hyphenation: Hybridization Of Identities And Politics In Mizoram*. Darjeeling: St. Joseph's Publication.
14. Anup Shekhar Chakraborty. (2009b). *Op.cit.*

15. This has been the dream of every Mizo and ever-political party in Mizoram. Even though India boasts of being a secular democracy and so also Mizoram, the speeches and the pre-electoral promises made by every political party in Mizoram tends to be overlaid with religious overtones (ASC).
16. Frederick. S. Downs. (1983). *Christianity in North East India.* Delhi: ISPCK, pp. 14-15; E.J. Thomas. (1993). *Mizo bamboo Hills Murmur Change (Mizo Society Before And After Independence).* New Delhi: Intellectual Publishing House.
17. The Mizo society serves as a good example for Bentham's Panoptic Society. In the Zo/Mizo society people live under the specter of the Pan-optics i.e. constant surveillance of the church and the moral agencies. The only difference being that in the case of the Mizo society the observer can be seen and sometimes partially invisible (ASC).
18. Hubert. L. Dreyfus & Paul Rabinow. (1982). *Michel Foucault: Beyond Structuralism And Hermeneutics.* Chicago: The University Of Chicago Press. pp. 213-215.
19. I have used the terms 'Being a Zo, Being a Christian' extensively in my PhD thesis "The Evolution of 'Zomi' Identity and Politics in Mizoram" (2005-2010) Department of Political Science, University of Calcutta, and also in my series of publications between 2007- 2013. I am not influenced by the similar sounding title of Joy Pacchua's book '*Being Mizo*' (2014). New Delhi: Oxford University Press.

20 Pi Vanramchhuangi ('Ruatfelanu'), Director HRLN Mizoram, Social Activist, *Personal Interview*, Chaltlang, Aizawl: 28th& 29th January 2008.

21. Henry L. Khojol. (2018). *Governor asked to leave Mizoram.* 31.05.18. The Telegraph. https://www.telegraphindia.com/states/north-east/governor-asked-to-leave-mizoram/cid/1450422 (retrieved on 12.12.2018).
22. Megha Varier. (2018). 'Drive out radical Hindu Governor': Campaign in Mizoram against Kummanam Rajasekharan. *The News Minute.* Friday, June 01, 2018. https://www.thenewsminute.com/article/drive-out-radical-hindu-governor-campaign-mizoram-against-kummanam-rajasekharan-82294 (retrieved on 12.12.2018).

22. ENS. 'Mizoram's church leaders urge flock not to observe yoga day.' 17 June 2015. *The Indian Express.* Aizawl. https://indianexpress.com/article/india/india-others/mizorams-church-leaders-urge-flock-not-to-observe-yoga-day/ (retrieved on 01.01. 2019).

23. Aniruddha Dutta. (2014). 'Contradictory Tendencies: The Supreme Court's NALSA Judgment on Transgender Recognition and Rights.' *Journal of Indian Law and Society.* Vol. 5 (Monsoon). pp. 225-236.

1

A General Discussion on Indian Secularism: Revisiting Old Debates, Re-raising Old Questions

Post-independence entanglements of the State in India have engaged on two competing issues: first, communalism and second, integration (via democratic development of various religious communities into a harmonious society). The framers of the Indian constitution were certain that 'Secularism' and the 'Secular state' do not necessitate the elimination of either religion or religiosity and therefore, the word 'Secular' was conspicuously absent in the original text of the Indian Constitution. The centrality of religion in societies in India and plural cosmology handed over generations had evolved into a lived experience of 'temperaments of tolerance' quintessentially understood as '*sarva-dharma samabhava*'.[1]

The Indian state is secular in the sense that its constitution guarantees full religious liberty to all individuals and groups and forbids discrimination against any citizen on grounds only of religion, and caste.[2] It is just as well that it is not secular in the western sense of complete separation between church and state, for the state reserves to itself the right to intervene in the interest of necessary social reforms in matters which customarily come under the preview of religion. The Indian constitution thus guarantees individual and corporate freedom of religion, citizenship rights and the state is not constitutionally connected with any particular religion nor does it deliberately seek to promote or interfere with it.[3]

Unravelling Indian Secularism

In India, secularism in its widest sense stands for tolerance. Indian secularism subscribes to the Hindu philosophical tenet that all religion has elements of truth and no religion can claim the monopoly of truth. Hinduism has never put forth the claims that it alone is the true religion.[4] The spirit of toleration is the foundation of the theory of secularism. Max Weber pays a similar tribute to the spirit of tolerance which has permeated India. He says, 'It is an unabated fact that in India, religious and philosophical thinkers were able to enjoy perfect, nearly absolute freedom for a long period. The freedom of thought in ancient India was so considerable as to find no parallel in the west before the most recent age'. Hinduism was never a militant religion.[5] It is in essence, a way of life evolved from diverse experiences to the great, each trying to reach the realization of the ultimate reality.

Secularism as one of the cornerstones of Democracy in India is contested on two lines: (a) One on the Nehruvian vision of separating religion and politics manifesting in the concept of 'dharmanirpeksata'. (b) The other on the Gandhian rejection of the idea of separation of religion and politics manifesting in the principle of equal respect of all religions that is the concept of 'sarva dharma samabhava'. The tug of war between these two 'Visions' marked the debates in the Constituent Assembly and later in academic circles in India.

Opinions on 'Indian Secularism' maintain that given the pervasive role of religion in the lives of the Indian people, secularism, defined as the separation of politics or the state from religion, is an intolerable, alien, modernist imposition on the Indian society. This, argument is a misreading of the Indian constitutional vision, which enjoins the state to be equally tolerant of all religions and which therefore requires the state to steer clear of both theocracy or fundamentalism and the 'wall of separation' model of secularism. What is distinctive to Indian secularism is the complementary articulation between the democratic state and the politics of satya and ahimsa, whereby the relative autonomy of religion and politics from each other can be used for the moral-political reconstruction of both the religious traditions and the modern state. Indian secularism has remained deeply problematic in contemporary Indian political discourse.

Throughout the 1980s and into the 1990s the debates on Secularism in India and also 'Indian Secularism', has found newer interpretations that have further groved the contests into the idea of '*Being Secular*'. For instance, the Bharatiya Janata Party (BJP) and the *Sangh Parivar* have been insisting on a distinction between their own 'positive secularism' and the 'pseudo-secularism' of the Congress. According to them, 'positive secularism' stands for 'justice for all and discriminations against none' while the Congress' 'pseudo-secularism' vilifies Hindu categories and symbols while to pampering Muslim minority communities as "Vote banks."[6] Nandy observes that Nehruvian secularism signaling the separation of state and religion has been imposed on the Indian people. This interpretation of Secularism packages with itself notions of modernity, western rationality, scientific growth, nation-building, national security and development. These constitute a 'modern demonology, a tantra with a built-in code of violence.' Whereas secularism demands of the members of religious communities to dilute their faith so that they can be truly integrated into the nation-state. It guarantees no protection to them against the sufferings inflicted by the state itself in the name of its 'secular, scientific, amoral' ideology of nation-building, security, development, etc. As a handy adjunct to these 'legitimating core concepts,' secularism helps the state-elites to legitimize themselves as the sole arbiters among traditional communities, to claim for themselves a monopoly on religious and ethnic tolerance and on political rationality. To accept the ideology of secularism is to accept the ideologies of progress and modernity as the new justifications of domination, and the use of violence to achieve and sustain the ideologies as the new opiates of the masses.[7]

Nandy's critique of Nehruvian Secularism points aloud the failed attempts to either eliminate religion from politics or to promote greater religious tolerance. Hence, it can 'no longer pretend to guide moral or political action.' Nandy therefore has no hesitation in calling himself an anti-secularist. By so criticizing secularism, Nandy does not mean to privilege the communalist ideology of either the majority or minority religious communities. To the contrary, these communalist ideologies are, in his view, the pathological by-products of modernity; they are the dialectical 'other' or counter-players of modernity's secular state. He notes that khaki shorts of the RSS cadres are modeled on the uniform of the colonial police. According to Nandy, the ideology of Hindu nationalist revivalism or fundamentalism, with its borrowing of the models of semiotic religions and of the modern Western nation-state, is 'another form of Westernization'[8] in the sense that it seeks to decontaminate Hinduism of its folk elements, turn it into a classical Vedantic faith, and then give it additional teeth with the help of Western technology and secular statecraft, so that the Hindus can take on, and ultimately defeat, all their external and internal enemies, if necessary, by liquidating all forms of ethnic plurality-first within Hinduism and then within India. Nandy's draws a distinction between two conceptions of religion.

(1) Religions as tolerant and accommodative faiths or folk ways of life and

(2) Religions as politically constructed monolithic, communalist ideologies of sectarianism and intolerance. The former, he says, characterized the pre-modern and pre-liberal way of life in India, whereas the latter is a product of modernity's nationalism, statecraft, and developmentalism.

The next move in Nandy's argument is to suggest that it is the very package of modern nationalism and its statecraft and scientific developmentalism which generate and nourish religious communalisms, which the state elites combat by resorting to the use of the ideology of the secular or nonreligious nation-state. This counter posing of the tyranny of the modern secular state and the violence of modern communal organizations is, in Nandy's view, nothing but the internal dialectics of modernity's nation-state paradigm. By this reasoning, communalism can be the majoritarian or the minoritarian variety, and the secular state stand condemned as the perverse gifts or, rather, the inevitable products of Western modernity. In Nandy's view, the ethico-politically appropriate alternative to them lies in the non-modern, pre-secular conception of religions as accommodative, tolerant faiths or ways of life as was practiced, in exemplary manner, by Asoka, Akbar and Gandhi. They derived their religious tolerance not from secular politics but from Buddhism, Islam and Hinduism, respectively. Gandhi's religious tolerance, he writes, 'came from his anti-secularism, which in turn came from his unconditional rejection of modernity.'

Accordingly, Nandy writes: 'As far as public morality goes, statecraft in India may have something to learn from Hinduism, Islam or Sikhism; but Hinduism, Islam, and Sikhism have very little to learn from the Constitution or from state secular practices.'[9] Nandy locates the cause of new religious violence in secularism and modernity. A 'gift of Christianity' and child of modernity and colonialism secularism is a product of western science and rationality and function as the ideology of modern State which according to Nandy is a source of most contemporary problems. Nandy's rejection of secularism is rooted in a twofold critique of modern culture and society and critique of secular state. Indian secular State has much to learn about morality from Hinduism, Islam and Sikhism while Hinduism, Islam and Sikhism have nothing to learn from the secular state in this respect. As an alternative to secularism Nandy pleads for the recovery of India's traditional religious tolerance.[10] Nandy's critique of the ideology of secularism is against western state centered version which has been adopted by India's westernized intellectuals. In this version of secularism religion should be abolished from the scientific management of the public sphere. In contrast is the non-western religion centred understanding of secularism that supports equal respect for all religions and suits South Asian realities.

Nandy defines religion in South Asia has split into two, '*Religion as faith*' and '*Religion as ideology.*' Faith means religion as non- monolithic, operationally plural way of life. Ideology means religion as sub national, cross national or national identifier of population protecting political or socio-economic interests. Religion as ideology is usually identified with one or more text and become the final identifier of the pure forms of religions and modern state prefers to deal with this form of religion. This idea is the product of modernity, statecraft and developmentalism. Secularism which is an imported idea from west does not use religion to link up different faiths or way of life which has its own principle of tolerance. The idea of secularism that give state the role of ultimate arbiter among different religions and communities is incompatible with understanding and role of religion in life of people in South Asia.

Nandy discusses two different meaning of the word in modern India, the first meaning of secularism demarcate two distinct sphere public life and private life and one's religion is not admitted in public life. According to Nandy, one can be a good Hindu or a good Muslim within one's home or at one's place of worship but when one enters public life, one is expected to leave one's faith behind. This ideology believes that public realm is dominated with vision of science and universal and bringing religion may lead to potential threat to modern polity. Pitched against this is the non - western meaning of secularism that believes in the principle of equal respect to all religions. Implicit is the idea that public sphere must have space for continuous dialogue among different religions because each include within it "an in house version of the other faith, both as an internal criticism and as a reminder of the diversity of the theories of transcendence."[11] This version of secularism is compatible with Indian understanding of secularism but India's westernized intellectuals have opted for abolition of religion from the public sphere. For instance, Nehruvian secularism which separates state and religion is a part of modern western package of scientific growth, nation building, national security and development. These according to him constitute a 'modern demonology a tantra with a built in code of violence'. The idea of secularism creates rigid separation of two spheres – state and religion. Religion enters politics through different means in the form of ideologies and instrumentalized religious exclusivism. Thus even threat of Hindu right has to be coped with religious and not secular means through reactivating traditional forms of tolerance. Secularism is also insensitive to politics of culture and believer is treated as person with inferior political consciousness. In this process traditional culture based on tolerance is eroded and tendencies of extremism increases and generates communal politics. Thus he suggests Gandhian path of inter-faith dialogue.

Similarly T. N. Madan maintains that religious zealots, who contribute to fundamentalism or fanaticism by reducing religion to mere political bickering, are provoked to do so by the secularists who deny the very legitimacy of religion in social life. To Madan, Nehru's secularism denies the immense importance of religion in the lives of the peoples of South Asia. Secularism is in this region an impossible credo, an impracticable basis for state action and an impotent remedy against fundamentalism or fanaticism. Ruling out the establishment of a Hindu state as an utterly unworkable proposition, Madan concludes that 'the only way secularism in South Asia, understood as inter-religious understanding, may succeed would be for us to take both religion and secularism seriously and not reject the former as superstition and reduce the latter to a mask for communalism or mere expediency.'[12] He applauds Gandhi not only for emphasizing the inseparability of religion and politics but also for opening up avenues of inter-religious understanding and of a spiritually justified limitation of the role of religious institutions and symbols in certain areas of contemporary life.

Madan complicates and criticizes the idea of secularism and cautions against unproblematic adaption of secularism in south Asian realities. Taking the case of Bankim Chandra Chatterjee, Madan argues how translations are difficult because words can be translated but it is difficult to translate an idea that the word denotes if that idea does not exist among people whose language translation is required. The idea of secularism as transferred to countries of South Asia also poses many difficulties. South Asia is a multi-religious society and the majority of people living in this region are active adherents of some religious faith. While Secularism is impractical for State action because Buddhism and Islam have been declared as State religion, Policy of equidistance is also difficult to maintain since religious minorities do not share the majority's view of what this entails for the State. It has failed to bring under control divisive forces which resulted in the partition of the subcontinent in 1947 and also failed to counter religious fundamentalism. Madan argues that it was possible to privatize religion in the West because of developments internal to Christianity such as reformation that facilitated the process. Whereas In South Asia major religious traditions do not assume any radical antinomy between the sacred and the secular. Religion covers all aspects of life and its impact is totalizing in nature thus it was impossible to restrict it to private domain. Religion as the doctrine of overarching ends is the most important factor in the lives of the people of India and South Asia. Religion gives meaning to lives of most of the people and also determines their place in society. Thus to impose secularism on believers is wrong in the words of Madan "an act of moral arrogance and political folly."[13] Religion and the belief of people must be taken seriously and should be given its place in society as non- religions because denial of legitimacy to religion in society of believers provokes fundamentalism on the part of religious zealots. Through religious pluralism inter religious harmony could be established. Secularism and religious faith must be recognized to be compatible with each other. The alternative conception in Madan's views is Gandhism because it has the possibilities of inter religious understanding.

Though Nandy dismisses secularism altogether Madan suggests that state practices of secularism have to be based on the recognition of religious practices. This has to be buttressed by discovering and strengthening the internal resources of religious pluralism and tolerance. Since India's civil society is deeply religious Nehru's concept of secular ideas poses a problem as state project. But in the end both theorists ground their understanding of tolerance in largely undefined and unarticulated lived practices. That these practices may have changed or degenerated in the context of competitive electoral politics and an equally competitive market economy is something that they would rather not take into account.

Partha Chatterjee too finds that the ideology of secularism is not an adequate or appropriate political perspective for meeting the challenge of Hindu majoritarianism. In his view, the official model of Indian secularism and the present campaign of the Hindu right for setting up a 'positively' secular state have brought India to a 'potentially disastrous political impasse.'

Turning to the recent shift in the ideological articulation of Hindu nationalism, Chatterjee points out that its present championing of 'positive secularism' is meant not only to deflect accusations of its being anti-secular but also to rationalize, in a sophisticated way, its campaign for intolerant interventions by a modern, positively secular state against the religious, cultural or ethnic minorities in the name of 'national culture' and a homogenized notion of citizenship.[14] In this role, writes Chatterjee, the Hindu right in fact seeks to project itself as a principled modernist critic of Islamic or Sikh fundamentalism and to accuse the 'pseudo-secularists' of preaching tolerance for religious obscurantism and bigotry. The quandaries generated by the career of the secular state in India and the potentially disastrous nature of the new politics of 'positive secularism' lead Chatterjee to the conclusion that the theory and practice of the secular state cannot bring about what, according to him, is really needed in India, namely, the toleration of religious, ethnic and cultural differences.

In so denouncing secularism, Chatterjee is in agreement with Nandy. They share the view that the politics of interventionist secularization is part of the same practices of the modern state which promotes religious communalism or religious intolerance. While Nandy's 'anti-secularist manifesto' of religious tolerance is couched in terms of the non-modern, pre-liberal philosophy, symbolism and theology of tolerance in the everyday faiths of Hinduism, Islam, Buddhism and Sikhism, Chatterjee's search is for a 'political' conception of tolerance as part of a non-Western form of modernity in India.[15] Finding that the liberal-democratic state can only recognize individual rights, and not the collective rights of cultural or religious groups, Chatterjee directs his intellectual efforts not to secularize the state in the name of any universalist framework of reason, but to defend minority cultural rights and to underscore the duty of the democratic state to ensure policies of religious toleration.

According to Chatterjee to assess the proper relationship between the state and the religious, ethnic and cultural groups, we need to go beyond the 'state sovereignty vs. individual rights' model. Following Foucault, he maintains that the specifically modern form of power, which cuts across 'the liberal divide between state and civil society,' exercises itself through forms of representation and through technologies of governmentality, that is, the self-disciplining of its subjects. He notes that this modern form of power is characterized by 'an immensely flexible braiding of coercion and consent'.[16] Hence, according to him, the secularization of the state cannot be taken as a non-coercive or power-free politics of pure (secular) rationality. Rather, under modernity, the religious, cultural and ethnic communities as well as the secular state are to be seen as institutional sites or strategic locations of the politics of identity and difference. This being so, according to him, arguments for a universal framework of governance based on so-called pure secular-rational grounds (e.g., the principle of the equal rights of all regardless of their religion or caste) which ignore their context of cognitive-political struggles over issues of identity and difference. Hence, Chatterjee calls for a conception of tolerance which recognizes that there will be political contexts where a group could insist on its right not to give reasons for doing things differently provided it explains itself adequately in its own chosen forum. In other words, toleration here would be premised on autonomy and respect for persons, but it would be sensitive to the varying political salience of the institutional contexts in which reasons are debated.

Contrary to Nandy's non-modern, religious conception of tolerance, Chatterjee directs his search to finding a 'political' conception of tolerance which will set out the practical conditions in order to demand and expect tolerance from others. According to him, if a religious community seeks to gain or preserve its autonomy and respect from other groups or from the state, it must conduct its own affairs through representative public institutions insofar as those affairs are not confined to simple matters of innocent beliefs or holy rituals. Those affairs or practices of any religious group which have a regulative power over its members must rest on the publicly secured consent of those members. In other words, writes Chatterjee, 'even if a religious group declares that the validity of its practices can only be discussed and judged in its own forums, those institutions must have the same degree of publicity and representativeness that is demanded of all public institutions having regulatory functions'.

Chatterjee observes that the duty of the democratic state is to ensure policies of religious tolerance within the constitutional vision. So is the case with the principles of respect for persons and of the consent of the governed, which he rightly takes to be the basis for the toleration of religious differences. The activity or policy of giving equal tolerance to all religions is not a strictly religious activity or policy. It is also not and a moral political activity in which the end is taken to justify any means adopted for its realization. It is rather a moral-political activity or policy, which is predicated on the relative autonomy of the political and the religious from each other. It assumes not only that a pluralism of religious and or nonreligious beliefs is ineradicable under the conditions of modernity but also that political institutions and political policies can be constructed and operated in different ways and for different purposes from those of religious institutions or religious doctrines. Indian secularism cannot be said to be situated entirely outside the problematic and thematic of the Western discourse on secularism. The problematic relationship between religion and politics in the West had its analogies in India too. What we mean is that despite important philosophical or metaphysical differences between them, both European Christianity and Indian Hinduism legitimized, in their own ways, analogous systems of social inequalities during the pre-modern period. The latter was complicit in the 'social construction' of the social evils mentioned above, namely, sati, untouchability, etc. Hence, an ethico-political reform of the socio-religious sphere was taken to be an integral part of the Indian movement for *swaraja* and *sarvodaya*. Government has also intervened in the matters of conversion. In the constituent assembly conversion as an issue was discussed and the constitution grants right to propagate but word conversion was not included. After Independence different State government made these acts to prohibit force, fraud and inducements for conversion. When matter relating to conversion was discussed in the Court, Supreme Court differentiated propagation of religion from conversion and viewed it as contrary to freedom of conscience.

Chatterjee observed that the post independent India model of secularism adopted by India's westernized elites implied exclusion of Indian alternative to Western secular modernity. It also introduced direct involvement of state in religious and social matters especially in Hindu religious matters. Chatterjee problematize implementation of secular principles in Indian realities in this context. If secularism is interpreted as strict separation of religion and politics this can prove fairly compatible with the discrimination against minorities. If secularism is interpreted as equidistance from all religious groups then its practice in India raise some doubts because State has intervened selectively in personal laws of different communities making laws to reform Hindu personal laws but the same reformist agenda has been absent for other communities like Muslims, Christian and Parses. Hindu right describe this as appeasement of minorities. Chatterjee refers to the exceptionality of India though he does not call for a new version of secularism. Chatterjee favoured the idea of political tolerance that incorporates autonomy, respect for persons and accommodates different reasons coming from different cultural and traditional institutions. He seems to be in agreement with the idea that minorities resist homogenization from outside but may introduce democratization within the community.

Achin Vanaik critiques the ideas positioned by Nandy and Madan.[17] Acknowledging their 'anti-secularist' position and theoretical soundness Vaniak argues that they legitimize politics of religious identity. According to Vanaik, Nandy's idea of replacement of secular state and secular public morality with religion based public morality of tolerance is dangerous. While for Nandy Secular state is imposed from above on traditional society Vanaik proposes that traditional beliefs and practices are responsible for undermining the secular state and democratization of society. The root cause of religious communalism is religion itself. The struggle against religion should not be limited to setting up a state equally tolerant of all religions but extend to the secularization and diminution of religion in civil society. To secularize civil society religious influence, importance of religious identity in everyday life and increasing privatization of religious commitments has to be reduced. Secularism means three things - right to freedom of worship, primacy of citizenship and non- affiliation of State to any religion. The secular State must separate state and religion, secularize state laws and policies. Recognizing due importance of Gandhian legacy Vanaik argues that though Gandhi did not separate religion and politics his role was indeed remarkable in giving principle of equal respect to all religions. But many of Gandhi's perspectives were against modern conception of secularism. Secular democracy requires rights centered relationship between individual and society. Vanaik interprets Gandhi's mixing of politics with religious idioms of *ahimsa*, trusteeship etc. as a strategy of class accommodation[18] for preventing any socialist revolution against capitalism. Gandhi mobilized masses in the Indian national movement but this contributed to a conservative though anti communalist, religious nationalism in contrast to a secular, democratic and egalitarian nationalism.

Akil Bilgrami criticizes Nehruvian form of secularism and also rejects Nandy's views on secularism.[19] He criticizes Nandy for practicing both nostalgia and skewed historiography. While Nandy is right in arguing that different religious traditions have their specific source of the realization of a tolerant way of life his ideas of the rise of Hindu Nationalism is oversimplified. According to Bilgrami, Nandy's anti secular proposal have flaws in it because the condition for different religious traditions and communities has changed in the modern India. In Bilgrami's opinion Nehruvian secularism stands in a conceptual and political space that lies outside the sphere of substantive political commitments. Secularism did not emerge as the product of a negotiation and dialogue between religious communities. It was adopted from above as an Archimedean point. If it would have been the result of debate and understanding of different communities then different groups would have subscribed to it. Presence of different communities in State is important and these communities could play very important role in designing secular principles. Bilgrami presents the model of negotiated or emergent secularism which is based on moderate religious persons embracing principle of secularism not on the basis of universalistic rationality but on their own internal value system.[20] Secularism should also incorporate clarification of those principles that belong to illiberal religious persons also. Instead of seeking neutral common agreement communities should contribute to a secular outcome for different reasons from within their different substantive value economies. Instead of being imposed it should emerge from bottom up incorporating moderate political voices and assumptions of different communities.

Nehru's notion of secularism *dharamnirpekshata* did not mean a state where religion is discouraged. It rather meant a State where people have freedom of religion and conscience and freedom for those as well who have no religion. Nehru himself said it is perhaps not very easy to find a good word for 'secular'. Some people think it means something opposed to religion. That obviously is not correct. What it means is that it is a state which honors all faiths equally and gives them equal opportunities, that as a state, it does not allow itself to be attached to one faith or religion, which then becomes the State religion.[21] Nehru's secularism was understood as freedom of religion or irreligion, no state religion and due honour of all religion equally. Different articles of our constitution define the Secular character of the State. Constitution guarantees freedom of religion to individual, also to religious denomination, guarantees equality of citizenship, equality of opportunity in public services, no discrimination in educational institutions, no communal electorate, although there is provision for reservation of seats for Schedule Castes and Schedule Tribes , no special taxes for promotion of religion, no religious instructions in state educational institutions. Through principle of '*sarva dharma sambhava*' Gandhi tried to bring people from different religions together. It was also a way to form mass movement in a religiously divided plural society. Gandhi also realized and recognized value of religion in people's lives and believed in equal respect of all religions. Nehru's concept of secularism is based on the principle of '*Dharmanirapekhsata*' or religious neutrality.

According to Chandhoke, Nehru's idea of secularism '*dharmanirapekhta*,' preferred that the state would not be influenced by religious consideration in policy and decision making. [22] Yet Nehru was convinced that in the Indian context religion could not be banished from the political and public spheres. Indian secularism is related to the constitutional values of democracy and fundamental rights. Thus secularism is important for India because (a) it enables people of different religions to live in civility with respect for all faiths, (b) it is a part of democracy which grants equal rights, (c) it safeguards democracy by limiting the powers of the majority and (d) it protects the equal rights of minorities to citizens. Nehru's secular ideal is important for India because it regulates the relation between the state and various religious groups on the principle of equality that the state shall not discriminate against any religion. Otherwise people will be subjected to oppression and denial of their right to freedom of belief. The majority is to be told that it does not have the right to control the country and the minority is to be assured of equal treatment. Thus secularism is the only alternate to maintain religious harmony in plural society.

The character of the Indian constitution on the other hand was decisively shaped predominantly in response to the deteriorating Hindu-Muslim relations. Indian state excluded religion on contextualist grounds for example by refusing to allow separate electorates, reserved constituencies for different religious communities, reservations for jobs on the basis of religious classification and the organization of states on the basis of religion.

Gleaning the Indian Constitution for locating the Secular Features of the State and Society in India

A secular state ideally ensures: – (a) 'liberty' to members of all religious community and to possess their core beliefs and practices. (b) non-preferential treatment to all members of every religious community so that the state respects multiple establishments. (c) 'freedom' to individuals to criticize the religion to which they belong and to reject or embrace it or to embrace another religion of their choice or to remain without anyone. (d) No specific religion will tend to dominate the other religions. (e) Physical security, material well-being of the individual and no individual should interfere in the private sphere of other. State promotes the value of equal citizenship where every individual irrespective of religion will be treated equally. (f) All citizens are recognized as equal participants in the public domain. Secularism tried to convey a community wide acknowledgement of equal respect for everyone in the political domain. (g) In multi-religious society, a secular state gives maximum liberty and equality to all its citizens. The Indian Constitution appears to possess all the above features.[23]

Article 25(1) of our constitution specifies the right to freedom of religion. All Indian citizens are allowed freely to choose their own religion, to profess and practice it, as well as to propagate it to others. Freedom not as an absolute but subject to the orders of the state regarding public order, morality and health. Religious customs such as human sacrifices and widow burning ('Sati') are therefore unacceptable to the state. In *Commissioner H.R.E, Madras vs. L.T. Swamiar, 1954*, the Supreme Court held that religion is a matter of faith and it should lay down a code of ethical rules for its followers to accept, it may prescribe rituals, ceremonies, modes of worship, dress code which will be regarded as integral part of religion.[24]

Religious demands and accommodations have been made possible in the Indian constitutional provisions in a myriad ways. The state in India has adjusted the demands and wants to Religious communities through a series of formal and informal provisions without demarcating a neat provision. A recapitulation of the several provisions of the Indian Constitution would unearth these formal and informal ways of accommodations, adjustments and circumvents.

For instance, Article 26 extends collective religious rights[25] beyond individuals to religious denominations. Religious denomination are allowed to establish and maintain institutions necessary to practice their religion, to own property and administer such property and it permits a denomination to manage its own affairs in matters of religion. Supreme Court held that Arya Samaj, Anandamarga, Vaishanave, the followers of Madhawacharya and other religious teachers though not separate religions yet they are separate religious denomination and enjoy the protection under Article 26 of the constitution.

Similarly, Article 30(1) gives to all religions or linguistic minorities the right to establish and administer their own religious educational institutions. This adheres to the principle that religion is not a matter of the state, but is purely individual and private.

Article 27 of the constitution forbids the state to collect taxes for the purpose of promoting or maintenance of any particular religion or religious denomination. State cannot support economically any specific religion hence we can say there is no official state religion.

Article 28(1) implies that no religious instruction shall be provided in any educational institution wholly maintained out of state funds. Thus we can say religion is prohibited in state supported or funded institutions. Article 28(3) states that no person attending any educational institution shall be required to take part in any religious instruction or attend any religious worship that may be conducted in such institution.

Article 14 and 15(1) both deal with equality of the citizens of India. It states that the state shall not discriminate against any citizen on grounds only of religion, race, caste, sex, place of birth or any of them. Every person has free access to all public places and to use public goods (well, tanks, roads, public resort) maintained partly or wholly out of state funds or dedicated to the use of the general public.

Article 16(1) and (2) prohibits discrimination with regard to employment or appointment to any office under the state and Article 29(2) prohibits discrimination with regard to admission into any educational institution maintained by the state or receiving aid out of state funds.

Article 325 of the constitution declares a general electoral roll for all constituencies and states and no one should get priority on the grounds of religion. Hence Articles 14, 15(1), 16(1) and (2), 29(2) and 325 deals with equality of citizenship.

Indian Constitution aims not only to give the Indian citizen freedom of conscience and choice of religion, but also it keeps religion and religious affairs out of the business of the state, whether state employment or education. Constitution also aims at keeping the state out of matters of religion. Despite its clarity on the separation of state and religion the constitution contains several inconsistencies on the matter of religion and state. Aim of Indian state is to secure to all its citizens social, economic and political justice, as well as equality of status and of opportunity. India traditionally was a very stratified society, in which social differences have been considered by the religiously legitimated caste system which hinders upward social mobility of the lowest social classes of Indian society. To ensure justice and equality is a complicated and difficult task.

Though Article 25 confers freedom of conscience and religion to the individual citizen Article 25(2) allows the state to limit the freedom of religion. This article may regulate or restrict any economic, financial, political or other secular activity which may be associated with religious practice to provide scope for social welfare. The other reason given for the state's interference in matters of religion centres on social welfare and reform and the opening of Hindu religious institutions to all classes of Hindus. Accordingly Articles 25(2) provides broad sweeping power of interference to the state in religious matters and reflect the peculiar needs of Indian society. It is important to mention here that law providing for the very extensive supervision by the state about temple administration has been enacted by virtue of this provision. Here it would not be out place to state that the extensive modifications of Hindu personal law (marriage, divorce, adoption, succession), has been affected by legislation based on the provision permitting measures of social welfare and social reform. For the validity of the Bombay Prevention of Hindu Bigamous Marriages Act of 1946, High court delivered its judgement that polygamy is an integral part of Hindu religion, Hindu religion recognizes the necessity of a son for religious efficacy and spiritual salvation, the religion also recognizes the institution of adoption and hence provides for the continuation of the same. The state is empowered to legislate the practice of monogamy among Hindu as a measure of social reform though it interferes with the right of a citizen freely to profess, practice and propagate religion. Harijan temple entry laws have been enacted, the *Central Untouchability (Offences) Act of 1955*[26] provides that any attempt to prevent Harijans from exercising their right to enter the temple is punishable with imprisonment or fine or with both. Therefore it must be clear that a secular civil law is equally applicable to all Indian citizens.

Though Article 26 guarantees to every religious denomination the right to manage its own affairs in matters of religion. In *Venkata Ramana Devaru vs. State of Mysore*,[27] the *Madras Temple Entry Authorization Act* threw all Hindu public temples including the Venkata Ramana temple to Harijans. The trustees of these denominational temples refused admission to Harijans on the ground that people of low caste were not allowed to enter the temple premise and under Article 26(b) of the constitution they had the right to manage their own affairs in matters of religion. Intervening in the inter-religious conflict, Supreme Court approved a compromise arrangement tilted in favour of rights of Harijans with a token concession to the rights of a religious denomination to exercise internal autonomy. Further Article 26(c) and (d) recognize the right of a religious denomination to own, to acquire and administer both movable and immovable property in accordance with law. However it was held in *Suriya Pal Singh vs. State of Uttar Pradesh* in the context of UP Abolition of Zamindari Act that the State could expropriate agricultural land dedicated to the maintenance of a Hindu deity with some compensation paid to the landlord and the High court held that there was only a change in the form of the property.

Article 17 debases the centrality of caste system by abolishing its practice and by making the enforcement of any disability arising out of it an offence punishable by law. Interestingly, Article 17 and 25(2) also intervene in the religious affairs of the citizen that the State promises to shelter.

Article 30(2) commits the state to give aid to educational institutions established and administered by religious communities. It also permitted religious instruction in educational institutions that are partly funded by the state.

These are significant departures from the 'wall of separation', view of the secular state. Even Article 30(1) recognises the rights of religious minorities to administer educational or religious institution, but it is a community based right and may be taken away for the interest of the greater. These features of the Indian constitution depart from the stereotypical western model – first, unlike the strict separation view that renders the state powerless in religious matters, they enjoin the state to interfere in religion and second, more importantly by giving powers to the state in the affairs of one religion, they necessitate a departure from strict neutrality or equidistance. Article 17, 25(2), 30(1) and (2) compromise the secularity of the Indian state. According to scholars like T.N. Madan, Ashis Nandy and Partha Chatterjee, the presence of these features in the Indian constitution shows why the Indian state cannot be really secular. By accepting community based rights for religious minorities and endorsing state-intervention in religion, the constitution depart from secular principles.

Article 15(4) states that nothing shall prevent the state from making any special provisions for the advancement of any social and educationally backward classes of citizens or for the scheduled castes and the scheduled tribes. First Amendment Act of 1954 means that the state in fact is allowed to perform reverse discrimination especially on behalf of the scheduled caste and tribes which are among the lowest in India's social order.

The vexed issues of reservation and religion can be gleaned through the provisions of Article 16(4), Article 15(4) specifically which allows the state to favour scheduled castes and tribes and other socially backward classes with regard to employment in state institutions.

Likewise in Articles 330(1) and 332(1) normalize reservations that take the form of communal awards. Reservation though aimed at affirmative action in practice tends to fan sectarian feelings.

Finally we have already mentioned that the constitution prohibits the collection of taxes for any particular religion (Article 27). This however is challenged by Article 290A which has been inserted by the 7th Amendment Act of 1956 and which states that a specified yearly sum is to be transferred from the states of Kerala and Madras to two religious funds for the maintenance of Hindu temples in those states. This clear breach of the overall sentiment of the constitution can perhaps be explained as a remnant of the old princely states of Travancore and Cochin, in which it was customary for the king to support Hindu temples. After the integration of these states in the Republic of India this custom was allowed to persist first in the state of Travancore-Cochin in 1949 and later into the state of Kerala in 1956.

In the years 1955 and 1956, a series of laws regulating marriage, divorce, adoption and maintenance for Hindus were passed by Indian state like Universal's Hindu Laws, 2004. This regulation and codification of Hindu personal law codified the right to divorce and cancelled the right of Hindu men to marry more than one wife. This act was severely criticized by orthodox Hindus as well as secular minded people who argued that it was not in accordance with Indian secularism. *Special Marriage Act of 1872* was passed in 1954 which specifies rules for a religiously neutral marriage (marriage in other religion) before a marriage officer. It may or may not accompany by religious rituals. Muslim personal laws have not, however, completely escaped codification by the state. As a result in 1985, Shah Bano a divorced Muslim women applied to Supreme Court and in contrast to Sharia law, won the right to maintenance. The Rajiv Gandhi government in order to please the Muslim opinion in 1986 succeeded in getting the so-called Muslim Women (Protection of Rights on Divorce) Act passed in parliament. The *Dissolution of Muslim Marriages Act from 1939* for the first time codified an aspect of Muslim Sharia law (Universal Muslim Laws, 2004).[28] Hence all these cases depict the state's intervention in religious or personal matter of the community which justifies the contra-secular features of Indian secularism – a departure from western secularism.

Studies on Secularism, accommodations of diversities in India have failed to look into the cases beyond the caged perspectives of communalized Hindu-Muslim relations. The operation of religious politics in the North East of India thus has remained 'uninteresting' or 'unimportant' for the intelligentsia from New Delhi and other metropoles. The discussions in the following chapters of this book attempts to fill the lacunae in the studies on Secularism and understanding secularism in India by drawing the attention to the Northeastern state of Mizoram.

Notes and References

1. Karan Singh. (1993). *Essays on Hinduism*. New Delhi: Ratna Sagar Publication. pp.99-101; Gerald James Larson. (2001). 'Introduction: The Secular State in a Religious Society' *in* Gerald James Larson. (ed.). (2001). *Religion and Personal Law in Secular India: A Call for Judgement*. Bloomington: Indiana University Press. pp.1-14.
2. Eugene Donald Smith. (1967). *India as a Secular State*. Princeton, USA: University of Pennsylvania Publications. p.5; Shabnum Tejani. (2008). *Indian Secularism: An intellectual History 1890-1950*. Bloomington: Indiana University Press.
3. R. S. Misra. (1996). *Hinduism and Secularism- A Critical Study. Delhi.* Motilal Banarsidass Pub. Pvt. Ltd. pp.101-103.
4. Saral Jingram. (1995). *Secularism in India, A Reappraisal*. New Delhi: Har Anand Publications. p. 35.
5. *Ibid.* pp. 84-85.
6. Thomas Pantham. (1997). 'Indian Secularism and its Critics.' *The Review of Politics*, Vol.59, No.3 (Summer), pp.523-524.
7. Ashis Nandy. (1998). 'The Politics of Secularism and the Recovery of Religious Toleration', *in* Rajeev Bharghav. (ed.) (1998). *Secularism and its Critics*. New Delhi: Oxford University Press Publications. pp.324-25; Ashis Nandy. (2007). 'Closing the Debate on Secularism: A Personal Statement', *in* Anuradha Dingwaney Needham and Rajeswari Sunder Rajan. (ed.). (2007). *The Crisis of Secularism in India*. New Delhi: Permanent Black Publications. pp.107-117.
8. *Ibid.*
9. *Ibid.*
10. *Ibid.*
11. Pantham. *Op.cit.*
12. T. N. Madan. (1998). 'Secularism in its Place', *in* Rajeev Bharghav (ed.) (1998). *Op.cit*. pp.298-99.
13. Pantham. *Op.cit.*
14. Partha Chatterjee. (1998). 'Secularism and Tolerance', *in* Rajeev Bharghav (ed.) (1998). *Op.cit.*; Partha Chatterjee. (2007). 'The Contradictions of Secularism' *in* Anuradha Dingwaney Needham and Rajeswari Sunder Rajan. (ed.). (2007). *Op.cit*. pp. 141-150.
15. *Ibid.*

16. *Ibid.*
17. Achin Vanaik. (1997). *Communalism Contested: Religion, Modernity and Secularism*. New Delhi: Vistaar Publications. pp. 306-308.
18. *Ibid.*
19. Akeel Bilgrami. (1998). 'Secularism, Nationalism and Modernity', *in* Rajeev Bharghav (ed.) (1998). *Op.cit.* pp.408.
20. *Ibid.*
21. Sayeed Abu Ayyub. (1968). 'Secularism and Jawaharlal Nehru' *in* V.K. Sinha (ed.) (1968). *Secularism in India*. New Delhi: Lalvani Pub.House. pp.127- 129.
22. Neera Chandhoke. (2004). 'Representing the Secular Agenda for India', *in* Hasan Mushirul (ed.) (2004). *Will Secular India Survive*. New Delhi: Imprint One Publication. pp.57-61.
23. T. N. Madan. (1997). *Modern Myths, Locked Minds; Secularism and Fundamentalism in India*. New Delhi: Oxford University Press. pp.116-118.
24. The Commissioner, Hindu ... vs Sri Lakshmindra Thirtha Swamiar ... on 16 April, 1954. https://indiankanoon.org/doc/1430396/ accessed 10/10/2017. Also, *See*, Rononjoy Sen.(2007). 'Legalizing Religion: The Indian Supreme Court and Secularism'. *Policy Studies 30*. Washington: East-West Centre.
25. Shabnum Tejani. (2007). 'Secularisms Historical Background', *in* Anuradha Dingwaney Needham and Rajeswari Sunder Rajan. (ed.). (2007). *Op.cit.* pp.82-86.
26. The Untouchability (Offences) Act, 1955, Act No.22 Of 1955. http://theindianlawyer.in/statutesnbareacts/acts/u14.html accessed on 10/10/2017.
27. Sri Venkataramana Devaruand ... vs The State Of Mysore And ... on 8 November, 1957. 1958 AIR 255, 1958 SCR 895 https://indiankanoon.org/doc/1896039/ accessed on 10/10/2017. Also, *See,* Granville Austin. (2001). 'Religion, Personal Law, and Identity in India', pp.15-23; Susanne H. Rudolph and Lloyd I. Rudolph. (2001). 'Living with Difference in India: Legal Pluralism and Legal Universalism in Historical context', pp. 36-68 *in* Gerald James Larson. (ed.). (2001). *Op.cit.*
28. *See*, for details Neera Chandhoke. (1999). *Beyond Secularism: The Rights of Religious Minorities.* New Delhi: Uxford University Press; Craig Duncan. (2009). *Shah Bano: The Dilemma of Religious Liberty and Sex Equality.* Ithaca: Cornell University; Sylvia Vatuk. (2001). 'Where will she go? What will she do? Paternalism towards Muslim Women in the administration of Muslim Personal Law in Contemporary India' *in* Gerald James Larson. (ed.). (2001). *Op.cit.* pp. 226-250.

2

Proselytisation and the Zo Hnahthlak

Proselytisation never engages in an empty space, like an encounter it engages in multifaceted layers in a living space, a space where cultures are constantly in the process of making and unmaking. The colonial encounter experienced in the then Lushai Hills actively engaged in the process of 'taming the wild tribes' from 'head-hunters' to 'soul hunters'. Needless to say the colonial encounter was marked by the project of understanding the 'oriental'. This underlying concern can be located in the several colonial documents and memories of colonial administrators and missionaries who worked endlessly among the *Zo hnahthlak*.

The encounter with Colonialism initiated two marked process among the *Zo hnahthlak*: one threw open the process of Proselytisation, Education, Medicine and an alien style of life and belief system; second threw open the process of the assimilation of the chauvinistic traditional[1] Zo practices into the Judeo-Christian, and internalization of the Victorian influences that can be summed up as the 'Localization of the Gospel'. Among many things the chapter first attempts to engage in locating the commonalities and differences in the outlook of Christianity[2] and the traditional Zo way of life. Second, it attempts to chart the spread of Christianity and the many revivals in the Lushai/Mizo Hills. Third, it attempts to accentuate the marked indigenization and emergence of Zo Christianity and practices such as 'spontaneous dancing and singing' (*'Hlim Rui'* (Intoxicated with bliss), spiritual healings etc. Fourth, it attempts to chart the contestations over the idea of Zo Christianity and the shifts and faults underling cultural revivalism and mushrooming of 'faith healers', self styled free churches among the *Zo hnahthlak*. The colonial encounter injected western ideas concerning

Map 2.1
Map depicting the Zo Territory

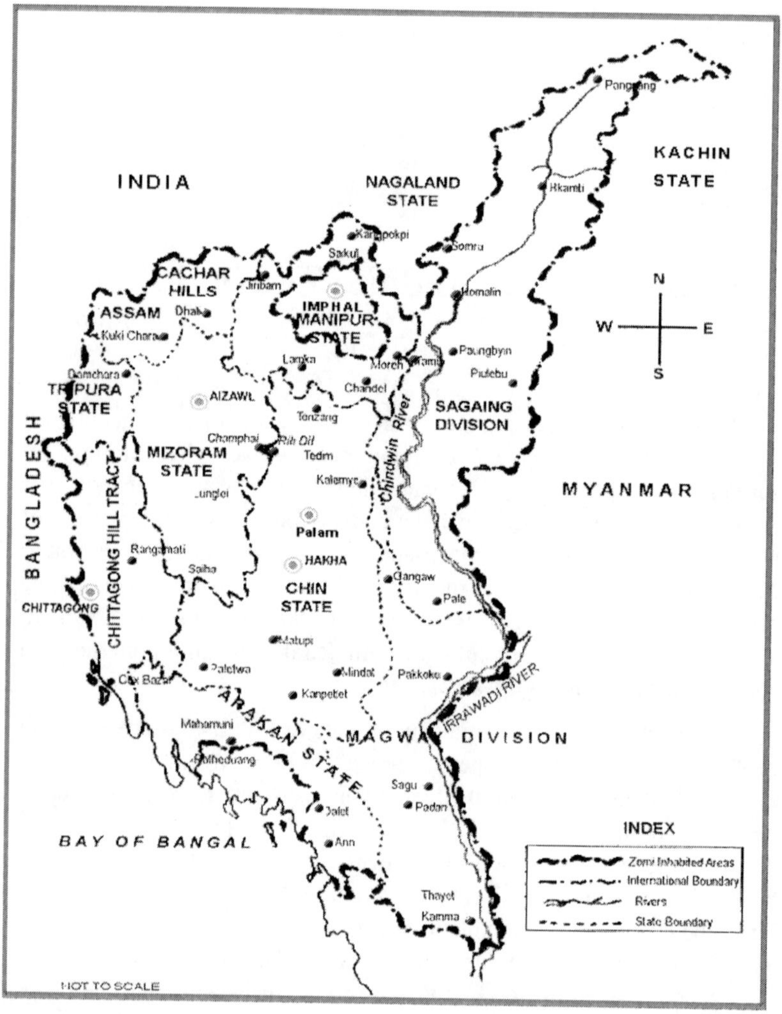

Source: http://www.zogam.org. (Official website of the Zo Reunification Organisation) (accessed on 18 June 2006; 29 January 2010; 15 December 2016).

The 'Ethnic Maps' of the numerous tribes in the region shows interesting trends first, they reflect the contest over territorial claims; second, there is a strong urge to usurp and override rival claims; third, the cartographic engagement unravels the notion of memory, folklore, botanical metaphors, places and sites as markers of the imprints of the concurrent wave of tribal migrations in time and space.

education, health and medicine, hygiene and house-keeping, belief in Christianity and the unquestioned acceptance of the superiority of the white man's belief system and life style over that of the native's understanding and appreciation of their world system.[3] However, the white man's ideas and hegemony were not accepted without stiff resistance. The series of border skirmishes and 'wars' waged by the Zo chiefs and reciprocal British initiatives to tackle the troublesome wild tribes stand proof to this contest over territorial claims and ideas of belief systems.[4]

The Elites among the Zo hnahthlak

The emergence of the *'New Elites'* marked the birth of a 'Middle class'[5] which was conspicuously absent in the traditional Zo society. The creation of the *New Elites* at the administrative level and also the religious level was fuelled by the Missionary activities of education. 'A new class of educated Lushais came up under the sponsorship of the Missionaries. This middle class explanation is effective for understanding 'identity politics' among the tribes in Mizoram. The introduction of money economy thus boosted the emergence of the middle class in the Zo society.[6] The common people were gaining new status and acquiring purchasing power and in turn felt confident enough to challenge and raise their voices against traditional autocratic authority of the chiefs. The exposure to the outside world through foreign travel during the world wars[7] opened the gates of consciousness and began to have its ripples even in the Zo Hills.

Despite these structural-functional changes, the internal affairs were left to the chief and his elders who ruled their units according to the customary laws of the land and the British administration intervened only when the chiefs went beyond their jurisdiction. Initially, the British manipulated the traditional chiefs and their elders and later when these traditional power structures were fully under their control, they increased their numbers by acting as 'kingmakers' in the Zo hills or Lushai Hills as it was called then. When the Lushai Hills were taken over by the Raj, there were some odd 60 chiefs which by the 1940s increased to more than 400.[8] The increase in the number of new chiefs speaks in volumes about the divide and rule policy of the British and their role as 'King-makers'. This policy of the British towards the Chiefs in the Lushai Hills was a mirror-image of the policies followed elsewhere in the colonial world having tribal population.[9] For instance, initially the British supported and relied on individual Chiefs and after sometime they strategically created newer centres of power and gradually ousted the older traditional structures. The British skillfully manipulated both these elites to maintain its indirect hold over the Zo territory.[10]

In effect, the British Superintendent and the Zo/Mizo Chiefs continued to rule as virtual dictators, and no organised protest was possible due to the support provided by the District Superintendent to the Chiefs. Towards the end of colonial rule, the resentment against the Chiefs had gained momentum all over the Lushai Hills. Western education, occupational security along with a sense of economic confidence and the exposure to the foreign worlds[11] made the first generation youths confident to control their own destiny. They found it difficult to accept the traditional authority and the unquestioning obedience that it called for that is they wanted freedom from the chiefs and the customary discipline. This individualism was principally based on their superior academic qualification cemented by comfortable salaried jobs.[12] The formation of the Young Lushai Association (YLA)[13] in 1935 accelerated the anti-chief wave and also McCall's District Chiefs Durbar[14] (1941) helped shape the political consciousness in the Lushai Hills.

It is pertinent to note that the Colonial Administrators and Colonial Missionaries though often at crossroads due to the very nature of their goals/missions towards the 'wild tribes of the North East' of British India worked in a loose collaboration in the Lushai Hills. The loose collaboration was infact the operation of a convenient demarcation of areas or spheres where the two could independently prevail. The Superintendent or the political agent was considered more powerful in 'this world', while the Missionaries or the ecclesiastical agents were masters holding the key to 'that world'. The understanding of 'life while on earth' i.e., the life world, and 'life after death' i.e., the life either in heaven (*Pialral*) or hell (*Meidil*) defined the blueprints for the imagery of the realms of 'politics' and that of 'ecclesiastics', among the Zo/Mizo Christians.

The Missionaries both European/American (*Sap* (Whites)) and native were looked as those holding the key to the world of education, medicine and Heaven. The material progression that contact with any of these two sets of colonial power accelerated was very difficult for the Zo tribes to resist. For instance, accepting colonial educational drive and Christianity enabled the 'wild tribes' to get 'permanent salaried jobs' either in the colonial administration or with the Missionaries. In all cases the steady rise of salaried persons among the *Zo hnahthlak* introduced 'newer class categories' in the British sense of social stratification and changed the traditional ordering of things and peoples position which was largely birth based. The salaried class eventually shaped and positioned itself as the 'middle class', working class regular salaried persons with strong Christian morals and faith that is the '*Pathian ring*'[15] ('believers in the living God').

Commonalities and Differences: Christianity and the Traditional Zo Way of Life

The annexation of the Zo territory by the British brought about some structural-functional changes. For instance in the pre-colonial times the 'Traditional Elites'-the Lal (Chiefs), the Lalupas (Elders) and Village Officials were the medium through which, religion, culture, administration, jurisdiction, economy and politics were determined. The Village Officials like the *Puithiam*, the *Sadawt* and the *Tlakpawi*, who were different categories of priests, helped the Chief to perform the religious functions. The other officials like the *Khawchhiar*, the *Tlangau*, the *Zalen*, and the *Ramhual* etc. helped the Chief to perform administrative- judicial and socio-economic functions.[16] The twin process of the systematic replacement of the 'Traditional Elites' by the 'New Elites' i.e. the 'Black Coats' at the religious level and the retention of the Traditional Elites at the political-administrative level[17] took place as a result of colonial contact. However, this does not suggest that the traditional elites were totally uprooted or displaced from their positions of authority; it merely meant that a new centre of power was created by the British to counter-check the hold of the Traditional Elites. The Lushai Hills under the Government of India Act, 1935, was administered as an 'Excluded Area', over which the State Government of Assam had no jurisdiction. The district was administered by the special powers of the Governor, there was no representative from the district to the State Legislature nor was any political activity permitted. As a result the British Superintendent and the Mizo Chiefs continued their dictatorial rule. The end of colonial rule and the fear of the New Elites of reverting back to the Pre-Colonial system of administration of the Chiefs lead to a Commoners Movement, resulting in the birth of a political party called the Mizo Union on April 9, 1946.[18] This was one of the first instances of rebellion against tradition in the Mizo society, resulting in the permanent displacement of the Traditional Elites by 'the Politicians' (political parties) at the political level. The British skillfully manipulated both these elites to maintain its indirect hold over the Zo territory.[19] The New Elites were the direct product of British colonialism and their existence totally depended on their allegiance to the foreign rulers. Naturally the nouveau elites eulogized and emulated the colonial masters and in doing so they became the 'mimicked man', the '*kalasahebs*' (the coloured gentleman or the Anglicized native gentleman), the new privileged class in the Zo/Mizo society.[20]

Entanglements of Religion and Politics

The two external symbols of power, namely the British Superintendent (Politico-Administrative head) and Christian Missionaries were considered to be superior[21] by the primitive tribes because of numerous reasons.[22] Most evidently because the British were able to defeat and subdue the most powerful and revered Zo Chiefs at the physical level; and partly because the Whiteman's way of life and religion delivered them from fear of evil, death and uncertainty at the psychological level. As evident from the names given by the Zo tribes to these colonial symbols for instance '*Lal man tu*' (one who catches the chiefs) implying to the Superintendent; and '*Thlarau man tu*' (one who catches the spirit) implying to the Missionaries. Christianity thus began to play an overwhelming role in Mizoram because of these internal and external factors.[23]

Religion and Politics were thus considered superior, powerful and therefore more alluring, this led to the 'male-fying' of religion and politics as the domain of the superior and reserved for men. By the same token, the Mizo patriarchy under the impact of Christian traditions began to view economics and the notions of business and profit to be both sensuous and materialistic and linked them with the notions of original sin and sexuality. The arena of Economics was automatically ascribed a secondary existence and women being excluded from the realms of spirituality and politics became fit alongside the marginal groups i.e. the 'Vai'[24] and the Poi' (Burmese) to occupy it[25] and form the 'Triad of the Marginals'.[26] The 'Nexus of Patriarchy' associated the 'Triad of the Marginals'-women, Vai's and Poi's (Burmese) with moral degradation, sin, immorality and everything signified by the word 'Khawvel' (worldly).[27]

Christianity and the Missionary activities of the Welsh missionaries in the then Lushai Hills through 1894 and beyond, in some form, brought about 'temporal relief' to women[28] through the systematic decline of the traditional symbols of patriarchy namely, the *Zawlbuk*[29] and the Chieftainship.[30] The erstwhile oppressed section passively welcomed the change but failed miserably to understand the temporality of the underlying politics of proselytisation. For instance, the Colonizers initially supported the cause of women and the marginals; but once the mission of proselytisation was achieved, the cause of women and marginals was systematically sidelined. In other words the freedom from tradition was temporal; it was no more than eyewash and did not help in changing in the positionality of women, children and the minority tribes and other marginalized groups in the Zo society. Further reaffirming the argument that sole motive of the Christian Missionaries and the British Raj was not just proselytisation but largely to 'tame' the 'wild tribes' of the frontier regions and annex their land so as to serve the commercial interests of the British Tea Plantations in the North- East of India.[31] The Colonial economic interest constricted and eventually smothered the local economies of the native tribes in the region. For instance, the 'Indian rubber' that was a natural resource of the Lushai Hills and Chin Hills[32]; and 'Cotton' that was in abundance in the Chittagong Hills and Lakher Hills.[33] The encroachment of the Raj into the hills and plains of the region was strongly aimed at the possibilities of economic gains from the land beyond the frontiers of the region into Southeast Asia.

Drawing heavily from my earlier writings I argue that the purpose of a 'Customized-Localized Gospel'[34] was to suit the understandings of the 'primitive tribes'. The content of the Gospel was decoded into a language that was receptive to the 'savage tribes'. For instance, the missionaries and the New Elites/ native new converts i.e. the Black Coats often equated Pu Pawla with St. Peter's who had a similar function in the Christian belief system. The Missionaries and the 'Black-coats', in order to win over the natives, also began to simultaneously equate '*Pathian*' (the traditional Mizo/ Zo male divinity of the heavens) with the 'image' of the Biblical 'God' (Father ('*Lalpa*') of the Trinity; and projected Jesus as the 'son' ('*Fa-pa*') of '*Pathian*' (hereafter *Pathian* and *Lalpa* enmeshed into each other) etc. in order to suit the sensibilities of the Zo tribes. There were plethora of reasons for the passive acceptance of the Gospel by the marginalized sections and the active resistance of the hegemonic group i.e. the 'Traditional Elites' to defend their power within the traditional fold. The whole process of interpreting the Gospel according to local situations proved very useful to the western missionaries.[35]

The result of such a customized strategy was that the erstwhile enemies of the Raj namely the Chiefs and the Elders who posed as big boulders in the path of the steady encroachment and extension of the highway to Southeast Asia could be easily befriended and convinced to become 'believers'. 'Believers' in not just the benevolence of the Raj and become recognized/ permanent parts as agents of the extractive rental Colonial economy; but also in the sense of conversion to a new religion, and engage in conversation with Christ and the idioms of Christianity in the *everyday*. The everyday becomes webbed in the observation of rituals, prayers during '*Chhungkua eikhawm*' (family breakfast, dinner), tutored prayers and hymns in schools and the like, the everyday thus becomes a canvass for the praise of the Lord and thanks giving to the almighty. The penetration of the Christian notions of 'being one in/with Jesus' enters not just in everyday but even in the 'application of non-secular law and order, Civilian Policing, Magisterial judgements'[36] etc., often engaging in palatable and unpalatable conversations. For instance, officers of the Civilian Police in Mizoram have time and again found it easy to extract confessions from suspects by asking them to confess 'in the name of the Lord, who is all forgiving'. Similarly, offenders and rapists have been pardoned all 'in the name of Christ/God' ('*Isuah/Lalpa hmingin ngaihdam*'). The inter-weaving of Christianity with Politics surfaced pronouncedly during the high tide of insurgency led by the MNF. The MNF interpreted every act of the Central Government from New Delhi to be 'anti-Christian' for instance holding of Public examinations on Sundays, or official dignitaries' visits on Sunday etc. Nehru's visit on 3rd April 1953 which happened to be a Sunday construed as hurting Christian sentiments. Likewise the curbs and restrictions[37] imposed by the Government of India on the foreign Missionary activities in the region were interpreted as a deliberate move to hurt and stall Christianity. The MNF instilled the idea that Mizoram and the Christian people of Mizoram were not safe in India: 'Like the Muslims have been fighting for their 'Jehad', the MNF had propagated that they are fighting a war for God.'[38]

The following extract from the 'Mizoram Municipal Steering Committee, 2006' reflects the emotional appeal of that Christianity has on governance in the state:

> *Pathianin duh taka a siam Khawvela Mizoten ram kan neih chhun Mizoram hi chen rengna tlak siam tur chuan kan chenna khua theuh enkawl thei thuneihna nei ENKAWLTU kan mamawh a.*[39]
> (Mizoram, the only territory allocated by the Christ for the Mizo needs a better administrative mechanism so as to make it fit for living for the future generations).

The Colonial encounter and the Localization of the Gospel contributed to dual process of the assimilation of the chauvinistic traditional Zo practices into the already male centric Christian religion[40] and vice versa. There were many commonalities as well as differences in the outlook of Christianity and the traditional Zo way of life.[41] The missionaries sidelined the cause of women and the marginalized as they found this strategy to be more useful for their goal of mass proselytisation. In order to gain the confidence and support of the patriarchal mindset, the church introduced Victorian morality, which became the guiding beacon for judging everyday Mizo social relations. Thus in a way the language of the mission became sexualized and gendered[42] fusing the elements of patriarchal chauvinism inherent in the Mizo socio-religious system with that of the patriarchal biases in the Judeo-Christian traditions.

With the introduction of Christianity and the internalization of the abstracts from the Old Testament like the story of the Creation-Genesis, the fall from Eden and Original Sin etc., controlling the sexuality of women and mapping their spatial domain[43] became the holy goal of the Zo Christian world. In other words notions of spirituality, divinity and God[44] began to be used as weapons to oppress Mizo women.

The transition from the indigenous traditional religion to Christianity had both liberating as well as oppressing effects on women and the marginalized sections of the Mizo society.[45] Most writers focus on the positive effect of proselytisation on the primitive Zo tribes and turn a blind eye on the wholesale slaughter of the indigenous Zo/Mizo culture.[46] No doubt Christianity accelerated the momentum of change in the Mizo society from a primitive stage economy to a modern one and had evangelical effects on the Mizo society ushering in the high tide of western enlightenment, rationality, education -scientific temper, morality, politics, and the power to read and internalize the 'Holy Gospel'. [47] It however failed to end the conservative attitudes and bring about a change in the position of women and the marginalized.[48]

The inherent contradictions between 'tradition and modernity' in the Zo society continue to undermine the very existence of women and the marginalized. For instance, the criteria requisite for entry into heaven (*Pialral*) while the Traditional Mizo society required that men (married or single) should have sex with as many women as possible during one's lifetime for attaining '*Pialral*' while in the case of women, it was just the opposite. Women had to preserve her virginity and incase she lied about her sexual purity she would anyway be caught by *Pu Pawla*, who like St. Peter's would be waiting at the gates of '*Pialral*' (heaven) and detect all illegal entry. Here, it must be noted that no single women (even if virgin) could enter heaven alone, she was to be escorted either by her father or husband i.e. male relations because women were believed to be directionless, just like the crab and therefore would lose her way. Moreover, spinsterhood was not respected and marriage was a norm expected for women and the pivot around which the life of women revolved[49]

The spread of Christianity and the Revivals in the Lushai/Mizo Hills

The Lushai Hills (Mizo Hills) witnessed a series of revivals: 1906, 1913, 1918, 1930, 1935, 1948, 1984, 1988 and 1990 that enveloped the Zo tighter into the mould of Christianity. 'Becoming one in/with Christ', 'spontaneous dancing and singing' ('*Hlim Rui*'), 'bouts of fits' etc., marked these revivals. Interestingly women played a significant role in the display of uninhibited dance in their calling for the divine during these revivals. Fanon's understanding of 'dance as liberation for the colonized' maybe employed to understand the reasons why Mizo women who in normal everyday situations play such a timid role of silent spectators take refuge to uninhibited display of dance during these revivals and spiritual healings.[50] Change in the Mizo society has been considered to be a change for convenience rather than progress and naturally it has been caught in the dilemma of tradition and modernity. For instance, changes in the laws of Inheritance[51], which can be considered to be reflective of modern democracy culminating in the new found 'Economic independence' of women, has not resulted in changing the power relations in the Mizo society. The *Mizo Hnam Dan*[52] i.e. traditional laws continue to dictate the terms of Marriage price[53], dowry and divorce. Even though Mizo women enjoyed considerable freedom[54] in '*Nula-rim*' (courting), marriage, sex, and divorce, they somewhat played a muted role when it came to the matters of property, decision-making, and politics. These freedoms granted to Mizo women are not backed by evangelical motives but are accepted merely for the fact that they are advantageous to men.[55] Women face challenges even in the field of the Mission and find it difficult to break the glass ceiling even in the field of being ordained. In order to gain the confidence and support of the patriarchal mindset, the church introduced 'Victorian morality', which became the guiding beacon for judging everyday Zo/Mizo social relations. Thus in a way, the language of the mission, fused the elements of patriarchal chauvinism inherent in the Mizo socio-religious system, with that of the patriarchal biases in the Judeo-Christian traditions.[56]

Proselytisation replaced indigenous way of life including past time games, everyday life activities such as evening chats/gossips among peer groups of both sexes etc., by activities like attending Sunday schools, choir practices, church services etc. The proselytisation to Christianity has added another dimension to contradictions at the level of 'social conduct' and 'private conduct'. The Zo/Mizo society today is in a dilemma whether to opt for the glitters of the contemporary globalized liberal societies or to tread the path of the Holy Gospel and strive for the life beyond or strike a balance between the two. This dilemma is specially found among the young educated youths who have completed their education in other states of India and have returned back to Mizoram to work in their home state. It becomes very difficult for the Zo/Mizo youths to digest the dictates of the church and the moral police especially, when it comes to dress code and watching television programmes etc. There are instances where the church has imposed restrictions[57] on inter-community relationships, using the internet for chatting, surfing (pornographic material), listening to 'heavy metal' music etc. The overwhelming encapsulation of the everyday of Zo/Mizo life by the Church and its agencies can be absorbed from the following details of a news item in Times of India dated January 9th, 1989:

> In a state where 85 percent of the population is Christian, the Church is playing a vital role in the 21st January elections to the State Assembly and has even indirectly supported the Congress in a significant message to the people of the state, ten denominations

of the Church, active in the state, have laid down guidelines for the voters and candidates, to be followed during the election. The message, issued shortly after the imposition of President's Rule on September 7th last year (1988), however, does not name any party or individual. During the last (1987) elections, the MNF was voted to power, as the Church had given a call to vote for that party which would bring peace to the State… "In the course of the campaign, we (*the Church*) deem it best that no public feast be held under the name of any party. The different parties, instead of campaigning from house to house, may launch their campaigns through public meetings. Party politics with its potential to create antagonism loosened the solidarity of the Mizo community and is also a stumbling block for the Churches."[58]

Our Church, Their Church: Emergence of Hybrid Christianity

The *Zo hnahthlak* post proselytisation began to absorb the teaching of the Church and the obnoxious presence of the 'Black covered, Red bordered Bible' marked the 'Christian piangthar Zo/Mizo'. The notion of *piangthar* that is 'born again' Christian was both intoxicating and contagious. Proselytisation also injected a close affinity to the institution of the Church and an identification with the materialization of the Church in the form a building. The early converts invested their time in terms of days ('*Ni*') and

Pic 2.1: shows children, women and men in the Vantlang hnatlang (Voluntary communal service) displaying tlawmngaihna for building the house of the God. Mission Veng Church construction under Rev John Meirion Lloyd

labour in terms of able bodied persons ('*Tha*') including women and children of both sexes to volunteer in the project of building the Churches on every hill. The result was an emotional connect with the Church and its paraphernalia. The ever mobile people were tied to the sentimentalities of the Chruch- their prayer hall, the House of their new found God. Such a connectedness swept the erstwhile marauding wild tribes to a more settled life close to 'their Church'. The notion of *Kan Kohhran* that is 'Our Chruch' began to evolve steadily and rootedly into the cosmology of the *Zo hnahthlak*.

Pic 2.2: shows men in the Vantlang hnatlang (Voluntary communal service) displaying tlawmngaihna for building the house of the God. Mission Church construction under Rev John Meirion Lloyd.

The encounter with Christiandom and the realignment of the earlier/ traditional Zo belief system introduced a strange concoction of practices and clannish cults further complexifying the Zo Christian Cosmology. Instances of the 'clannish cult Churches'[59] such as the 'Lalzahavara-Nu Diheli' (around Sangau Khua/Village)[60], 'Enoka Pawl' (around Salem Veng), 'Channa Pawl' (around Baktawng Khua/Village) can be cited as reflecting the same. These clannish cult Churches incorporated strong elements from the traditional Zo practices while claiming to be the new Churches among the *Zo hnahthlak*. The indigenization of Christianity also marked the evolve of resistance to both Christianity and the Colonial ways as emphasized by the Missionaries. For instance, the Channa Pawl which evolved in Baktawng

Pic 2.3: shows women and men in the Vantlang hnatlang (Voluntary communal service) displaying tlawmngaihna for building the house of the God. Mission Veng Church construction under Rev John Meirion Lloyd.

Village some 100 kilometers from Aizawl derived its existence to the use of the traditional drum i.e. *Khuang* as an item of worship among the ancestors of the cult founders. The Welsh Missionaries had strongly voiced their concerns over such practice and banned the worship of the *Khuang* as practiced by the ancestors of Challianchanna. Challianchanna and his brother then founded the rebel church grounding their ancestral practices into the mould of Christianity as preached by the Welsh Missionaries and styling the cult church as 'Channa Pawl' or 'Lalpa Kohhran' in the early 1930s.

Christianity manifests itself very differently in different places conditioned by specific social realities. The Christian experience among each of the Zo tribes intune with the experience of Christianity elsewhere throughout South Asia shows points of convergences and manoeuvrings of those receiving the 'new religion' and way of life. Clannish, intra-tribal, inter-tribal, animistic/traditional practices coupled with cartographic zoning of the Zo people have largely affected the moorings to the same. Christianity amidst the ostensible homogeneity among the *Zo hnahthlak* is veritably fragmented. Heterogeneity with a projected homogeneity is one of the marked paradoxes of Christianity among the *Zo hnahthlak*.

The Cartographic zoning for instance injected a sense of marked difference among Zo tribes in the region. The Welsh Presbyterian actively worked among the Northern tribes while the London Baptist Missionary Society worked among the Southern tribes. It is very interesting to note that the cartographic zoning also affected the projection and degree of belief in Christianity for instance Northerners began to stereotype Southerners as 'less believers'; and Southerners stereotyped the northern Christians as 'less believers' while retaining and claiming the position of 'strong believers' for their respective tribes. The denominational divide also worked very interesting complexities among the Zo Christians. For instance, from the Colonial times the Roman Catholics were considered to be non-Christian in belief system because of the relegated position of Mary; and interestingly the localized Christianity as practiced among the Zo does not proscribe divinity to women.[61]

Being a Zo, Being a Christian: Hybridization in the Everyday

It is interesting to note that *'Being a Zo'* and *'Being a Christian'*[62] are the two issues around which religious identity politics in Mizoram is developed. The first issue has problems of parameters of definitions and it remains contested. While the second issue has elements of experiential-ness embedded to it as evident from the casual everyday use of language *'Khristian nilo in an hrethiam lovang'* ('Non-Christians will not be able to understand') to brush side those who do not belong to the Church as not being able to understand the Bible and its teachings. Both these issues are projected in the state-building process of an *'Ideal Zo Christian State'*.

The use of traditional musical instruments like the *Khuang* (traditional drum), *Dar* (Burmese brass bell), alongside western instruments like the guitar or the option of wearing of traditional '*puanchei*' (wrap around worn by Mizo women) for Zo/Mizo women as an alternate to the wedding gown as many such examples to show the marked indigenization of the practices of Zo Christianity. The Whiteman's way of life and religion[63]delivered the tribes from fear of evil, death and uncertainty of a war prone migratory life at the psychological level.[64] 'Religion and Politics' thus began to play an overwhelming role in Mizoram[65] and began to be considered superior, powerful and therefore more alluring.

A great force in the process of *Zo* integration has been the Christian faith, which in fifty years turned Mizoram and many *Zo* inhabited areas into a Christian land. The newly zealous *Zo* converts took it as their privileged burden to tell the 'Good News' to their kindred tribes and many had volunteered to go to the heathen *Zo* areas to preach the Gospel. These apostle-like preachers carried the good tidings along with new Christian hymns in the Lushai dialect, which the pioneer missionaries employed as a vehicle to spread the Gospel. As a result, Lushai (*Duhlian*) dialect quickly developed into a rich language to become an effective instrument for spreading the gospel and *Zo* integration. The first Bible translation and many other pioneering publications among the *Zo* tribes were in Lushai that subsequently came to be known as the 'Mizo language', a language that became the link language of the *Zo* people. Wherever *Zo* preachers carried the Gospel and new churches were planted, they also implanted *Zo*-ness, thus paving the way for a re-unification. Therefore, next to their common ethnic root, Christianity has become the most important bonding force of the *Zo* people. A *'Zo'* professing any other faith except the traditional religion (animism) is considered by the majority *Zo* Christians as not only a renegade but an alien. Being a *Zo* and a Christian is like a coin with two faces.[66]

The Church's influence is really deep and daily life is encircled by it. The church has become Mizoised through *ruaithre* (community feasting) and *'zai leh lam'* (song and dances). Zaliana observes:

> Alongside religion, the 'Denominational' factor has greatly influenced the Zo/Mizo politics. The undivided Aizawl district had a more welcoming attitude. While in the south *(chhim)* one had to have a local network or local connections to have a footing into the politics of that region. Most of the political leaders in Mizoram come from *Chhim* (southern). Excluding Lalthanhawla most leaders from Ch. Chhunga, Dengthuama, Laldenga, T. Sailo and others all had *Chhim* (southern) links and were under London Baptist influence. They also were the first set of Mizos to come under the influence of western education, religion and politics.[67]

The influence of religion can also be understood why the early leaders decided to do away the clannish affiliations and its markers for creating an egalitarian political identity cutting across clan and sub-tribe identity. For instance, politicians and people at large in Mizoram hardly use their clan names or tribe names and instead use their first names. Politics in order to survive and create an *'Ideal Zo Christian State'*, therefore crucified clannish identity and its markers at the altar because 'if there is no crucifixion there is no rising'.[68] The church leaders in turn maintain a dignified, respectable and non partisan stand. It is because of the role of the Church and its agencies that the Election Commission labelled Mizoram as a role model for other states in India. Humour at times reflects the societal actuality for instance a popular aphorism: *'Mizoram-ah chuan Sawrkar a lalber a, Kohhran a thuber'* ('In Mizoram the Government is the highest authority, and the

Church has the final say') well sums up the dominance of the Church and its agencies. 'The government and the bureaucracy have not been able to touch the masses as the Church. The elites try to go with the tide and without any spirituality they enter the Church activities in order to gain popularity and mass appeal. So in short, they dictate terms in their interest through the church.'[69]

Christianity spread like forest fire in Mizoram after the 60s MNF rebellion precisely because the post-rebellion psychological trauma compelled people take refuge in culture and religion in order to find solace. The post-rebellion trauma was exploited by the evangelists to convert because to convert more people to the fold of Christianity meant a more secured life for the evangelist in the next world.[70] Similarly there was a growth in music and education in the post-rebellion times. The growth and rise of music and education can be seen as 'healing' the Zo/Mizo society. Christianity, Education, Music, in other words, "Religion" and "Culture" became important markers of *Zo Identity*. The predominance of religion in *Zomi* politics reflects itself through the constant references made to God (*Pathian*).

Contestations over the Idea of Zo Christianity

Healing and spirituality have transcendental commonalities and links. The experience of proselytisation and the waves of revivalist movements coupled with the lament for the loss of a nostalgic past resulted in the emergence of paradoxes in Christianity among the Zo people. The emergence of faith healers or '*khoithei dam thei*'/'*Chul dam thei*' (healing through touch), and self styled free churches or indigenized churches with clannish practices are interesting offshoots of proselytisation among the *Zo hnahthlak*.

The open reception that the 'wild tribes' gave to the alien region infused enthusiasm in the Colonial Administrators who in turn began to employ suitable tactical moves to suit the psychology of the tribes and their understanding of the divine. For instance, the introduction of the *'Customised-Localised Gospel'* facilitated to an extent the unification of the different warring clans under a common 'Lushai' identity and common *'Duhlian'* dialect in the Zo/Mizo Hills. The introduction of the 'Localised Gospel' was not easy for the Missionaries as is evident from the B.M.S. Report presented by R.A. Lorrain in 1913 where he mentions:

> Our first message as soon as we could speak the language was a Saviour from Sin. But the people had no sense of sin and felt no need for a Saviour.…We proclaimed Jesus as a vanquisher of the devil…This to the Lushais was "Good News" indeed and exactly met with great need.

The Christian Church rendered three major services among the tribes of the region: first, it liberated the tribes from the fear of evils spirits and from the evils of head-hunting and continuous war-fare and blood-revenge; second, it established centres of education and; third, it provided extensive medical service at a time when no Government or other private agency bothered about the tribals.[71] Christianity, through the weapons of Education and Medicine, attracted the savages, mostly in the case of the Zo Hills as is evident from the accounts of Missionaries like Lorrain ((1912)1988). The attraction to 'Western Medicine', on the part of the 'wild tribes' can be rationalised through the logic of 'Social healing' and 'physical healing'.[72] Medicine brought about emancipation from 'pain' which had always been the innate desire of the tribes lacking indigenous medicinal knowledge. For instance, the Zo/Mizo tribes had limited knowledge of 'herbs and cure', and relied more on the 'ritualised nature of treatment', that is sacrifices and appeasing evil spirits/demons.[73] These 'ritualised treatment' were slow and the success rate were poor. On the other hand western medical science provided instant remedy to physical ailments. Naturally, western medicine began to have is large following and the Missionaries exploited this faith and ready acceptance of 'western Medicine' to their advantage. For instance, D.E Jones in the 1st Years Reports mentions that 'Some are ready to believe in Christ if they will be kept from illnesses'. And the attraction to 'Education' can be rationalised through the logic of the incentives added to the education process in the initial stages. For instance, Lorrain ((1912) 1988) mentions about the 'free food', 'free lodgings' etc. provided to the tribes as incentives to attract them to schools. Such incentives like 'free food', 'free shelters' would mean great things for tribals residing in the remote inaccessible hilly terrain without a permanent economy and limited productive agricultural know how.

The most important factor that contributed to the popularity of Christianity among the *Zo* tribes was the psychological emancipation that it promised. These tribes were not 'demon worshippers' but 'demon appeasers' as is evident from their rituals and practices. The Gospel with message of a powerful male God and promise of emancipation from pain not just in this life but also the next attracted the wild tribes all the more. Naturally the Missionaries were successful in winning the confidence of the tribes of the region. The Khasis were the first among the tribes of the region to have converted to Christianity way back in 1812-13 and the Missionary activities were initiated in the Naga Hills in 1840s and in the Zo/Mizo/Lushai Hills in 1894-95.[74] In this sense of time frame the Zo/Mizo were late arrivals to the Evangelical missions. However, the success rate in the Zo Hills has been the maximum in terms of mass proselytisation.

The spread of Christianity in the Zo Hills was partly due to the waves of revivalism[75] which, paradoxically, converted more people in a wave than could be done by sustained proselytisation. In these revivalist movements large number of people would profess their oracle-like powers. There would be great mass dancing, with drum beats, hysterical singing of hymns and sometimes, also bouts of *Zu* (rice beer) drinking. These moves made Christianity more adoptable to the people with their age-old superstitions, habits and customs, and provided the meeting grounds of the new religion with the old animism, drawing more and more people to the new faith.[76] The missionaries by highlighting the issues of exploitation, oppression and domination and by addressing the issues of health, disease, education and language, tried to construct or help construct the contrasting nature of tribal-'non-tribal' identity/culture. The Missionaries and the Colonial Raj thus helped in the construction or imagination of a distinct tribal identity. All geared to accelerate the dual process of proselytisation of tribes and taming of the 'head-hunters' so as to benefit their larger interests that is 'Tea Gardens (Tea Industry)' and the security of 'its people' (natives; and immigrant labourers (who today form the category of 'Tea-Tribes') in the adjoining territories of the Raj.

The colonial encounter contributed towards the process of injecting Christian code of life into the core body of the *Nexus of Patriarchy* among the Zo/Mizo[77] tribes. The resultant effect of which was that the nostalgia of a romanticised past, crowded by visions of a once brave and honourable people, who practiced the code of *'tlawmngaihna'*[78] in letter and spirit, began to be strongly nurtured, alongside the notion of a progressive and enlightened Christian society. The desire to create an *Ideal Zo Christian State* has been strongly portrayed and at times has led to the voyeuristic intervention of the church and its agencies in both the private and public arena. The dual operation of Proselytisation and Colonialism introduced marked structural and functional changes in the everyday life of Zo/Mizo society.[79]

In 1951, during a Revivalist Movement in an obscure village 'Buallawn', a local headman fell into a trance, and had a vision that persuaded him that the Zo/Mizo were Jews and descendants of one of the lost tribes of Israel.[80] A group of believers then set off on foot for the *Promised Land*, thinking it might be just over the horizon. Some went north, to see a train for the first time and got as far as Assam the neighbouring Indian state. Others went northeast and reached Nagaland. No one made it to Israel, but the story of the vision and the abortive journey to *'Zion'* continues to inspire believers. The belief in the vision eventually led to the formation of a Mizo Israel Zionist Organisation (MIZO) in 1974 which sought the Israeli Premier to recognise their 'new-found identity'. Eversince, there has been a substantial following of the new found identity. The 1991 Census records 792 Jews in Mizoram and 373 in Manipur, and lists another 497 persons under "Enoka Israel" living in the area aptly named 'Salem Veng'. What is interesting about this is the "socio-political manifestation of the Zo/Mizo search for identity which reinforces their regional feeling to a great extent".[81]

The Zo Re-unification Organization (*ZORO*) demanded recognition of the Zo/Mizo scattered in various states of India and neighbouring countries as one 'ethnic race' and unite all Zo/Mizo under one umbrella.[82] The demand was supported by the 'Mizo National Front' and the 'People's Conference Party' at different times.[83] This Zo-Reunification movement was paralleled by a movement to unite the Zo/Mizo with the state of Israel. Controversy exists, however, as to when exactly the Zo/Mizo first claimed ancestry from a lost tribe of Israel. What is known is that in the 50s, a villager in Northern Mizoram named Kawla visioned that 'an angel revealed to him that the Zo/ Mizo were descendants of the lost tribes of Israel and should return to the land of their forefathers.' Kawla developed a following and gradually the belief evolved among some of his followers that the Mizo should not only return to their ancestral land, but also practice their ancestral faith of Judaism.

The Zo/Mizo attracted special attention of a Jewish Rabbi, Eliyahu Avichail of Jerusalem, who had set up an organisation in 1975 called Amishav, to seek the return of the descendants of the lost tribes to Israel. Upon hearing the claim of the Zo/Mizo, the Rabbi began to teach them the rudiments of the Jewish faith, and prepare them for their return to Israel. Gradually a movement towards embracing Jewish practices grew and by 2003, thousands of Zo/Mizo had embraced the Jewish faith and/or had moved to Israel.[84] The Chhinlung Israel People's Convention (CIPC)[85] founded by Lalchanhima Sailo[86] in 1994 uniquely combined two claims: one that the Zo/Mizo were the *'Lost Tribes of Israel'* and the second, a call for independence. In 1994, the Centenary year of the first Christian Missionary visit to Mizoram, Lalchanhima Sailo met an old Mizo Sabbath observer Sanzoa, who strongly believed in the 'Israel Theory' and had always, preached that the children of Israel should be unified. Under his inspiration, Sailo decided to publish an advertisement in the newspaper calling all Zo/Mizo who believed they were the children of Israel to gather together.

Initially the CIPC called for establishing a 'State Human Rights Commission' in Mizoram and distributed magnetic cassettes purporting the claim of the Zo/Mizo as the 'Lost Tribe of Israel'. It campaigned against the Indian government on several economic issues and demanded wavier on loans made to the state of Mizoram. It protested against the inundation of Zo/Mizo territory by dams built across the border in Bangladesh and asked the Indian government to demand compensation. It helped refugees from Myanmar settle in Mizoram and in the rest of India and Zo/Mizo who wanted to move to Israel. The CIPC in 1994 submitted a thirty-page memorandum to the United Nations, India, Israel and a number of other countries. The memorandum demanded recognition of the Zo/Mizo as a lost tribe of Israel, on the basis of oral history, and political independence and unification of all Mizo areas in India and neighbouring countries. It also claimed that the Mizo were never part of British India or Burma as they had lived in a legally defined, 'excluded area' divided arbitrarily by the British and that as a separate administrative area it had a right to independence when the British de-colonised the South Asia region. The popularity of the CIPC surged after 1998, when the CIPC organised its 'identity referendum' in which thousands of Zo/Mizo from the adjoining areas voted in favour of the CIPCs 'Lost Tribe' identity and the call for independence and unification of the *Zohnahthlak*.

As the CIPC grew, a nexus developed between its belief in descent from a lost tribe of Israel and Jewish movements.[87]Lalchanhima Sailo maintained a warm relationship with Rabbi Avichail and the Israeli embassy which eased the process of immigration for the Mizo to Israel.[88] Individuals like Lalchanhima and researchers like Zaithanchhungi[89]continue to defend the lost tribes' theory, so much so that the *'Zo-Israel-Chhinlung Identity'* movement has mass appeal and is steadily contesting though not directly confronting the *'Zo-Christian-Chhinlung Identity'*.[90]

The Presbyterian Church's concern was not only that Zo/Mizo were adopting an Israelite and Jewish identity in large numbers. There was the fear that the Israelite identity movement would upset the status quo of peace and prosperity in Mizoram in the changed times. For instance, life in the post-Peace Accord Mizoram under India was good with large flow of finances into the state from the Central Government making Mizoram one of the wealthiest states in India. The multifold development in and around the capital Aizawl, and its elevation from a small town to a 'City' connected by air within a short span of the Peace Accord, impressed upon the Zo/Mizo people the positives of living with India.

The growth in education and rise in literacy (third highest in India); the reservation policies in Medical Colleges, Engineering, the accelerated pace of development all brought about a mellowing down of attitudes at both ends. The Zo/Mizo constantly began to contrast the grim memories of the insurgency times and the continuing turmoil in the neighbouring North-

Eastern states of Manipur and Nagaland with that of the changed wave of peace and development in Mizoram. The Church feared that call for an independent Mizoram by the supporters of the *'Lost Tribes'* could develop into an insurgency like situation. The Church felt that Mizoram as an independent country would be weak and defenceless. Likewise, an independent Mizoram would weaken the Indian Union as a whole and it would set an example for other Indian states to follow.[91] The Church in Mizoram and the Indian State put a check on the Jewish missionaries in the North-East India as it could affect Indo-Arab and Indo-Palestine relations. Individual efforts have also been directed to counter the *Chhinlung-Israel movement*. One such critical voice was that of P.C. Biaksiama, who argued that 'there was no similarity between Mizo and Israelite custom'.[92] The belief about being a tribe of Israel arose out of a religious revival, out of a dream in a remote village in Mizoram. The Bible constantly spoke about the Israelites and the Mizo held them in high esteem. From this developed a tendency among certain Zo/Mizo to identify with the Israelites.

Lalchanhima Sailo countered Biaksiama's criticism in a televised programme by arguing that 'the Mizos do have customs that resemble those of the Ancient Israelites'.[93] 'Building an independent Mizoram was possible by non-violence. The mistake of the Mizo National Front was that they had not used international law and diplomacy to achieve their aim. Lalchanhima argued that he was following 'the provisions of the Indian constitution, the United Nations and Gandhi. Resolution 242 could apply to the Mizos as a lost tribe of Israel and an independent Mizoram would not be landlocked. It would include the port of Chittagong in Bangladesh as well as the Arakan region of Myanmar.'

Over the years, the *'Zo-Israel-Chhinlung Identity'* has invited protracted arguments and counter-theorisations on lines of the *'Zo-Christian-Chhinlung Identity'*. The controversy over the 'lost tribes of Israel' is clearly visible from the newspaper and book stalls which continue to sell Biaksimia's book *'Mizo leh Israel'* alongside the pro-Jewish newsletter, *'Israel Tlangau'* with pictures of Amishav's new President Michael Freund, a supporter of the lost tribe theory of the Mizos. The Zo/Mizo in the streets are divided over whether to adopt a *'Zo-Israel-Chhinlung Identity'* or a *'Zo-Christian-Chhinlung Identity'*.

Both contested theories of the *'Zo-Christian-Chhinlung Identity'* and the *'Zo-Israel-Chhinlung Identity'* remain open to contestations and newer interpretations. The tussle between an overtly Christian Identity and a Jewish Identity continues to resonate in public debates.[94] The Biaksiamas and Lalchanhimas in Mizoram are yet to solve the riddle of Identity and the 'double helix' of the DNA continues to be a contested strand. Interestingly, both contested theories build up their narratives in and around the 'Memory of *Zopui-Chhinlung*' (Traditional Myth-Memory of the Zo people). The 'Zomi movement' belongs to the genera of the *'Zo-Christian-Chhinlung Identity'* while the *'Zo-Israel-Chhinlung Identity'* stretches and links the *'Chhinlung Theory'* to that of the *'Lost Tribes of Israel'*; and provides a solution in the form of either creating an independent 'Israel State in and around Mizoram' or migrate back to the 'promised homeland'.[95] 'Questions of racial roots aside, the Bene Menashe serves as an example and metaphor of subterranean crisis of identity'.[96] The confusion over identity is plainly visible in the narrow and precipitous streets of Aizawl the capital city. One side is Bethlehem, the other Salem, another side is Cannan and mid-way is Zion Street, with an intersection called Israel Point. Shops, schools, homes and institutions carry names such as Israel Stores, Zion Tailors, Solomon's Cave, Exodus Press, Bethesda, Beer-seba, Nazareth School, Mount Carmel School. Names and identities randomly plucked from the entire Judeo-Christian spectrum continue to exhibit the contest between the New and the Old Testaments.

Conflations in Memory: Remembering and Forgetting in Identity Construction

'Why do we remember some events?' even in trans-generational mode and conversely, 'why do we forget?' few closer events in time and space with the blink of an eye. The relevance of remembering and forgetting is tightly multibraided into the 'Politics of Memory', more so among ethnically charged communities, the politics of memory retaining, commemoration, and re-living events in historically contested narrations forms an intrinsic part of inventing vexed 'Time, Space and History' and prefix the three with the highly coveted, exclusivist word 'Our'. This enterprise of rewriting, revisiting, reinventing, renarration is supposedly closer to the concerned community and presented as 'the authentic, the emic'. The following sub-sections would unfold this aphoristic enterprise of memory making and retention among the *Zo hnahthlak.*

Memory of the Lost Territory, Lost Space and the discovery of a 'New One'

'Places have multiple meanings for their inhabitants. They are constructed spatiality… (and) need to be understood apart from their creation as the locales of ethnography… (More crucial is to) raise questions about how the anthropological study of place relates to experiences of living in places.'[97] Malkki (1990; 1992) shows how an identity between people and territory is created and naturalised through the visual device of the map, which represents the world of nations "as a discrete spatial partitioning of territory" with no "bleeding boundaries": Each nation is sovereign and limited in its membership. The enclosure, measurement, and commodification of space have been key for the production of the modern notion of a national territory bounded by frontiers that sharply distinguish *inside* from *outside*: Baptised with a proper name, space becomes national property, a sovereign patrimony fusing place, property, and heritage, whose perpetuation is secured by the state.

This identity between people, heritage, territory, and state is also brought about by the use of botanical metaphors that 'suggest that each nation is a grand genealogical tree, rooted in the soil that nourishes it'. The Zo/Mizo or *Zomi* also use the metaphor of a tree to link up their rooted-ness with the claimed territory; the Zo/Mizo claim that their folksongs and folklores speaks of a grand tree planted by their fore-fathers before they migrated from *'Zopui'*, west of Tiau valley. For instance, the *Kuki-Chin-Zo-Mizo Folklore* suggests that their 'family tree' is at *'Khampat Bungpui'*[98] and that when the ariel roots of the great *'Bung'* (Banyan tree) will touch the ground the children of *Zo* will return to the mother village *'Zopui'* and the dispersed *Zo* clans will be re-united. The memory of the ever blessed village *'Zopui'* symbolic of the grandeur of *Zo* history serves a purpose: a purpose of providing a unifying thread for the great collection of ethnic tribes living in and around present day Mizoram, Chittagong Hills Tracts, the Chin Hills in Burma to the areas around Tripura, Cachar (Assam) and Manipur. The memory of the lost village, lost territory directs the urgency to re-claim the lost land and re-establish the lost *Zo* heritage and 'Honour' of the once brave and powerful, *head-hunting*, *Pasaltha* that rode through the hills and valleys of the region of Zoram. The metaphor of a grand genealogical tree limits the membership of the shared memory to the *Zo* people alone and by the same logic serves the purpose of de-limiting the membership or proximity of the other tribal groups in the region. 'Myth-making'/'Myth-building' forms an important part of the ethnic-national identity building process as evident from the several theories of the origin and history of Zo/Mizo tribes.

The above metaphors like a map also configure the nation as limited in its membership, sovereign, and continuous in time. Maps are critical for conceptualising the state as 'a compulsory organisation with a territorial basis', as 'the stable centre...of [national] societies and spaces'. The partition of the *'Zo territory'* and the memory and mythification of *Zoram/Zopui* became embedded in the collective imagination systematically entering into the debates and discourses of nation-building, identity, statecraft, insider-outsider, inclusion-exclusion, migration/trans-border movement and the whole process of 'Othering'. The issue of a territory, a boundary thus remained highly contested: 'A boundary does not only exist in the border area, but manifests itself in many institutions such as education, the media, memorials, ceremonies and spectacles.

These are effective expressions of narratives linked with boundaries and border conflicts and serve as reference to the other'.[99] The spatial matrix materialised in the operation of the state system shapes the imagining of personhood as well as place. The bounding of the nation as a collective subject, as a super-organism with a unique biological-cultural essence, replicates the enclosure of national territory. Tropes of territorialised space are articulated with tropes of substance in the imagining of collective and individual national bodies. The Botanical metaphor that is the 'family tree' becomes symbolic of the cohesiveness of the group; it's imagined commonness and lived in memory. The idiom of kinship, Brown (2000) comments, has a 'special potency as a basis of community' because 'it can draw upon the past not simply to posit a common origin but also to claim substantial identity in the present.' The solidarity of kinship rests on reproduction of memory, a distant past: a history (usually of loss or pride), "shared substance" (biogenetic and psychic), and "codes for conduct".

How the identity of a place and its people get shaped and reaffirmed in the midst of the growing encapsulating homogeneity and the fragmentation of space. How the concreteness of the territory and its visual markers is secured through material forms in everyday life and language and as well as in scholarship are the pertinent issues that I attempt to explore in this sub-section. What really makes the Zo/Mizo construction of a 'Memory of the Lost Territory, Lost Space' even more interesting is the convenient hybridization of the 'Memory of *Zopui* and *Chhinlung*' with that of the *'Lost Tribe of Israel'*.

Tracing the Fossils of the Ten Lost Tribes of Israel

A small group of people living between Myanmar and Bangladesh have been practicing Judaism for more than 25 years. They call themselves *Bene Menashe*, descendants of the Tribe of Menashe, one of the ten lost tribes.[100] Also known as the *'Chhinlung-Israel'*, the Bene Menashe relates their history of exile from the Northern Kingdom of Israel in 721 B.C. across the silk route finally ending up in India and Myanmar.[101] The oral traditions of the Zo/Mizo tribes in special the Hmar oral sources appear to indicate their Jewish origin and on the basis of these sources, some writers even go to the extent of saying that Hmar and their brethrens, Kuki and Mizo could perhaps be one of the ten lost tribes of ancient Israel.[102] Interestingly the beliefs disseminated by European travellers, Jews and Christians, have been internalised by some of the ethnic communities in the region to such an extent that the 'myth' became an integral part of their ethos and identity.

Hybridization of the Memory: 'Zopui -Chhinlung' to 'Chhinlung-Israel'

In 1951, during a Revivalist Movement in an obscure village 'Buallawn', a local headman fell into a trance, and had a vision that persuaded him that the Zo/Mizo were Jews and descendants of one of the lost tribes of Israel.[103] A group of believers then set off on foot for the *Promised Land*, thinking it might be just over the horizon. Some went north, to see a train for the first time and got as far as Assam the neighbouring Indian state. Others went northeast and reached Nagaland. No one made it to Israel, but the story of the vision and the abortive journey to *'Zion'* continues to inspire believers. The belief in the vision eventually led to the formation of a Mizo Israel Zionist Organisation (MIZO) in 1974 which sought the Israeli Premier to recognise their 'new-found identity'. Eversince, there has been a substantial following of the new found identity. The 1991 Census records 792 Jews in Mizoram and 373 in Manipur, and lists another 497 persons under "Enoka Israel" living in the area aptly named 'Salem Veng'. What is interesting about this is the "socio-political manifestation of the Zo/Mizo search for identity which reinforces their regional feeling to a great extent".[104]

The Zo Re-unification Organization (*ZORO*) demanded recognition of the Zo/Mizo scattered in various states of India and neighbouring countries as one 'ethnic race' and unite all Zo/Mizo under one umbrella. The demand was supported by the 'Mizo National Front' and the 'People's Conference Party' at different times.[105] This Zo-Reunification movement was paralleled by a movement to unite the Zo/Mizo with the state of Israel. Controversy exists, however, as to when exactly the Zo/Mizo first claimed ancestry from a lost tribe of Israel. What is known is that in the 50s, a villager in Northern Mizoram named Kawla visioned that 'an angel revealed to him that the Zo/Mizo were descendants of the lost tribes of Israel and should return to the land of their forefathers.' Kawla developed a following and gradually the belief evolved among some of his followers that the Mizo should not only return to their ancestral land, but also practice their ancestral faith of Judaism.

The Zo/Mizo attracted special attention of a Jewish Rabbi, Eliyahu Avichail of Jerusalem, who had set up an organisation in 1975 called Amishav, to seek the return of the descendants of the lost tribes to Israel. Upon hearing the claim of the Zo/Mizo, the Rabbi began to teach them the rudiments of the Jewish faith, and prepare them for their return to Israel. Gradually a movement towards embracing Jewish practices grew and by

2003, thousands of Zo/Mizo had embraced the Jewish faith and/or had moved to Israel.[106]

The Chhinlung Israel People's Convention (CIPC)[107] founded by Lalchanhima Sailo[108] in 1994 uniquely combined two claims: one that the Zo/Mizo were the *'Lost Tribes of Israel'* and the second, a call for independence. In 1994, the Centenary year of the first Christian Missionary visit to Mizoram, Lalchanhima Sailo met an old Mizo Sabbath observer Sanzoa, who strongly believed in the 'Israel Theory' and had always, preached that the children of Israel should be unified. Under his inspiration, Sailo decided to publish an advertisement in the newspaper calling all Zo/ Mizo who believed they were the children of Israel to gather together.

Initially the CIPC called for establishing a 'State Human Rights Commission' in Mizoram and distributed magnetic cassettes purporting the claim of the Zo/Mizo as the 'Lost Tribe of Israel'. It campaigned against the Indian government on several economic issues and demanded wavier on loans made to the state of Mizoram. It protested against the inundation of Zo/Mizo territory by dams built across the border in Bangladesh and asked the Indian government to demand compensation. It helped refugees from Myanmar settle in Mizoram and in the rest of India and Zo/Mizo who wanted to move to Israel. The CIPC in 1994 submitted a thirty-page memorandum to the United Nations, India, Israel and a number of other countries. The memorandum demanded recognition of the Zo/Mizo as a lost tribe of Israel, on the basis of oral history, and political independence and unification of all Mizo areas in India and neighbouring countries. It also claimed that the Mizo were never part of British India or Burma as they had lived in a legally defined, 'excluded area' divided arbitrarily by the British and that as a separate administrative area it had a right to independence when the British de-colonised the South Asia region. The popularity of the CIPC surged after 1998, when the CIPC organised its 'identity referendum' in which thousands of Zo/Mizo from the adjoining areas voted in favour of the CIPCs 'Lost Tribe' identity and the call for independence and unification of the *Zo hnahthlak*.

As the CIPC grew, a nexus developed between its belief in descent from a lost tribe of Israel and Jewish movements.[109] Lalchanhima Sailo maintained a warm relationship with Rabbi Avichail and the Israeli embassy which eased the process of immigration for the Mizo to Israel.[110] Individuals like Lalchanhima and researchers like Zaithanchhungi[111] continue to defend the lost tribes' theory, so much so that the *'Zo-Israel-Chhinlung Identity'* movement has mass appeal and is steadily contesting though not directly confronting the *'Zo-Christian-Chhinlung Identity'*.

The Presbyterian Church's concern was not only that Zo/Mizo were adopting an Israelite and Jewish identity in large numbers. There was the fear that the Israelite identity movement would upset the status quo of peace and prosperity in Mizoram in the changed times. For instance, life in the post-Peace Accord Mizoram under India was good with large flow of finances into the state from the Central Government making Mizoram one of the wealthiest states in India. The multifold development in and around the capital Aizawl, and its elevation from a small town to a 'City' connected by air within a short span of the Peace Accord, impressed upon the Zo/ Mizo people the positives of 'living with India'.

The following stanzas from James Dokhuma's poem *'Aw Delhi'* (translated in English by Rev. Zairema) reflect the changed attitude towards New Delhi (Symbolic of India):

Aw! Delhi (Oh! Delhi) While nations poised for spoils, Plan destruction for imagined wrongs; Count their armies and cannons, 'Might is right' said they. But you. O! Delhi, city of peace;

Sits serene indisposed to aggression; Messenger of peace to all nations, With your watch-word- 'peace on Earth'. Mizo, Naga, Garo and Khasi from the east,

Down to wave-tossed boulders of Kumari on the south
From the Gate of India on the West, To the snowy mountains on the north. With one Accord we march together, We drink your nectar, oh how sweet! Should your enemies attack you,

We shall sing a victory song under your flag.

…

…

…

Source: Laltluangliana Khiangte (ed.).(2002). *Mizo Songs and Folktales (Indian Literature in Tribal Languages).* New Delhi: Sahitya Akademi. pp.62-65.

The growth in education and rise in Literacy (second highest in India); the reservation policies in Medical Colleges, Engineering, the accelerated pace of development all brought about a mellowing down of attitudes at both ends. The Zo/Mizo constantly began to contrast the grim memories of the insurgency times and the continuing turmoil in the neighbouring North-Eastern states of Manipur and Nagaland with that of the changed wave of peace and development in Mizoram.[112] The Church feared that call for an independent Mizoram by the supporters of the *'Lost Tribes'* could develop into an insurgency like situation. The Church felt that Mizoram as an independent country would be weak and defenceless. Likewise, an independent Mizoram would weaken the Indian Union as a whole and it would set an example for other Indian states to follow.[113] The Church in Mizoram and the Indian State put a check on the Jewish missionaries in the North-East India as it could affect Indo-Arab and Indo-Palestine relations. Individual efforts have also been directed to counter the *Chhinlung-Israel movement*. One such critical voice was that of P.C. Biaksiama, who argued that 'there was no similarity between Mizo and Israelite custom'.[114] The belief about being a tribe of Israel arose out of a religious revival, out of a dream in a remote village in Mizoram. The Bible constantly spoke about the Israelites and the Mizo held them in high esteem. From this developed a tendency among certain Zo/Mizo to identify with the Israelites.

Lalchanhima Sailo countered Biaksiama's criticism in a televised programme by arguing that 'the Mizos do have customs that resemble those of the Ancient Israelites'.[115] 'Building an independent Mizoram was possible by non-violence. The mistake of the Mizo National Front was that they had not used international law and diplomacy to achieve their aim. Lalchanhima argued that he was following 'the provisions of the Indian constitution, the United Nations and Gandhi. Resolution 242 could apply to the Mizos as a lost tribe of Israel and an independent Mizoram would not be landlocked. It would include the port of Chittagong in Bangladesh as well as the Arakan region of Myanmar.'

Over the years, the *'Zo-Israel-Chhinlung Identity'* has invited protracted arguments and counter-theorisations on lines of the *'Zo-Christian-Chhinlung Identity'*. The controversy over the 'lost tribes of Israel' is clearly visible from the newspaper and book stalls which continue to sell Biaksimia's book *'Mizo leh Israel'* alongside the pro-Jewish newsletter, *'Israel Tlangau'* with pictures of Amishav's new President Michael Freund, a supporter of the lost tribe theory of the Mizos. The Zo/Mizo in the streets are divided over whether to adopt a *'Zo-Israel-Chhinlung Identity'* or a *'Zo-Christian-Chhinlung Identity'*. Both contested theories of the *'Zo-Christian-Chhinlung Identity'* and the *'Zo-Israel-Chhinlung Identity'* remain open to contestations and newer interpretations. The tussle between an overtly Christian Identity and a Jewish Identity continues to resonate in public debates. The Biaksiamas and Lalchanhimas in Mizoram are yet to solve the riddle of Identity and the 'double helix' of the DNA continues to be a contested strand. Interestingly, both contested theories build up their narratives in and around the 'Memory of *Zopui-Chhinlung*' (Traditional Myth-Memory of the Zo people). The 'Zomi movement' belongs to the genera of the *'Zo-Christian-Chhinlung Identity'* while the *'Zo-Israel-Chhinlung Identity'* stretches and links the *'Chhinlung Theory'* to that of the *'Lost Tribes of Israel'*; and provides a solution in the form of either creating an independent 'Israel State in and around Mizoram' or migrate back to the 'promised homeland'. Questions of racial roots aside, the Bene Menashe serves as an example and metaphor of subterranean crisis of identity.[116] The confusion over identity is plainly visible in the narrow and precipitous streets of Aizawl the capital city. One side is Bethlehem, the other Salem, another side is Cannan and mid-way is Zion Street, with an intersection called Israel Point. Shops, schools, homes and institutions carry names such as Israel Stores, Zion Tailors, Solomon's Cave, Exodus Press, Bethesda, Beer-seba, Nazareth School, Mount Carmel School. Names and identities randomly plucked from the entire Judeo-Christian spectrum continue to exhibit the contest between the New and the Old Testaments.

Some Closing Observations

The colonial encounter experienced in the then Lushai Hills actively engaged in the process of 'taming the wild tribes' from 'head-hunters' to 'soul hunters'. Needless to say the colonial encounter was marked by the project of understanding the 'oriental'. This underlying concern can be located in the several colonial documents and memories of colonial administrators and missionaries who worked endlessly among the *Zo hnahthlak*. The colonial encounter injected western ideas concerning education, health and medicine, hygiene and house-keeping, belief in Christianity and the unquestioned acceptance of the superiority of the white man's belief system and life style over that of the native's understanding and appreciation of their world system. The issues discussed in this chapter accentuate the skillful manouverings of the traditional element of the Zo religion for survival amidst the onslaught of proselytisation. Also, the discussions show how Christianity traverses through slippery 'Zo paths'[117] and circumvents its hold over the 'Savage mind'. The enmeshing of faith and identity along with an encryptic evangelical zeal can be best summed up in the strong emphasis in the goodness of 'being believers' as reflected in the ever reverberating melodious composition by Roliana Chhangte '*Mitdel kan awm toh lo Jerusalem thar ah*' ('there are 'no blind persons' (i.e., non-believers who fail to see the Glory of Christ) in the 'new Jerusalem' (referring to the Zo hills)'.[118] Such manouverings reflect the specific discomforts and comforts in the process of engagements in proselytisation and simultaneously 'being Zo' among the *Zo hnahthalk*. What is to be retained and displayed, or showcased as 'hybrid', and what is to be forgotten and quarantined in this engagement is not an unconscious enterprise rather an intensely loaded choice making enterprise driven by the *Nexus of Patriarchy*.

Notes & References

1. Following Rowena Robinson. (2003: 172) I firmly believe that 'Churches have traditionally though, been sites for the articulation and maintenance of inequalities of caste, class and gender.' Chapter 6 'Cults, Cures and Challenges to the Church' *in* Rowena Robinson. (2003). *Christians of India.* New Delhi: Sage Publications. pp. 172-205.
2. Presbyterianism is the major Christian denomination in the state of Mizoram, India. The Mizoram Presbyterian Church was established by a Welsh Missionary named Rev. D.E. Jones and is one of the constituted bodies of the General Assembly of the Presbyterian Church of India, which has its headquarters at Shillong, Meghalaya (India). The administration of the Presbyterian Church is highly centralised. The Synod, with its headquarters at Aizawl, is the highest decision making body of the church with considerable influence. The financial operation, personnel (including selection of missionaries), administration, management and operation of the church are directly or indirectly controlled by the Synod Headquarters. Other Christian churches in the state of Mizoram include the Baptist Church of Mizoram (BCM),United Pentecostal Church (UPC), the Salvation Army (SA), the Seventh-day Adventist Church (SD), Kohhran Thianghlim (KT), Roman Catholic (RC), Lairam Isua Krista Baptist Kohhran (LIKBK), Congregational Church of India (Maraland), Evangelical Church of Maraland, Independent Church of India (ICI) and Evangelical Free Church of India (EFCI) etc.
3. For details *see*, A.G. McCall. (1949). (2003). *Lushai Chrysalis*. Aizawl: Tribal Research Institute.
4. For instance, captain Blackwood's expedition with the parties of the Sylhet Infantry and the Armed Civil Police 1844; Captain Lister's expedition 1847 and 1849; the Lushai-Kuki raids of 1845 and 1847 etc. just to single out few prominent events relating to the same. It is interesting to note that the Raj skilfully engaged and recruited/appointed small sections of the Lushai-Kuki tribes to engage in tackling and taming the non-confirming Lushai-Kuki chiefs and bring them to the fold of the Colonial scheme of administration and regular uniformized tax regime. *See*, L.W. Shakespear. (1927). (1977). *History of The Assam Rifles*. Calcutta: Firma KLM Pvt. Ltd. Aizawl: Tribal Research Institute; R.G. Woodthorpe. (First print UK 1873). (First Indian reprint 1980). *The Lushai Expedition 1871-1872*.Guwahati: Spectrum Publications.
5. For details, *See,* B. Datta Ray. (1983). *The Emergence and Role of Middle Class in North-East India*. Delhi: Uppal Publishing House.
6. 'A new class of educated Lushais came up under the sponsorship of the Missionaries. Western Education of the middle class made their entry into government and non-government services easy. Tribes were ably aided into this through the provision of reservation, which were available not only for employment purposes but also in higher education and politics. These measures and avenues made possible the emergence of the middle class. Christianity meant medical care, education, English language and a richer material life.' The education policy generated a feeling that 'education' and 'Christianity' were the only means to salaried jobs, which would bring freedom from the drudgery, toil and uncertainty of cultivation. Having a missionary education thus began to

signal the sure possibility of securing government jobs or such other modern salaried occupation. This permanent 'paid-in-cash' ('pawisa'/'sum chhuana' in Mizo) occupation seemed to be a readymade solution to all ailments of semi-migratory tribes and Jhum economy.

7. The Zo tribes were recruited by the British Government as labour forces to load military equipments and rations into train compartments, keep the supply chain of coal to the train engines, as well as unloading train coaches in the war zones of Europe and Mesopotamia. The British carried the recruitment drive in the Lushai Hills and mustered the youths in Aizawl, 1917 and divided them in four labour companies. They were paid in cash on their return from the Great War (World War I). Many of the youths used the cash to pay for their bride price. The war returns had popular following among the women in the region. However, the recruitment drive for the War was not easy as it has been projected. Few areas showed stiff resistance to the call of the British Government for instance in the Hakka and Falam areas of the Chin Hills the Thado-Kuki group openly revolted. The Colonial administration took a fisted step to tame the uncivilized uprising and forcibly engaged the labour of these tribes to part-take in the Imperial projects such as road making (Falam Tuangpat/ tlanghel), creation of an artificial lake (Ralkap Tili/ Soldier's Lake), Falam Cinmual football field etc.

8. A.G. McCall. *Op. cit.*

9. The Colonial strategies in Africa show striking resemblance and reapplication of the same among the now banal categorization 'tribal' in South Asia. For Colonial encounter and tribal societies in Africa see, Mair Lucy. (1963). *New Nations*, London: Widenfeld & Nicholson.

10. A.C. Ray. (1982). *Mizoram Dynamics of Change*. Calcutta: Pearl Publishers/ ICSSR, p. 65; N.N. Acharyya, (1984). 'Modernisation of Mizoram.' *Proceedings*. NEIHA. 5th session; Lalchungnunga. (1994). *Mizoram: Politics Of Regionalism And National Integration,* New Delhi, India: Reliance Publishing House, pp.35-36; C.R. Nag. (1998). *Mizo Polity And Political Modernisation,* Delhi: Vikas Publishing House, pp. 67-72.

11. Similar trends took place in Africa where experience in Foreign Service during the wars increased the political consciousness among the people. The discontent of the returned soldiers led to the demands of the Africans for control of their own destiny. *See*, Mair Lucy. *Op.cit.*

12. A.C. Ray. (1982). *Op. cit*. p.66.

13. For further details on the role of youth and students movements in politics in Mizoram *See*, Anup Shekhar Chakraborty. (2013a). 'Elementary Aspects of 'Otherness' in Mizoram: An Enquiry into the Nature and Processes of Social Inclusion and Exclusion in a North East Indian State'. *Occasional Paper VII*, Department of Sociology, University of North Bengal. Shivmandir, Siliguri: The University of North Bengal Press.

14. McCall's Durbar had a strong impact on politics in Mizoram; First, it united the Chiefs (traditional as well as ascribed) on a common platform, made them coordinate and voice their feelings against the British and also it led to a new found oppressive psychology among the chiefs. Second, the main objective of McCall was to keep down agitation of the commoners and New Elites and Neo-rich in Mizoram. But the British objective boomeranged and the voices of

commoners' had to be given an outlet in the form of political self-assertion in the 1946 Durbar elections under A.R McDonald. The commoners' were given right to elect their own representatives (A.C. Ray. (1982). *Op.cit.*). The British objective also boomeranged at another level that is at the level of the unity among the two types of chiefs namely 'traditional chiefs' and 'ascribed chiefs'. The British did not apprehend the possibility of a unity between the two types of chiefs.

15. Pathian was the traditional male Zo/Mizo God. Interestingly post proselytisation the image of the Pathian was transmuted with that of the figure of the God in Christendom. '*Pathian ring*' (believer) in contemporary Zo/Mizo cosmology of Divinity undoubtedly refers exclusively to the latter transmuted figure i.e., Christian God has become incorporated with strong identifiers of the traditional Zo/Mizo Pathian. This is very much what the crux of this paper engages in i.e., the Localization of Christianity.
16. Lalrimawia. (1982). 'The Lushai Chiefs under the British Rule', *Proceedings,* NEIHA. 3rd session; E. J. Thomas. (1993). *Mizo bamboo Hills Murmur Change (Mizo Society Before And After Independence).* New Delhi: Intellectual Publishing House; A. C. Ray. (1993). *Mizoram,* New Delhi: National Book Trust, pp. 72-74; C.R. Nag. *Op.cit.* pp.15-21.
17. Lalrimawia. *Ibid.*; E. J. Thomas. *Ibid.* ; A.C. Ray. (1993). *Ibid.*; C.R. Nag. (1998). *Ibid.* pp. 25-29.
18. N. N. Acharyya. *Op.cit.*; C.R. Nag, *Ibid.* p. 72.
19. N. N. Acharyya. *Ibid.*; Lalchungnunga. *Op.cit.* pp.35-36;C.R. Nag. *Ibid.*, pp. 67-72.
20. Here again we observe that mimicry is the effect of hybridity. First, the metonymy of presence supports the authoritarian voyeurism, but then as discrimination turns into the assertion of the hybrid, the sign of authority becomes a mask, a mockery.
21. The Zo tribes used the word 'Sap' a corrupted form of the Hindustani word 'Sahib' to refer to the Europeans i.e. white men. B.B Goswami observed during his field work and interaction with the local people in Mizoram that 'There is not a single Mizo either in urban or in rural areas who told that the Mizos in general can become better or superior than saps'; and also that 'the saps are better than the Mizos for they have golden hair, beautiful eyes, tall and white complexion' etc. For detailed reading on the construction and imagery of the Superiority of the white races in the minds and psychology of the Zo tribes Mizoram, *see* B.B. Goswami, "out-group from the point of view of In-group: A Study of Mizos", *in* S. M. Dubey. (1978). North East India: A Sociological Study. pp. 99-110.
22. B.B. Goswami *in* S.M. Dubey. *Ibid.* pp 104-109.
23. Frederick. S. Downs. (1983). *Christianity in North East India*. Delhi: ISPCK. pp. 47-48.
24. The term *'Vai'* is a Zo/Mizo word and refers to the people of India who have Aryan features (Goswami *in* Dubey. *Op.cit.* pp. 99-110). The category of the *'Vai'* is again categorised as *'Vai chhia'* (bad/inferior *'Vai*) and *'Vai thra'* (good/ superior *'Vai'*). The *'Vai'* from Silchar/Cachar speaking *Sylheti Bengali* fall under

the first category. The *'Vai'* from North India and elsewhere with lighter skin tones fall conveniently under the second category. The *'Vai'* thus also has racial overtones attached to it. In Mizoram, the term *'Vai'* evokes mixed feelings of contempt, distrust, mockery and envy. The inflow of the *'Vai'* in present day Mizoram has a strong colonial linkage. The gradual yet sure, entry of the *'Vai'* into the Zo/ Mizo economy provided for a greater degree of interaction between the *'Vai'* and Zo/Mizo especially Zo/Mizo women. For details, Anup Shekhar Chakraborty. (2012). 'Construing And Gleaning The Vexing Notion Of The 'Outsider' In Mizoram: Pre-Statehood To Post-Statehood Times', *QUEST- The Journal of UGC Academic Staff College, Nainital, Kumaun University*. Volume 6, Issue. 2. pp. 297-304.

25. Gurpreet Mahajan. (2000). 'A Gendered Diary: Subject Dharma Kumar', *Economic and Political Weekly*, (June 3, p. 1899), gives a similar explanation for the exclusion of women from the realms of spirituality. My argument carries forward Mahajan's lines and locates the ultimate option left for the women in the Mizo society i.e. the realms of economics, which according to the Mizo patriarchy is both sensuous, and materialistic. Typically signified by the word '*Khawvel*' (worldly).
26. Anup Shekhar Chakraborty. (2007). 'Politics of Silencings: Echoes of the Margins from Mizoram', *Indian Journal of Political Science (IJPS)*, Vol. LXII, No. 4, Oct.-Dec.; Anup Shekhar Chakraborty. (2008a). 'Emergence of Women from 'Private' to 'Public': A Narrative of Power Politics from Mizoram'. *Journal of International Women's Studies*. Bridgewater, Vol. No. 9, 3 May; Anup Shekhar Chakraborty. (2008b). 'Manufacturing of Spaces: The 'Others' in Zo/Mizo Politics'. *South Asian Journal of Socio-Political Studies (SAJOSPS)*. Vol.9, No.1, July-Dec.,; Anup Shekhar Chakraborty. (2008c). "Mustering Empowerment experiences from Mizoram: A Leap from 'Private' to 'Public' Living Spaces", *Global South SEPHIS e-magazine*. Vol.4, No.4, July.
27. The stereotyped depiction of women as greedy, materialistic, vain and immoral (sexual) and the projection of Vai's as cunning, shrewd, lustful and the Poi's as greedy, rich and foolish in most of the folktales and sayings reflect the underlying patriarchal biases acting against the 'Triad'. The attitude of placing women at the periphery in the post-colonial situation can be traced to these internal factors and external factors.
28. Lalrinawmi Ralte. (1993). *Crab Theology: A Critique Of Patriarchy-Cultural Degradation And Empowerment Of Mizo Women*. Episcopal Divinity School, UMI Dissertation Services, Michigan, U.S.A: A. Bell & Howell Company.
29. The 'Zawlbuk' was the male dormitory and symbolized male hegemony and vigour in the Mizo society. It was one of the pillars that upheld the chieftainship in traditional Mizo society; however, it was not practiced among all the Zo tribes. The members or the 'Tlangvals' (boys, men) of the Zawlbuk could act in a high-handed manner for instance, if a girl of the village refused to entertain these men during the ritualized practice of '*Nula-rim*'. They would go in a group and shake the posts or the stilts of the hut in which the girl and her family lived till it fell down. This practice was known as '*Bang Sawi*' and not even the Chief could intervene; to avoid such social embarrassment no girl dared to displease her suitors during the routine '*Tlaileng*' (evening stroll) '*Nula-rim*' process.

Westernization contributed to its decline and eventual extinction from the Mizo society.

30. Lalrimawia. (1982). *Op.cit.*; Lalrimawia. (1983). 'A Brief Survey of the Administrative Development in the Lushai Hills (1890-1947)', *Proceedings,* NEIHA, 4th session; N. Chatterji, *The Mizo chief & his Administration.* Aizawl: Tribal Research Institute, 1975; Sangkima. (1987). 'Zawlbuk and its abolition: A significant event in the history of the Mizos', *Proceedings,* NEIHA, 8th session.
31. Zairema. (1978). *God's Miracle In Mizoram (Glimpse of Christian work among Head-Hunters),* Aizawl, Mizoram: Synod Press. p.1; B.C. Allen, E.A. Gait, H.F. Howard, & C.G.H. Allen, (ed.). (1979, (2001)) *Gazetteer of Bengal & North-East India.* New Delhi: Mittal Publications; Suhas Chatterjee. (1990). *Mizoram Encyclopaedia,* Vol. I, Bombay: Jaico Publishing House. p.144.
32. Suhas Chatterjee. (1985). *Mizoram Under the British Rule.* Delhi: Mittal Publications. pp.185-86.
33. The Chittagong Hill Tracts was known as the '*Kapas Mahal*' (Cotton Country) and the Lakher Hills was an extension of the natural cotton reserve. Infact, the northerner tribes (Lushai/Lusei tribes) in Mizoram use the Lushai term 'Lakher' to denote one of the southern tribes which literally translates as 'those who extract cotton.' For details on the '*Kapas Mahal*'/Chittagong Hill Tracts *see*, Tamina M. Chowdhury. (2016). 'Raids, annexation and plough: Transformation through territorialisation in nineteenth-century Chittagong Hill Tracts'. *The Indian Economic and Social History Review*, Vol. 53, 2. pp.183-224.
34. I use this term to stress on the indigenization of the Christianity into the Mizo belief system and vice versa, i.e. Christianity as practices and preached in Mizoram. (Stress intended to include all tribes professing Christianity in Mizoram: A.S.C). I owe this insight on the tactics of indigenization of Christianity & its usefulness in the Mizo society, identity etc., to my supervisor Dr. Bonita Aleaz, Professor· Department of Political Science, University of Calcutta. For a detailed reading on uniqueness of Mizo Christianity, *see*, Lalrinawmi Ralte. (1993). Chapter-VII, "Dance: An Example Of Crab Theology", *Op.cit*. pp. 193-209.
35. Anup Shekhar Chakraborty. (2009b). 'Where are 'Our women'? Locating Women through the History of Proselytisation in Mizoram', *Dharma Deepkia- South Asian Journal of Missiological Research- issue on Mission In Contexts Of Violence And Uncertainty*. Issue 30, Vol.13 No. 2 July-December.
36. For details, Anup Shekhar Chakraborty. Forthcoming: 'An Account of the Customary Laws and CRPC in Mizoram'.
37. J.V. Hluna. (1985). 'Mizo Problem Leading to Insurgency'. *Proceedings of North East India History Association (NEIHA)*. Sixth Session, p. 445.
38. C.G. Verghese and R.L. Thanzawna. (1997). *A History of the Mizos*. Vol. II. New Delhi: Vikas Publishing House. p. 21.
39. Cited in preface to Vanlalruata (ed.). (2006). *Zoram Nghahfak (Municipal Sorkar Leh Village Council Thuneihna Sang Nei Kalphung*. Aizawl: Mizoram Municipal Steering Committee (MMSC) Hqrs.
40. Christianity as a religion is male centric it moves around the pivot of the Trinity- the Father, Son and the Holy Spirit. Christianity revolves around the 'Father-

Son Axis' and this axis gets filtered into the individual family system itself. Thus the male gets to play a more prominent role while the female get to play a subservient role. In case of the Mizo society this filtering of the 'Father-Son Axis' psychology led to the further male-ifying of the already male society.

41. Sangkima. (1988). 'Position & Status of women in the Traditional Mizo Society', *Proceedings.*NEIHA. 9th session; Rami Sena Samuelson. (1990). *The Mizo People: Cultural Analysis of life in a Mizo village in the 1980s,* Ann Abhor, U.S.A.: University of San Francisco, UMI. p. 22; Lalrinawmi Ralte. (1993). *Op.cit.*
42. Shelly Mathews. (2001). *First Converts- Rich Pagan Women & The Rhetoric Of Mission In Early Judaism &Christianity,* Stanford, California: Stanford University Press. p 7.
43. I owe this insight to Professor Rudo B. Gaidzanwa. 'Silence becomes useful to both- those who inflict it as well as those on whom it is inflicted. That is to say 'silence' becomes a weapon for male hegemony (maintained through 'Fear Psychosis') and at the same time it also becomes a weapon for women in her own domain- the household, the private arena. (At the CODESRIA/SEPHIS Extended Workshop, Dakar, 2006). (ASC).
44. Mary Daly. (1973). *Beyond God The Father- Towards a Philosophy of Women's Liberation,* Boston, U.S.A: Beacon Press. pp.19, 20.
45. Lalrinawmi Ralte. (1993). *Op.cit.*
46. Frederick. S. Downs. (1983). *Op.cit.* pp.14-15; E. J. Thomas. *Op.cit.*; Lalrinawmi Ralte. (1993). *Ibid.*
47. Anup Shekhar Chakraborty. (2009b). *Op.cit.*
48. Lalrinawmi Ralte. (1993). *Op.cit.*
49. Lalrinawmi Ralte. (1993). *Ibid.* pp. 25-29, 43-49.
50. Saurabh Dube's paper: Chapter 12 'Issues of Christianity in Colonial Chhattisgarh' *in* Rowena Robinson. (ed.). (2004). *Sociology of Religion in India.* New Delhi: Sage Publications. pp. 231- 255, shows similar experiences of spiritual healings among the Satnami's in Colonial Chhattisgarh.
51. Women have the right to inheritance under the Lushai District Act, No.1, 1956 (Inheritance of Property). A daughter or a wife can inherit property only if the deceased has no heir on the male side. Women, however, are entitled to their own property i.e. the dowry, called 'thuam', which she gets during her marriage from her parents. A written 'will' formally executed may now confer woman the right to inherit the family property.
52. The traditional laws or the '*Mizo Hnam Dan*' (Mizo Customary Laws) are a novel attempt of combining the British laws and the traditional Kuki-Chin-Lushai customary laws. They were compiled by B.C Carey and famously known as the Chin Hills Regulations of 1896.
53. The Indian Christian Marriage act in not applicable in Mizoram and the customary law has fixed the bride price at rupees 420/- reducing women to a cheap purchasable commodity.
54. This freedom however does not suggest that the terms of justice for men and women are equal nor does it enable women to enjoy an advantaged position in

the Mizo social system. It basically provides freedom of choice as determined by the patriarchy. This has to be understood in the light of the Engelsian debate. I owe this insight to Dr. Samita Sen, Reader, then associated with the Department of History, University of Calcutta. (At the CODESRIA/SEPHIS Extended Workshop, Dakar, 2006). (ASC).

55. E. J. Thomas. *Op.cit,* p.16.
56. Anup Shekhar Chakraborty. (2009b). *Op.cit.*
57. I consider the voyeuristic attitude of the church and its agencies to be a contributory factor to the rapidly increasing rate of corruption, drug abuse and sexual liaisons in the Mizo/Zo society. 'People want a way out of the oppressive restrictive social system' and the easiest route to flow away into the realms of fantasy is by taking refuge to drugs (keeping in mind the regions easy proximity to the international drug smuggling routes) and other means to enjoy the life they have been denied by the moral police (ASC).
58. Prasun Sonawalkar. (1989). 'Church playing vital role in Mizo polls'. The Times of India News Service. Aizawl. *The Times of India*. Ahmedabad: 09 January.
59. I am of the opinion that these 'Clannish Cult Churches' (3C) should not be confused with what we so often hear/read in Sociological/Theological studies as 'Popular Religious Movements' (PRM). Though much like PRM's the 3C's stress on healing, fighting evils and miracles but the similarity abruptly moves no further. The 3C's I observe harps closer to the pulse of the clan and clannish lineages. Also, their popularity tends to be around specified zonal areas maybe a part of a village and not the entire village, a closed group phenomenon. In that sense the 'popularity' is much limited. The official Christian Churches do not consider these 3Cs to be Christian in any sense and sneer their practices such as polygamy, communism of wives, institution of '*Chi thlak*' (practice of selecting a male or the leader of the cult to be the biological father or the 'sperm donor'. The objective of such a practice is to create a reservoir of 'pure progeny' that can be directly linked to the cult leader and future leaders could be selected from that reservoir) etc.
60. The 'Lalzahabara- Nu Diheli' cult church evolved in the late 1970s and retained popularity through the 80s in Sangau village in Southern Mizoram. Lalzahabara declared himself as the god incarnate and the new Christ. Nu Diheli was his primary wife and the entire women in his cult were his wives. The men served as support systems to put the Zahavara cult into order. For details, Anup Shekhar Chakraborty. *Forthcoming*: 'Lalzahabara-Nu Diheli cult: The Sangau Experiential Clannish Cult Church'.
61. Anup Shekhar Chakraborty. (2009b). *Op.cit.*
62. I have used the terms 'Being a Zo, Being a Christian' extensively in my PhD thesis "The Evolution of 'Zomi' Identity and Politics in Mizoram" (2005-2010) Department of Political Science, University of Calcutta, and also in my series of publications between 2007- 2013. I am not influenced by the similar sounding title of Joy Pacchua's book '*Being Mizo*' (2014). New Delhi: Oxford University Press.
63. David Hardiman. (2007). 'Healing, Medical Power and the Poor: Contests in Tribal India', *Economic And Political Weekly*. (April 21- April 27), pp. 1404-1408. Also *See,* George Mark Moares. (1964). *A History of Christianity in India:*

From early times to St. Francis Xavier A.D 52- 1542. Vol. I, Bombay: P.C Manaktala& Sons Private Ltd. pp. 246-264.

64. R.A. Lorrain. (1912). (1912). (Reprinted 1988). *Five Years in Unknown Jungles: For God and Empire.* London, Guwahati: Spectrum Publications. pp. 222-224.
65. Frederick. S. Downs. (1983). *Op. cit.* pp. 47-48.
66. Anup Shekhar Chakraborty. (2009b). *Op.cit.*
67. Pu Zaliana. Senior Research Officer, Tribal Research Institute, Art & Culture Department, Government of Mizoram, McDonald Hill. *Personal Interview.* Zarkawt, Aizawl: 22nd, 23rd& 24th January 2008.
68. Pu Zaliana. *Personal Interview. Ibid.*
69. Pi Vanramchhuangi ('Ruatfelanu'), Director HRLN Mizoram, Social Activist, *Personal Interview*, Chaltlang, Aizawl: 28th& 29th January 2008.
70. Pu Lallianchhunga, Lecturer, Department of Political Science, Mizoram University, .*Personal Interview,* Chaltlang Campus, Aizawl: 19th January 2008.
71. Stephen Fuchs. (1973). *The Aboriginal Tribes of India.* London/Madras: The Macmillan Press Ltd. p.236.
72. George Mark Moares. (1964). *Op.cit.*
73. *See*, G.H. Loch's letter to R.A. Lorrain, dated April 18th 1911 cited *in* R.A. Lorrain. (1912). *Op.cit.* p.262.
74. Stephen Fuchs. *Op. cit.*
75. The administration and the mission were both equally adverse to revivalism. McCall thought that the periodic revivalist movements showed that the Lushais had a tendency to fall back upon irresponsible behaviour. He suggested that the mission should be able to keep these movements under control. Much would depend "upon the ability of the Missionaries and their supporters to correlate Christianity and Lushai agriculture, homes, industry, schools and infact, every and all the practical experience of Lushai life. This task will be difficult. But if the Mission do fail, great lawlessness may prevail". A.G. McCall. *Op.cit.* pp. 49, 228.
76. A.C. Ray. (1982). *Op.cit.* pp.60-61.
77. The great debate on whether to be called 'Mizo' or *'Zomi'* has shadowed the politics of identity building in Mizoram for a long time. The general accepted term to refer to their identity is *'Zofate' or 'Zohnahthlak' (children of the Zo people).*
78. Unconditioned service to people or community based on 'good will', sympathy, empathy, courage and honour.
79. Frederick. S. Downs. *Op.cit.* pp.14-15; E.J. Thomas. *Op.cit.*
80. S. K. Mukherjee. (1998). 'Jewish Movement in the Hills of Manipur and Mizoram', *in* M.N. Karna (ed). (1998). *Social Movements in the North- East India.* New Delhi: Indus Publishing Company/NEICSSR, Shillong, pp.189-198.
81. Lalchungnunga. (1994). *Op.cit.*
82. Anup Shekhar Chakraborty. (2013b). 'Identity And Virtual Spaces among the *Zo Hnahthlak*: Emergent Zo Cyberpolitics' *in* Gaurav Desai. (ed.). (2013). *The Virtual Transformation of the Public Sphere: Knowledge, Politics, Identity.* 3

Critical Interventions in Theory and Praxis. New Delhi/ London: Routledge Publications. pp.169-193.

83. For details *See*, Prasun Sonawalkar. (1990). 'Uncertainty grips Mizoram Govt.', The Times of India News Service. Guwahati: 07 June. *The Times of India*. New Delhi: 08 June; *The Times of India*. (1990). 'JD decision shocks Mizoram', The Times of India News Service. Aizawl: 16 June. New Delhi: 17 June.

84. Despite the lack of scientific evidences Israel is keen to bring Bene Menashe back to Israel. One of the evident reasons being that Israel is facing crisis of human resources and declining birth rate has raised its difficulties. The current birth rate in Israel is far below that of Palestine which has the highest birth rate in the world. It means Israelis fear to be dominated by growing Palestinian population in the coming decades. The Zo/Mizo are also suffering from an identity crisis in India. The protracted insurgency and the disgruntled-ness over the post-Peace situation made it a breeding ground for spiritual adventurers offering salvation, identity and the prospect of emigration and riches abroad. Given all these facts, it cannot be refuted that Israel is expanding its occupation, and involving other nations also in this game. New Delhi's *'don't disturb them'* policy unfortunately fails to see the hidden agenda of the Zionists.

85. The Chhinlung-Israel Peoples Convention is campaigning across the state to change the name of the Mizo tribe to Chhinlung-Israel. It also talks of a greater Chhinlung-Israel state that would include the Mizos of neighbouring Burma and Bangladesh.

86. Lalchanhima Sailo a Shillong born, descendant of a Mizo chief, former employee of the Food Services Corporation of India, and holder of law and history degrees from JNU in Delhi and Osmania University in Hyderabad joined the Mizo People's Conference Party in 1990 (Brigadier T. Sailo's Party). In 1992, while attending an International Seminar on 'Studies on the Minority Nationalities of North-East India: the Mizos' (7th-9th April) at Aizawl, he argued against efforts by Indian intellectuals to assimilate Mizo identity with that of the Assamese. In 1993, he was initially projected as a candidate for the state legislature but the People's Conference withdrew its support, disgruntled, he was forced to run as an independent.

87. This became evident when LalchanhimaSailo decided to adopt the faith of the Bet-Israel sect (a Jewish sect was founded by Jonathan Kahn an American Jew, who believed in the restoration of Israel and Jesus Christ). In 2000, an Indian Christian preacher, P.P. Job spoke in Mizoram on an invitation by Jonathan Kahn. Kahn blew the 'shofar' (the traditional Jewish ceremonial ram horn) in the Assam Riffle field of Aizawl. He said that, 'the stick of Ephraim and Judah should stick together', suggesting a connection between the Jews and Mizos. Sailo, who was till then a nominal member of the Presbyterian Church felt that Jonathan Kahn's talk on the restoration of Israel could be understood to mean the restoration of a lost tribe of Israel, the Zo/Mizo, in an independent Israelite state in South East Asia. The connection between Lalchanhima Sailo and the CIPC with Jewish movements was not limited to Jewish-Christians.

88. Although Lalchanhima Sailo himself did not convert to Judaism, he did not deny that there was a possibility of him doing so in the future, saying, 'Let time tell who I am'. He admitted that his movement was a stepping stone for Zos/

Mizos to convert to Judaism 'as our movement grew more and more people became Jewish or started to follow Judaism.

89. Zaithanchhungi was a relative of one of the members of the original group that went to seek or reach Zion following the vision of the headman in 1951. Formerly a successful insurance agent and the wife of a state legislator, and a former teacher she went to Israel in 1983. There she met Eliyahu Avichayil, an Orthodox rabbi whose Amishav organization engages in tracing and locating the descendants of the lost tribes. He showed immediate interest in her story, saying Jews had been scattered as far as China. He urged her to return to India to catalogue Mizo history. She came up with a list of apparent similarities, including the building of altars, the sacrifice of animals, burial customs, marriage and divorce procedures, a belief in an all-powerful deity and the symbolic presence of the number seven in many festivities. Zaithanchhungi saw other links in musical instruments and household practices. 'I was a non-believer, but after my research I now believe very firmly that the Mizo are of Jewish descent'. Yet she herself remains a Presbyterian.
90. Anup Shekhar Chakraborty. (2013b). *Op.cit.*
91. These concerns of the Church in Mizoram further stand as proof that the Church is not against India and is not the cause of insurgencies and secessionist movements in the Northeast as commonly perceived by many Indians.
92. In June of 2003, Biaksiama presented his report on the CIPC before the church elders in the Presbyterian Pastorate of Champhai. He claimed that the CIPC assertions, both about being a lost tribe of Israel and independence were full of lies. The elders who had become members of the CIPC were taken aback. Attacked harshly by Mr. Biaksiama, they said that they only sympathized with the CIPC call the independence and unification. P.C. Biaksiama continued his movement against an Israelite identity for the Mizos and the CIPC. He conducted a seminar at his home church in Cannan Veng area of Aizawl and in November of 2003, he published a book called, 'CIPC leh Mizo Israel' dissecting the positions of the CIPC and condemning them for their wrong teachings.
93. Lalchanhima Sailo countered Biaksiama's arguments by pointing that 'the high priests did not sacrifice with pig and the lower priests who sacrificed with pig would not eat the meat. A kind of Sabbath was observed. They had a kind of circumcision as well. They buried their dead by first bathing and clothing the body before burial. 'They had always referred to Menashe who is Menashe, the son of Joseph, their great ancestor.
94. Anup Shekhar Chakraborty. (2015b). *Hegemony To Hyphenation: Hybridization Of Identities And Politics In Mizoram*. Darjeeling: St. Joseph's Publication.
95. Anup Shekhar Chakraborty. (2013b). *Op.cit.*
96. Mona Zote. (2006). 'Heaven in Hell: A Paradox', (Section IV: The Conflict of Identities) *in* Geeti Sen (ed.). (2006). *Where the Sun Rises When Shadows Fall: The North-East*, New Delhi: Oxford University Press/ India International Centre.
97. M.C. Rodman. (1992) 'Empowering place: Multilocality and multivocality'. *American Anthropologist.* 94(3): 640-56 cited *in* Seemanthini Niranjana (2001). *Gender and Space: Femininity, Sexualization and Female Body.* New Delhi: Sage Publications.

98. R. Zamawia. (2007). 'Bung-2, Kan Thlaltute Thlangtlak Dan' in *Zofate Zinkawngah: Zalenna Mei a Mit Tur a Ni Lo*. Aizawl: Lengchhawn Press. pp. 12-13.
99. A. Paasi. (1996). *Territories, Boundaries and Consciousness: The Changing Geographies of the Finnish-Russian Border*. Chichester: John Wiley & Sons. p. 76.
100. S.K. Mukherjee. (1998). *Op.cit.*
101. *See*, R. Zamawia. (2007). *Op.cit.* Then Khatna, Bung-1, Mizo (Zo) Hnam Tobul Leh Thlahtute. pp. 1-7.
102. Zaithanchhungi. (1990). *Israel- Mizo Identity.* Aizawl: J.R Bros offset Printer; Lalchungnunga. *Op.cit*; S.K. Mukherjee. *Op.cit.*
103. S. K. Mukherjee. *Ibid.*
104. Lalchungnunga. *Op.cit.*
105. For details *See*, Prasun Sonawalkar. (1990). *Op.cit*; *The Times of India*. (1990). 'JD decision shocks Mizoram'. *Op.cit.*
106. Despite the lack of scientific evidences Israel is keen to bring Bene Menashe back to Israel. One of the evident reasons being that Israel is facing crisis of human resources and declining birth rate has raised its difficulties. The current birth rate in Israel is far below that of Palestine which has the highest birth rate in the world. It means Israelis fear to be dominated by growing Palestinian population in the coming decades. The Zo/Mizo are also suffering from an identity crisis in India. The protracted insurgency and the disgruntled-ness over the post-Peace situation made it a breeding ground for spiritual adventurers offering salvation, identity and the prospect of emigration and riches abroad. Given all these facts, it cannot be refuted that Israel is expanding its occupation, and involving other nations also in this game. New Delhi's *'don't disturb them'* policy unfortunately fails to see the hidden agenda of the Zionists.
107. The Chhinlung-Israel Peoples Convention is campaigning across the state to change the name of the Mizo tribe to Chhinlung-Israel. It also talks of a greater Chhinlung-Israel state that would include the Mizos of neighbouring Burma and Bangladesh.
108. Lalchanhima Sailo a Shillong born, descendant of a Mizo chief, former employee of the Food Services Corporation of India, and holder of law and history degrees from JNU in Delhi and Osmania University in Hyderabad joined the Mizo People's Conference Party in 1990 (Brigadier T. Sailo's Party). In 1992, while attending an International Seminar on 'Studies on the Minority Nationalities of North-East India: the Mizos' (7th-9th April) at Aizawl, he argued against efforts by Indian intellectuals to assimilate Mizo identity with that of the Assamese. In 1993, he was initially projected as a candidate for the state legislature but the People's Conference withdrew its support, disgruntled, he was forced to run as independent.
109. This became evident when Lalchanhima Sailo decided to adopt the faith of the Bet-Israel sect (a Jewish sect was founded by Jonathan Kahn an American Jew, who believed in the restoration of Israel and Jesus Christ). In 2000, an Indian Christian preacher, P.P. Job spoke in Mizoram on an invitation by Jonathan Kahn. Kahn blew the 'shofar' (the traditional Jewish ceremonial ram horn) in the Assam

Riffle field of Aizawl. He said that, 'the stick of Ephraim and Judah should stick together', suggesting a connection between the Jews and Mizos. Sailo, who was till then a nominal member of the Presbyterian Church felt that Jonathan Kahn's talk on the restoration of Israel could be understood to mean the restoration of a lost tribe of Israel, the Zo/Mizo, in an independent Israelite state in South East Asia. The connection between Lalchanhima Sailo and the CIPC with Jewish movements was not limited to Jewish-Christians.

110. Although Lalchanhima Sailo himself did not convert to Judaism, he did not deny that there was a possibility of him doing so in the future, saying, 'Let time tell who I am'. He admitted that his movement was a stepping stone for Zos/ Mizos to convert to Judaism 'as our movement grew more and more people became Jewish or started to follow Judaism.

111. Zaithanchhungi was a relative of one of the members of the original group that went to seek or reach Zion following the vision of the headman in 1951. Formerly a successful insurance agent and the wife of a state legislator, and a former teacher she went to Israel in 1983. There she met Eliyahu Avichayil, an Orthodox rabbi whose Amishav organization searches the world for descendants of the lost tribes. He showed immediate interest in her story, saying Jews had been scattered as far as China. He urged her to return to India to catalogue Mizo history. She came up with a list of apparent similarities, including the building of altars, the sacrifice of animals, burial customs, marriage and divorce procedures, a belief in an all-powerful deity and the symbolic presence of the number seven in many festivities. Zaithanchhungi saw other links in musical instruments and household practices. 'I was a non-believer, but after my research I now believe very firmly that the Mizo are of Jewish descent'. Yet she herself remains a Presbyterian.

112. Anup Shekhar Chakraborty. (2015b). *Op.cit.*

113. These concerns of the Church in Mizoram further stand as proof that the Church is not against India and is not the cause of insurgencies and secessionist movements in the Northeast as commonly perceived by many Indians.

114. In June of 2003, Biaksiama presented his report on the CIPC before the church elders in the Presbyterian Pastorate of Champhai. He claimed that the CIPC assertions, both about being a lost tribe of Israel and independence were full of lies. The elders who had become members of the CIPC were taken aback. Attacked harshly by Mr. Biaksiama, they said that they only sympathized with the CIPC call the independence and unification. P.C. Biaksiama continued his movement against an Israelite identity for the Mizos and the CIPC. He conducted a seminar at his home church in Cannan Veng area of Aizawl and in November of 2003, he published a book called, 'CIPC leh Mizo Israel' dissecting the positions of the CIPC and condemning them for their wrong teachings.

115. Lalchanhima Sailo countered Biaksiama's arguments by pointing that 'the high priests did not sacrifice with pig and the lower priests who sacrificed with pig would not eat the meat. A kind of Sabbath was observed. They had a kind of circumcision as well. They buried their dead by first bathing and clothing the body before burial. 'They had always referred to Menashe who is Menashe, the son of Joseph, their great ancestor.

116. Mona Zote. (2006). *Op.cit.*

117. The traditional pathways to the Zo villages were almost inaccessible, the precipitous ranges and cliffs were used to the best advantage of its settlers. This was one of the reasons which provided the much needed security of the tribes and their world infested with insularity and intra and inter tribal contestations. For details, Anup Shekhar Chakraborty. *Forthcoming*: 'Examining the Look East and Act East Policy through the History of Colonial Expeditions, Surveys and Road Building into the Zo territory'.
118. Anup Shekhar Chakraborty. (2016). 'Localization of the Gospel, Cultural Revivals And Christianity: Colonial Encounter in South Asia and the Zo Hnahthlak'. *Asian Studies*. Vol. XXXIV. Nos. 1& 2. January-December. pp. 36-67.

3

Politics of Zo Christianity, Representational Leadership and 'Being Secular' in Mizoram

The discussion in this chapter attempts to weave seemingly polarised ideas into a knot of convergence and thereby attempt to understand the practices of borrowed[1] concepts of religion, institutional democracy (political representations) and secular politics alongside indigenous[2] religiosity, everyday democracy, and peoplehood.[3] The discussions by interloping three issues that is the 'notions of Politics of Zo Christianity', 'Representational Leadership' and 'Being Secular' in Mizoram attempts to address the 'constrictions, circumvents and collations' and critique the same.

Drawing heavily from the previous chapters I argue that the purpose of a 'Customized-Localized Gospel'[4] was to suit the understandings of the 'primitive tribes'. The content of the Gospel was decoded into a language that was receptive to the 'savage tribes'. 'Being a Zo/Mizo' and 'Being a Christain' began to be seen as being one among the *Zo hnahthlak*. The *Politics of Tlawmngaihna*[5] has by and large been one of the strong guiding principles/marker of Zo/Mizo identity politics.[6]

Through the post-colonial times the encounter with Christiandom and the realignment of the earlier/traditional Zo belief system resulted in the evolution of a strange concoction of practices and clannish cults further complexifying the Zo Christian Cosmology. Instances of the 'clannish cult Churches'[7] such as the 'Lalzahavara-Nu Diheli' (around Sangau Khua/ Village)[8], 'Enoka Pawl' (around Salem Veng), 'Channa Pawl' (around Baktawng Khua/Village) can be cited as reflecting the same. These clannish cult Churches incorporated strong elements from the traditional Zo practices while claiming to be the new Churches among the *Zo hnahthlak*. The indigenization of Christianity also marked the evolve of resistance to both Christianity and the Colonial ways as emphasized by the Missionaries. For instance, the Channa Pawl which evolved in Baktawng Village some 100 kilometers from Aizawl derived its existence to the use of the traditional drum i.e. *Khuang* as an item of worship among the ancestors of the cult founders. The Welsh Missionaries had strongly voiced their concerns over such practice and banned the worship of the *Khuang* as practiced by the ancestors of Challianchanna. Challianchanna and his brother then founded the rebel church grounding their ancestral practices into the mould of Christianity as preached by the Welsh Missionaries and styling the cult church as 'Channa Pawl' or 'Lalpa Kohhran' in the early 1930s.

All these 'deviations', reaffirms very strongly that Christianity manifests itself very differently in different places conditioned by specific social realities. The Christian experience among each of the Zo tribes intune with the experience of Christianity elsewhere throughout South Asia shows points of convergences and maneuverings of those receiving the 'new religion' and way of life. Clannish, intra-tribal, inter-tribal, animistic/traditional practices coupled with cartographic zoning of the Zo people have largely affected the moorings to the same. Christianity amidst the ostensible homogeneity among the *Zo hnahthlak* is veritably fragmented. Heterogeneity with a projected homogeneity is one of the marked paradoxes of Christianity among the *Zo hnahthlak*.

The Cartographic zoning for instance injected a sense of marked difference among Zo tribes in the region. The Welsh Presbyterian actively worked among the Northern tribes while the London Baptist Missionary Society worked among the Southern tribes. It is very interesting to note that the cartographic zoning also affected the projection and degree of belief in Christianity for instance Northerners began to stereotype Southerners as 'less believers'; and Southerners stereotyped the northern Christians as 'less believers' while retaining and claiming the position of 'strong believers' for their respective tribes. The denominational divide also worked very interesting complexities among the Zo Christians. For instance, from the Colonial times the Roman Catholics were considered to be non-Christian in belief system because of the relegated position of Mary; and interestingly the localized Christianity as practiced among the Zo does not proscribe divinity to women.[9]

The use of traditional musical instruments like the *Khuang* (traditional drum), *Dar* (Burmese brass bell), alongside western instruments like the guitar or the option of wearing of traditional '*puanchei*' (wrap around worn by Mizo women) for Zo/Mizo women as an alternate to the wedding gown as many such examples to show the marked indigenization of the practices of Zo Christianity. The Whiteman's way of life and religion[10]delivered the tribes from fear of evil, death and uncertainty of a war prone migratory life at the psychological level.[11] 'Religion and Politics' thus began to play an overwhelming role in Mizoram[12] and began to be considered superior, powerful and therefore more alluring.

Christian faith was a great force in the process of *Zo* integration and over fifty years turned Mizoram and many *Zo* inhabited areas into a Christian land. The newly zealous *Zo* converts took it as their privileged burden to tell the 'Good News' to their kindred tribes and many had volunteered to go to the heathen *Zo* areas to preach the Gospel. These apostle-like preachers carried the good tidings along with new Christian hymns in the Lushai dialect, which the pioneer missionaries employed as a vehicle to spread the Gospel. As a result, Lushai (*Duhlian*) dialect quickly developed into a rich language to become an effective instrument for spreading the gospel and *Zo* integration. The first Bible translation and many other pioneering publications among the *Zo* tribes were in Lushai that subsequently came to be known as the 'Mizo language', a language that became the link language of the *Zo* people. Wherever *Zo* preachers carried the Gospel and new churches were planted, they also implanted *Zo*-ness, thus paving the way for a re-unification. Therefore, next to their common ethnic root, Christianity has become the most important bonding force of the *Zo* people. A *'Zo'* professing any other faith except the traditional religion (animism) is considered by the majority *Zo* Christians as not only a renegade but an alien. Being a *Zo* and a Christian is like a coin with two faces.[13]

The Church's influence is really deep and daily life is encircled by it. The church has become Mizoised through *ruaithre* (community feasting) and *'zai leh lam'* (song and dances). Zaliana observes:

> 'Alongside religion, the 'Denominational' factor has greatly influenced the Zo/Mizo politics. The undivided Aizawl district had a more welcoming attitude. While in the south (*chhim)* one had to have a local network or local connections to have a footing into the politics of that region. Most of the political leaders in Mizoram come from *Chhim* (southern). Excluding Lalthanhawla most leaders from Ch. Chhunga, Dengthuama, Laldenga, T. Sailo and others all had *Chhim* (southern) links and were under London Baptist influence. They also were the first set of Mizos to come under the influence of western education, religion and politics.'[14]

The influence of religion can also be understood why the early leaders decided to do away the clannish affiliations and its markers for creating an egalitarian political identity cutting across clan and sub-tribe identity. For instance, politicians and people at large in Mizoram hardly use their clan names or tribe names and instead use their first names. Politics in order to survive and create an *'Ideal Zo Christian State'*, therefore crucified clannish identity and its markers at the altar because 'if there is no crucifixion there is no rising'.[15] The church leaders in turn maintain a dignified, respectable and non partisan stand. It is because of the role of the Church and its agencies that the Election Commission labelled Mizoram as a role model for other states in India.

Christianity had spread like forest fire in Mizoram after the 60s MNF rebellion precisely because the post-rebellion psychological trauma compelled people take refuge in culture and religion in order to find solace. The post-rebellion trauma was exploited by the evangelists to convert because to convert more people to the fold of Christianity meant a more secured life for the evangelist in the next world.[16] Similarly there was a growth in music and education in the post-rebellion times. The growth and rise of music and education can be seen as 'healing' the Zo/Mizo society. Christianity, Education, Music, in other words, "Religion" and "Culture" became important markers of *Zo Identity*. The predominance of religion in *Zomi* politics reflects itself through the constant references made to God (*Pathian*).

It is interesting to note that *'Being a Zo'* and *'Being a Christian'*[17] are the two issues around which religious identity politics in Mizoram is developed. The first issue has problems of parameters of definitions and it remains contested. While the second issue has elements of experiential-ness embedded to it as evident from the casual everyday use of language *'Khristian nilo in an hrethiam lovang'* ('Non-Christians will not be able to understand') to brush side those who do not belong to the Church as not being able to understand the Bible and its teachings. Both these issues are projected in the state-building process of an *'Ideal Zo Christian State'*.

Representational Leadership

The issue of leadership[18] and its role in construction of identities and consciousness among the *Zo hnahthlak* has been muted.[19] 'Leadership' and 'Politics' in the changed times relied heavily on the code of *Tlawmngaihna* and Social Welfare. At the same time, both these arenas remained the bastions of patriarchy due to the functioning of Christian Ethics and code of life. Interestingly, in the post-insurgency situation, leadership also began to mobilise identity consciousness around 'memory'.

Leadership among the *Zo hnahthlak* in the pre-colonial times was strictly clan and class assigned. The *Lal* and the various *Upa* were the source of direction for the community and naturally leadership was attributed to them alone. The others in the clan/tribe were the followers and assigned the duty of subservience and obedience. The chief was the central figure and as the linchpin, he could impress upon the villagers to provide their best, and also attract others from other villages to join his village.

> 'Each village is ruled over by a chief. Most of the Chiefs belonged to the Sailo clan, which had established itself as the ruling family before the British took over the hills. In addition there are a certain number of chief's, who do not belong to the ruling clan and who are known as Hnamchawm chiefs. These are mostly people who have been appointed as chief's over vacant lands by Government, usually as reward for services rendered in the Lushai wars. There are also a few Hualngo and Poi chiefs who formerly held sub-villages under Sailo chiefs and have since been recognised as independent chiefs. In Lungleh subdivision there are many Poi and Lakher chiefs whose forefathers have been chiefs for generations and who have never fallen under Sailo influence. There are also a few Fanai chiefs, most of these follow Sailo custom. The chief is the father of his people, he helps them when they are in distress and if he falls into difficulties, they also help him in turn.'[20]

On the reverse the Chiefs weakness and lack of maturity as a leader could result in wholesale abandonment of his village by the *hnamchawm*.[21] This audacious act of 'abandonment' could be construed to mark 'everyday democracy' among the 'primitive'. The everyday democracies among the *Zo hnahthlak* arose from the fact that the commoner was never tied to the soil as land was not a fixed asset in the traditional Zo society and correspondingly the allegiance to the Chief was also flexible and non-contractual, non-permanent. As land was not a property and was abundant, this situation favoured the commoner in that he/she was always guaranteed that amount of freedom. However, even so, the act was always undertaken with discretion.

Institutional democracy in the Lushai/Mizo hills witnessed the marked contest among the triumvirate- Lalthanhawla, Thenphunga Sailo and Laldenga These three men and the political parties they represented in Mizoram namely: the Congress, the People's Conference and the Mizo National Front (MNF) were concern as to who would be credited as to having succeeded in ushering in 'Statehood', a dream long cherished by the public in the Zo hills: a panacea which would solve or resolve all tensions and conflicts in the region and bring '*remna leh muanna*' (peace and prosperity).

As elsewhere in India around the mid 1970s 'ethnic consciousness' or 'ethnic exclusivism' and 'autonomy' came as added packages along with the growth in Regional Parties. The debate on the issue of authentic People's Representation in Mizoram in the form of the Congress Party ('*Vai*' Party) versus the MNF Party ('Zo' Party) reflects the lived experience of the contested nature of Centre-State relations in contemporary Indian politics.[22]

Laldenga advocated the secession from India following the great famine of the late 1950s when starvation stalked the hills following the 'Mautam'. Using the spirit of Christianity and *Tlawmngaihna* through the distribution of food supplies by 'Famine Front', he skilfully impressed upon the ill-informed villages his interpretation of the story of victimisation, neglect and cultural suppression.[23] The MNF used overtly Christian nomenclatures for their various activities during the insurgency. For instance, the simultaneous attacks at Aizawl, Kolasib, Champhai, Serchhip, Lunglei and other prominent places in Mizoram in March 1966 was named 'Operation Jericho' in line with the story of the defeat of Jericho and the occupation of the 'Holy land' by the Jews on their exodus from Egypt. The MNF declared independence after an audacious attack on the district's major towns.[24] This was followed by the counter-insurgency strategy of the Indian State. Thousands of villagers were uprooted from the hills and sent to Regrouped Villages built along the highways. For the next 20 years, violence continued in the Mizo hills with the MNF camping in East Pakistan. With the fall of East Pakistan in 1971, Laldenga's men scattered to Myanmar while he moved to Pakistan. Rajiv Gandhi in 1986 hammered out a deal to end the secessionist agenda. During these times of crisis 'the Churches role in peace process was mostly in the form of community prayers ('*twang tai*') and church services. In fact the underground MNF returnees say, 'the prayers of the public made them come back to the normal life in Mizoram.' 'We were fed up of the troubles of insurgencies.' 'The MNF used 'the prayers' of the public as an excuse to come back to mainstream politics.' Vanramchhuangi is of the opinion that 'the MNF themselves had realised the futility of their demands and Laldenga had come to realise that his movement was failing. Therefore he and his followers said that the call of the church was the reason why they gave up arms.' 'They needed an excuse to justify their calling to an end of their demands and secessionist movement. They publicly said that they surrendered to God (Jesus Christ) and not to anyone else.'[25] Mizoram attained statehood and Laldenga became its interim chief minister before his MNF won the first elections to the state legislature.[26]

Post Peace Accord Laldenga's leadership underwent a severe metamorphosis both at the level of authority and administrative tactics. The change in leadership tactics echoed the dynamics of the changed times.[27] The era of long-distance leadership being over, Laldenga had to taste the 'bitter sweet' nature of 'real power' exercised in constraints within the sphere of democracy. Laldenga began to realise the pushes and pulls of exercising power in a democratic set up and also the multiple stakeholders pressures', the most pronounced of which was 'the Church'. For instance, Laldenga found it difficult to cope up with the issue of 'Total Prohibition', and openly challenged the dictates of the Church but soon he had to bite his words because the Church started anti-Laldenga propaganda which led to his downfall. An abstract form a news item in the Times of India mentioned:

> 'Church sources said …its role in the political affairs had become more prominent during the liquor controversy …when the former CM Mr. Laldenga clashed with the Church leaders. He had gone to the extent of warning the Church not to interfere in temporal matters, "just as we do not interfere in spiritual affairs"'.[28]

The 'love-hate' relationship between Laldenga and the Church in Mizoram can be traced back to the 60s and 70s when the Church attempted to mediate between the MNF rebel leaders and Government of India.[29] Even though a general perception exists that 'Insurgency' in most cases in the North-East is sponsored or supported by the missionaries.[30] The case in Mizoram proves otherwise, 'infact, the Presbyterian Church, the most powerful of the 10 denominations in the state, had opposed the insurgency led by Mr. Laldenga' though the MNF was the first political outfit to serve a concoction of religion and politics by declaring itself as a party driven by the force of God (Isua/Pathian). Most of the Churches took a cautious stand and restrained themselves from openly accepting Laldenga's words. All through the insurgency and the counter-insurgency phase, the Churches maintained mixed responses to the MNF and read the messages of Laldenga with caution. The methods of intimidation, liquidation, arson etc., which the MNF adopted alarmed the Churches and the Presbyterian Church in particular felt it was their moral duty to take initiative for restoration of peace and normalcy. The Presbyterian Church thus issued pamphlets expressing disapproval of violent activities of the MNF as being against the teachings of Christ as well as against Human Rights.[31] The MNF reacted strongly against the Presbyterian Church Pamphlet of 1966 and warned the Church to keep to its ecclesiastical realms and refrain from worldly affairs of politics.[32] The other Churches like the Baptist Church Assembly undeterred by the warnings of the MNF to the Presbyterian Church issued similar pamphlets condemning the MNF activities and misuse of the name of Christ for its violent methods.[33] Later in September 1966 the two Churches namely the Presbyterian and the Baptist issued a joint circular[34] to its members expressing their disapproval of the violent methods of the MNF.

The Churches accused Laldenga of high-handed-ness and encouraging social evils and deviating from the code of a Zo Christian life and the vision of an *Ideal Zo Christian State*. In a direct reference to the MNF Supremo, the Church and its agencies accused Laldenga of encouraging various social evils like drinking, partying, sex, night-life, corruption and consumerism in the post-peace accord era.[35] The Church also stretched its accusations by blaming all vices in the Zo/Mizo society to the long years of disturbance and lack of guidance during the MNF led insurgency. The Churches in unison squarely pointed fingers at Laldenga for sustaining rampant corruption in Zo/Mizo politics and using money power to win over support from young voters and other quarters.

Post 1989 Laldenga realised that his challenge to the Church had cost him heavy electoral losses. For instance, the election code of conduct for the Mizoram Assembly Elections outlined by the Church:

> 'asked political parties not to nominate candidates who are known to consume liquor, another indirect reference to Mr. Laldenga whose fondness for the spirit is well known. Let all those who make nominations select only such persons who stay clear of sin. We appeal not to select any person who falls short of the Church's wishes and criteria, no matter which party he belongs to'.[36]

Laldenga had to re-think and re-formulate his take on Church-Politics relationship in Mizoram in the Post 1989 situation. Laldenga strategically crafted his *new* take on Church-Politics relationship in the new times though as a result he had to live a life of schizophrenic dilemma publicly defending the cause of Christianity and the Zo people's reunification and defending 'Total Prohibition' while privately challenging the same by ignoring the claims of the faith and indulging in booze and money-power. During its Ministry the MNF had ignored the demand of the Churches to discontinue the Excise Act (Licence for Selling Liquor) and its promise to discontinue the Excise Act in the election manifesto 1987.[37]

Laldenga, post-1989 was a changed man having succeeded in hiding the tragic news of his long battle with cancer from public life. Laldenga knew well that he would not survive long and showed apathy towards active political life as evident from the following piece of news in the Times of India: 'The 63 year old leader was, in fact more pre-occupied with completing his 3 storey house near Aizawl than campaigning for the MNF...'[38] The above cited news report seems to show a different picture of Laldenga as a 'family man', concerned for the welfare of his family and provide them with all comforts, wellbeing and all sort of financial security after he was gone.

The Electoral verdict of the Assembly Elections of 1989 led to the fall of the image of 'Laldenga' at the political front and the fading of the image of 'Pu Denga' at the social front. For instance, at the political front the fall of the MNF Ministry in 1989 led to further factionalisation of the MNF Party so much so that a section of the MNF began to have second thoughts about the Accord[39] and its leadership. At the social front the general message conveyed was that of Divine intervention/Divine punishment. For instance, Chawnghzuala, President of the MNF (D) faction of the MNF firmly believed that it was God who toppled Laldenga from power positions. Chawnghzuala said that 'Mr. Laldenga was neither with the Church nor with the people.'[40]

Laldenga was quick to re-affirm his take on the issue of political loss and made it loud and clear to his followers that the 'MNF would not go back to insurgency' just because it failed to handle the reigns of democratic power. Laldenga also brushed aside rumours that the MNF factions were having second thoughts about the Accord as being fabricated by other contending parties like the People's Conference; Lalthanhawla led Congress and the Governor of Mizoram Hiteshwar Saikia. Laldenga at a National Press Conference in New Delhi on 24th February 1989 mentioned that 'if we (MNF) ever take up arms again, it will be for the defence of India'.[41] Though critical of the Mizoram Pradesh Congress and its leader Lalthanhawla, Laldenga continued his good words for the Congress leader Rajiv Gandhi.[42]

Brigadier Thenphunga Sailo (AVSM)[43] a straight forward and educated senior army officer had entered Zo/Mizo politics at a time when Laldenga made an exit to Pakistan. The leadership vacuum impelled the Mizo people to look out for a suitable leader capable of handling the problems in Mizoram. After his retirement from the Indian Army in January 1974, Brigadier Thenphunga Sailo came back to Mizoram. Feeling the pulse of the people the retired Brigadier set up the 'Human Rights Committee' with the objective of rendering help in legal measures against mass rapes, the grouping of villages, to uphold civil rights of the 'oppressed' civilian population, and to educate the public in upholding their legal rights against the Security Forces. Thenphunga's intervention toned down the Army's brutal activities in Mizoram and the populist 'anti-Army' slogans and attracted a large fan following immediately. For a while, the sway of the ex-MNF people towards the Congress party was effectively stopped. Sailo milked the Human Rights issue to clear the ground for launching his political party the People's Conference (P.C) on April 17, 1974.[44]

Brigadier Sailo compiled details of incidents which were supposed to have taken place after March 1st, 1966 in the Mizo Hills District and submitted a report to Indira Gandhi. He also filed cases against various army officers who had carried out counter insurgency operations in Mizoram, including some who had been decorated posthumously. He filed a suit in Guwahati High Court against the Government of Mizoram for the grouping of villages, but lost the case. He then collected a large number of petitions against the Security Forces and forwarded them to the Central Government for action against the guilty. He criticised Government policies, Army actions as well as army in-actions, but failed to condemn the atrocities of the MNF and the brutality of the MNF. Brigadier Thenphunga Sailo earned the wrath of the Indian State and was detained under the infamous Maintenance of Internal Security Act (MISA) during the Emergency. Sailo thereafter, openly aligned with the Janata Party, which had ousted Indira Gandhi in 1977.

Two years, later Thenphunga's popularity eclipsed that of Ch. Chhunga the first chief minister of Mizoram. The use of the 'Human Rights card': Indian Army's violation of women; strategic extension of sympathy to the MNF leader in exile (Laldenga) and, the use of the *'Zo Christian Identity'* readily helped the People's Conference to convert the popularity of its leadership into electoral success and Brigadier Sailo became the Chief Minister of Mizoram in May 1978. Sailo's party also won the mid-term elections of 1979 and became the Chief Minister of Mizoram for the second time. Superficially, the defeat of the Congress was blamed on factors that had brought about the rout of the Congress and Indira Gandhi in the immediate post-Emergency phase. Sailo apparently rode the crest of popularity because of his anti-Security Forces stance, and his promise to bring the MNF and the Government of India into the negotiation table, and bring about peace and development. Union Territory Governments of Ch. Chhunga and also Sailo ushered in a relaxed atmosphere for instance, the dusk-to-dawn curfew, which had become a permanent feature of Mizo life for the past thirteen years, was lifted, and the movement-by-permit system was also abolished along with the de-grouping of select villages. The elevation to a UT status brought about multi-fold infrastructural developments and the insurgent hit people began to see a ray of hope in the PC Party. The Party in turn exploited all possible strategies including that of 'Social Welfare' to systematically convert popularity into electoral support through votes to secure their foothold in Zo/Mizo politics. The conditions during this period would, in all probability, have led to an accord, but Brigadier Sailo refused to hand over power to Laldenga. This adamant posturing of Sailo led to the failure of talks and renewed tensions in the region. The MNF and New Delhi squarely put the blame on Sailo naming him as the main stumbling block during the peace talks between the rebels and the Indian government. The loss of lustre in the persona of Sailo resulted in the loss of his party in the 1984 assembly elections, and the rise of Lalthanhawla's Congress.

By the time the Peace Accord was signed Sailo begun to realise his short-comings as a statesman and the need to develop newer strategies to attract the masses. The first step that Sailo initiated towards this end during the changed times was to realign with the 'Greater Zoram' movement which by then had matured to an organisation the *ZORO* (Zo-Reunification Organisation). However, Sailo found it hard to juggle with the numerous stakeholders in the post-peace situation and ended up earning the wrath of the most prominent stakeholder in post 1986 politics in Mizoram-the Church. For instance, the Church also indirectly rapped the methods of canvassing of the People's Conference Party whose *ZORO* Movement caught the imaginations of almost every youth in the State. Boys and Girls under 15 and college students can be seen almost everywhere sporting the *ZORO* headgear and waving *ZORO* flags. The giving of uniforms by the party to *ZORO* volunteers has come in for adverse criticism from many quarters. "We request that the parties and candidates carry out their campaign in a graceful manner as would befit the believers", the Church message said.[45]

Lalthanhawla as a prominent triumvirate of political leaders among the Zo hnahthlak serves an interesting case to observe and absorb the 'constrictions, circumvents and collations' in understanding the 'notions of Politics of Zo Christianity', 'Representational Leadership' and 'Being Secular' in Mizoram. Popular as the 'Durtlang Pa' he started his career as Recorder in the office of Inspector of Schools in the District Council. After that, he joined the Assam Co-operative Apex Bank as Assistant. In 1966, he joined the Mizo National Front as Secretary till 1967 when he was arrested and jailed in Silchar. Once released from jail, he joined the Indian National Congress Party and in 1973 he was elected Party President. In 1978 and 1979 he was elected as a Legislator in the Union Territory Elections. In 1984, under his leadership, the Congress party swept the elections in the state and he became Chief Minister. The results of the 1984 election in Mizoram were, therefore, more or less a foregone conclusion. Congress party fought the elections on the platform of peace and won with an overwhelming majority. Lalthanhawla became the first Congress Chief Minister of Mizoram in May 1984. In accordance with their election pledge, the first major action taken by the new government was to formally appeal to the Prime Minister to resume talks with the MNF. The Security Forces' operations against the MNF were suspended. Unfortunately, Laldenga returned to New Delhi from London on October 29, 1984, a day before the assassination of Indira Gandhi, and the talks could not be resumed for many months.[46]

The next two years saw the development of secret links between the Indian National Congress (I) and the MNF, evidently with the full backing of Indira Gandhi. The Congress Party in Mizoram was largely a party of ex-MNF operatives and sympathisers. Lalthanhawla, who headed the Congress in Mizoram, was a young, suave and sincere politician who enjoyed an enviable degree of trust and respect in the Prime Minister's inner circle. He was able to persuade the Prime Minister that, with her support, he and his ex-MNF colleagues in the party would be able to achieve what she herself desired most: a settlement in Mizoram leading to an end to insurgency and the ouster of Sailo and his People's Conference from power. The Mizoram Pradesh Congress Committee embarked on this mission and openly charged Sailo with sabotaging the peace process because of his personal ambition and love for power.

Throughout the insurgency period, the Congress in Mizoram emphasised on peace and tranquillity; though the Congress Manifesto during the elections of the said time frame did not openly promise Statehood, it did address the issue in a subtle manner. The Congress made it clear that once peace and tranquillity were established all things would automatically follow. The other issues that were highlighted by the Congress during the time were improvement in agriculture; industrialisation of the State, integration of territories inhabited by the Zo/Mizo (Zo territorial integration movement, *'Zomi leh sa'*, *'Zo hnahthlak'*) provided they were contiguous to Mizoram.

Lalthanhawla in 1986 abdicated his Chief Ministership as part of the Peace Accord agreement for Pu Laldenga. Through this gesture Lalthanhawla began to be held in high esteem in public memory as the true *'Tlawmngai Congress Pa'*. this gesture for initiating the era of peace made Lalthanhawla's popularity even more overwhelming than that of Sailo and next just to Laldenga. In fact, in the post-peace Accord Zo/Mizo politics, the contest for the 'Father of the Zo/Mizo nation' had two prominent contestants namely Laldenga (MNF) and Lalthanhawla (Congress). The ground was cleared for a clear tug of war between the two parties-the MNF and the Congress. The public attitude towards the Congress mellowed fast under the tactful leadership of Lalthanhawla. The Congress now began to be viewed as a party that could bring greater resources, finances and faster development to Mizoram and make the vision of an *Ideal Zo Christian State* realisable. The popularity of Rajiv Gandhi and his wife (Sonia Gandhi) also helped the Congress to make its hold in politics in Mizoram even stronger. The fear of the congress as being a *'Vai'* Party having its remote control in New Delhi (*'Vai ram'*, mainland India) began to easy off. The charisma of Rajiv Gandhi and the issue of his wife being a foreigner (Christian origin, Roman Catholic) were interpreted among the people of this Christian state and the Church as being advantageous for the Zo people. The Congress (I) in general and Rajiv Gandhi in particular (as indeed the Nehru-Gandhi family members[47]) have always exerted some fascination in the North-East, especially in the peripheral States of the North-East. The apparent ease and the lack of inhibitions with which the Nehru-Gandhi family have conducted themselves in the public in these predominantly tribal territories have made an impression difficult to contest. Also their western appearance (white skin/complexion, light eyes and doze of superficial western outlook made them, almost ostentatiously as it were, when they were in these regions, further predisposed the people of the region, so avidly attached to the most superficial and ersatz symbols of such 'westernisation', in their favour.[48] More than being a clash among contesting parties, the case in Mizoram reflected a contest between personality and leadership. The Zo/Mizo story of transition *from* insurgency and violence *to* constitutionalism and peace, to a large extent revolved around the *Politics of Tlawmngaihna*. Few instances to support this argument are: Laldenga organised the Famine Front to distribute food to the Mautam victims; Brig. Sailo put to use the power of the pen to write about the Human Rights violations during the insurgency in order to mobilize the Zo/Mizo consciousness and; Lalthanhawla abdicated his legally recognised post of the elected Chief Minister of Mizoram for Laldenga all for the greater cause of peace and stability and the realisation of the greater, long term goal of creating/building an *Ideal Zo Christian State*.

Lalthanhawla the *'Tlawmngai Congress Pa'* was quick to realise that collaborating with the Church and its agencies could enable the congress sound benefits and strong footage in Zo/Mizo politics in the peaceful times. In order to exhibit the spatial and psychological proximity of the Congress Party with the Churches in Mizoram tickets were given to people fulfilling the criteria mentioned by the Church. For instance, in the 1989 Assembly Elections in Mizoram, Mr. Vanlaltluanga, a senior church leader was made to contest the Aizawl South constituency on a Congress ticket.[49] Vanlaltluanga himself made it public that he was contesting elections for enabling a better co-ordination between the Church and the Government. He also said that many other Church leaders were contesting the 1989 elections because of the unsavoury tiff with the Laldenga Ministry. Accusing the Laldenga led MNF Ministry of corruption, Vanlaltluanga mentioned that 'the Church had asked the Laldenga Ministry for land to build structures for the Church but the Laldenga Ministry did not do anything' and that made the tug of war between the Church and Laldenga public. The 1989 Mizoram Pradesh Congress Election Manifesto clearly promised to 'establish a government in tandem with Christian Principles and pledged that as Christians it is our bounded responsibility to proclaim the Gospel… the Congress (I) policy of socialism is based on the Biblical teachings as well as the traditional ethos of the Mizos…'[50]

Lalthanhawla over the years faced several mounting criticisms and has often been said to have matured from *'Tlawmngai Congress Pa'* to 'Corrupt Congress Pa' (*Tlawmngai* Congress man to the Corrupt Congress man). Lalthanhawla has been accused of nepotism and placing his favourite people in important positions to make his grip firmer in Zo/Mizo politics. For instance, Lalthanhawla backed Lalchhunga his brother-in-law as the IGP of the state. Similarly the important posts of Chief Secretary and other important portfolios were handed to people having close proximity to Lalthanhawla.

He has been accused by the opposition of being corrupt. For instance when Lalthanhawla visioned the Lengpui Airport which officially began to function between 1999-2000 he was swamped with criticism from all quarters for dreaming it too big. The location and the site selected for the international size airport was highly contested and the opposition booed Lalthanhawla that 'not even a vulture would land in such a hilly terrain and wooded area'. Few felt that Lalthanhawla selected the site primarily because he would get compensated for his mother's property which was a large portion of the area demarcated for that purpose.

One blot in his career has been the charge sheet filed against him in October 2003 by a lower court. Lalthanhawla has been charged of cheating the state exchequer in collusion with some businessmen. However, Lalthanhawla brushed the charges aside and said:

> 'It is only an attempt by my political rivals to deny me the right to fight these polls and stop the Congress from coming back to power. There will be no more talk of this corruption case once we are back in power. I have immense faith in the Indian judicial system'.[51]

Lalthanhawla or Pu Hawla continues to be referred to as being soft and close to the '*Vai*', his proximity to the Delhi circles continues to raise eyebrows among contending politicians in Mizoram. He has been nicknamed 'Vaihawla', 'Vaithanhawla" (the prefix '*Vai*' strongly signifying his proximity to the abhorred '*Vai*' and his public gestures, body language which is atypically '*Vai*'). Critics of Lalthanhawla have been fast to criticize his

'*Vai*' ways of life and political public gestures. The opposition parties and the Churches have time and again accused him of converting to '*Vai* religion' i.e. Hinduism.[52] It is interesting to note that while performing seemingly 'Hindu' (*Vai*) practices like a 'namaskar', inaugurating a Durga Puja Pandal etc., Lalthanhawla is accused to be 'anti-Zo Christian', and 'non-secular' but while performing markedly Zo Christian practices like invoking the name of 'Jesus' before making political statements, partaking in '*ruaithre*' (community feasts in the Churches or elsewhere) etc., his 'secular' credntials were not suspected.

Pic 3.1: The controversial picture of Lalthanhawla and Pi Lal Riliani inaugurating a 'Durga Puja Pandal in Kolkata to mark the 25th Dushera Anniversary & Cultural Function at IB Block Sector III, Kolkata Salt Lake Lalthanhawla and his wife had attended the Durga Puja celebration which the MNF regarded as "betraying his God and forsaking his Christianity. Guwahati.* The Telegraph *Sunday 9 October 2011."

The perception of the 'Congress' as a 'Vai Party' and the contortions, and constrictions through which the Congress has cling to its hold in the region needs to be seen from the larger historical context and content of institutional democracy operative in the North East. The congress, it must be remembered, was not an unchallenged party in Assam during the national movement and the same argument goes for Mizoram or Lushai Hills as well. Almost all Political Parties in Mizoram were formed out of the 1st Political Party in Mizoram the 'Mizo Union'. The birth of the Congress in Mizoram also followed the same story. Defection and internal feuds within the Mizo Union led to the birth of the Congress in 1961 by A. Thanglura. After the formation of the Union Territory the local Congress (Mizoram

Pic 3.2: Lalthanhawla and Pi Lal Riliani visit to Mizoram University 2000. Lalthanhawla and wife admiring the 'alpana/rangoli' on the marbled floor. The 'Alpana/rangoli' was construed by many in the audience to be an invasive 'Vai culture' surreptitiously entering the reserved space of the Zo culture. Mamon Mazumdar: Aizawl.

Pic 3.3: Lalthanhawla and Pi Lal Riliani visit to Mizoram University 2000. The 'Namaste' by Lalthanhawla had created a stir among the hardliners of the Zo public. While those supporting the then CM felt that given the cosmopolitan nature of the university with students from other states the casual gesture of 'namaste' was considered appropriate. Mamon Mazumdar: Aizawl.

Pradesh Congress Committee (MPCC)) leadership was taken over by the young Lalthanhawla as its President. The initial days of the Congress were that of stiff resistance from the Zo/Mizo public and blunt criticism from the other Political leaders. For instance, the Congress for a very long time was looked as a *'Vai'* party having its core in Delhi (India).[53] In other words the Congress was an alien party trying to control the lost sovereign Zo territory through remote control and filtering *'Vai'* (Hindu) ethics to the sacred territorial space of *Zo Christianity*. The attitude towards the Congress was that of a mixed baggage. 1st at one level it was seen as an alien party trying to control the Zoram. At another level it was seen as a party that was the root cause of all mismanagement/mis-happenings in Zoram. For instance the Congress was blamed for all the misery caused by the great famine caused by the Mautam. At the 3rd level it continued to reflect and sustain the enigma of the Nehru-Gandhi parivaar.[54] At the 4th level it was also seen as a party that was rooting for filtering the Assamese hegemony through the process of Ahomisation and supporting the cause of the Sanskritised Ahom culture into the sacred territory of the Zo Christian space. For instance, the silence maintained by the Centre on issues such as language policy of Assam during the said period was taken to mean the unsolicited support of the Centre towards the B.P. Chaliha government.[55]

The Congress (at the Centre and in Assam) during the pre-Union Territory days for instance, sided Laldenga's 'MNFF' which was an organisation floated to combat the famine or Mautam[56] in the Mizo Hills. The Government of Assam led by the Congress Chief Minister B.P. Chaliha provided Laldenga's non-state actor full patronage to take up the role of an active actor to distribute food to the famine stricken people in the remote interiors of Mizo hills. The state patronage to Laldenga and his band enabled the MNF to gain easy popularity. The Assam Government relied on the non-state actor more than the rival State-actors that is, the Mizo Union led by Ch. Chhunga. The Congress government both in Assam and at New Delhi felt that such a move would check the Mizo Union's foothold in the Mizo hills. The Mizo Union at that time was venturing on the possibility of breaking up from the Assam Government and rallying behind the Eastern India Tribal Union for an independent Hill State. The other alternative of collaborating with the United Mizo Freedom Organisation (UMFO) was not feasible for the Congress led Assam Government for the simple reason that the UMFO was openly preaching separation from the Union of India. However, the politically motivated move of the Assam Government proved costly for the Chaliha Government. The Famine Front mutated itself into a political outfit- the MNF in 1961.[57] Laldenga made full use of technology (magnetic tapes)[58] and print nationalism through his paper *'Mizo Aw'* (Mizo

Voice)[59] to construct a new 'Political Identity' heavily laced with primordial overtones.

The Congress in Mizoram overtime had to strategically negotiate with the underground MNF forces and dislodge two prominent political rivals namely the Mizo Union and the PC Party. The post-Union Territory phase of Mizo politics shows the series of shrewd political bargainings carried forward by the Congress to chisel its space in terrain of Mizo/Zo politics. Congress in Mizoram began to grow in membership and political acceptance after the attainment of Union Territory status and the seal of recognition given by Indira Gandhi. The Congress made a systematic and calculated move by at times blaming the core Mizo Union and its leadership Lawrence Ch. Chhunga for all the problems in Mizoram and waving sympathy towards Laldenga's MNF. The political gain came in the form of defectors from both political outfits making a bee-line to the Congress. So much so that by 1973 the Congress almost looked like the demon that it denounced the arch political rival the Mizo Union.[60] The Mizo Union due to its stiff-lipped approach to the MNF and its anti-MNF stand was losing in popularity in the public. Ch. Chhunga was unable to match the image of a 'Hero' attached to the persona and leadership of Laldenga and his parallel 'Mizoram Sawrkar'.

Ch. Chhunga's anti-Laldenga stand and pro-India stand was by and large accepted by most members of the Mizo Union. The alliance with the Congress was seen by many within the Mizo Union as a sly strategy to dislodge the Chief Minister and the Mizo Union from power. This led to fissures and cracks within the Mizo Union. Ch. Chhunga the then Chief Minister of Mizoram realised that the Congress would soon out number it and so decided to merge with the Congress and gain from its proximity to the National Party. The unconditional merger of the Mizo Union with the Congress was sealed at the AICC meeting at New Delhi. The move further created factions within the Mizo Union and finally some consensus was achieved when the Congress High Command officially approved the merger of the two on 24th January, 1974. As per the merger Ch. Chhunga was allowed to continue as the Chief Minister and two members of the Congress were inducted in the Ministry. The merger had two pronounced effects in the public: first, the absorption of the Regional Party in the National Party was seen as threatening the indigenous Mizo way of life; second, it brought into power the Mizoram Congress which all along had been exploiting the Laldenga trump card to its advantage.

The Congress though being a partner of the Mizo Union exploited the issue and pointed fingers at Ch. Chhunga's leadership and his party's commitment to the anti-MNF stand. Ch. Chhunga succumbed to the strategies of the Mizoram Congress and finally on May 9th 1977 Ch. Chhunga resigned. The psychological pressure from within and without was too heavy to bear, though Ch. Chhunga said that his 'Ministry was resigning on the expiry of its five years term in the Assembly'.[61] The resignation of Ch. Chhunga was followed by imposition of President's Rule (Article 356) on 11th May 1977 (continued till 1st June 1978) a strategy which was later repeated even in 1988 when the Laldenga Government was toppled by the Mizoram Congress. The Mizoram Congress through the office of the Governor also exploited Article 356 to maintain the supremacy of the Centre in the State. Such a move, further substantiating the critique, that the wide discretionary powers of the Governor are in effect powers exercised by the Central Government by proxy through the Governor. [62]

The stiffest competition to the Congress and MNF partnership was given by Brigadier Thenphunga Sailo 'People's Conference' (PC). Sailo's immediate popularity through the Human Rights Committee was a direct result of the vacuum in leadership created by the exit of Laldenga on self-exile to Pakistan. The increased level of strained relations between the Indian Army and the public compelled Brigadier Thenphunga Sailo, a retired Indian Army Officer, along with some friends, to form the Human Rights Committee (HRC) in the month of June 1974 in Aizawl. The popularity of the HRC was converted into a Political Party and the following year (17th April, 1975) the People's Conference (PC) came into existence. Brigadier Sailo started on a note of clean politics, honest politics, to solve the political problems of the state. Sailo felt that on economic development Mizoram was lagging behind Meghalaya and Nagaland. He blamed Ch. Chhunga and the Mizo Union for all the failures of the state to bring the MNF to the negotiation tables. Coming from the 'Sailo Chiefs clan'[63], the Brigadier felt that he was superior to the earlier leadership of the Mizo Union which was very much middle class and mediocre. He targeted the leadership qualities of Ch. Chhunga and at times even exploited the issue of Ch. Chhunga's son who joined the MNF.[64] Ironically, Sailo forgot that while in service in the Indian Army he had to face similar personal attacks from his colleagues when his son, Lalsangliana, had joined the MNF.[65] Right from its initiation the PC tried to align itself with the Janata Party and maintained a strategy just the opposite of the Mizoram Congress. Though never officially recognised by the Janata Party at New Delhi, Sailo maintained his commitment to the national party. Sailo most probably felt that proximity to the national party would fetch it suitable gains. Sailo maintained a positive attitude towards the Centre.

At one stage Sailo hoped to act as the self appointed political advisor to the parallel government of the MNF. Sailo was well aware of the fact that most of the followers of the MNF were under educated, with very little expertise in statesmanship required to deal with the more polished *'Vais'*. With his experience in the Indian Army and prolonged contact with the *'Vai'*, Sailo felt that he was the right man to steer the unrest and lead Mizoram towards peace. The popularity of the PC topped the charts and the young educated masses flocked to it. Sailo strategically made a calculated move and toned down his anti-Indian Army stand as well as its pro-MNF stand. The PC before coming to power at this stage was largely welcomed by the MNF leadership. The President's Rule that followed Ch. Chhunga's resignation ended on 2nd June 1978 when Brigadier T. Sailo formed the Ministry. Sailo appealed to the people to help bring peace back to Mizoram. Brigadier Sailo had initially milked the issue of 'Human Rights' and atrocities committed by the Indian Army on the Mizo people. Sailo after assuming power realised the thorniness of the Chief Minister's position. Instead now Sailo played with the image of a *'Pa chang sipai anga ri-thlap'* (a tough military man) and conveyed the message that 'the need of the hour was a new set of leaders with good army background to check the excesses of both the Army and the MNF as well as provide quality leadership which both the Mizoram Congress and Mizo Union were 'unfit to provide'. Sailo realising the unhappiness of a section of his followers especially women due to the tuning down of the 'Human Rights card', felt the urgency to pull out a new rabbit from his hat. This time Sailo attempted to appease the Church and garner the support of the powerful Church. Sailo made a calculated move and declared his goal 'to cleanse the Zo/Mizo society which through external contacts had lost its way'. The first steps was to check 'fraud and liquor' a move welcomed by the Church.[66] This alliance between politics and religion further strengthened the influence of the *Nexus of Patriarchy* on Zo/Mizo identity politics.

Sailo through his strict handling of the MNF earned him the wrath of the MNF Supremo Laldenga so much so that Laldenga ordered the people not to vote Sailo.[67] The People's Conference by the end of 1977 had two clear groups: those inclined towards the MNF and the other having a neutral stand or anti-MNF stand. Throughout the Chief Ministership of Brigadier T. Sailo, the Mizoram Pradesh Congress made concerted efforts to dislodge the non-congress ministry by inclining itself towards the insurgent MNF supremo Laldenga. Lalthanhawla the Congress leader had by this time successfully won the confidence of the Laldenga. The erstwhile partners in the MNF movement were back in partnership. Sailo's second stint as Chief

Minister of Mizoram began on 8th May, 1979 and continued till 4th May, 1984. Sailo kept the option for peace talks open for bringing lasting peace in Mizoram. Sailo made it public that his party was in favour of stronger institutional safeguards and stricter implementation of the ILP which would govern the entry of the *'Vai'* in Mizo territory. Sailo also highlighted the sensitive issue of the 'Chakma influx'. The objectives of the PC started on the plank of development issues, improvement in power and communication, efficient administration. Laldenga felt offended by the verdict of thc Zo/Mizo people and claimed that the verdict was no verdict as it did not involve a larger section of the Zo/Mizo people who were beyond the borders of the Union Territory of Mizoram. To make situation tough for Sailo, the MNF issued 'Quit Mizoram' notices to the *'Vai'* ordering all outsiders to leave Mizoram by 1st July 1979 and threatened defaulters with death. The timings of the 'Quit Mizoram' notices was matched with the 'Peace Accord of 1976' and conveyed the message loud and clear that the MNF did not uphold the Accord and would not surrender arms. The MNF felt that Sailo was acting as a mouth piece of the Centre and was too close to New Delhi. The MNF impressed upon the public that Sailo was being remote controlled by the *'Vais'* in Delhi. The tensions between Laldenga and Brigadier Sailo had reached a level where political extermination was not shied away from. The arrest of Lalhminga (Hmingtea) a courier-cum-body guard of Major Lalrawna of the 'L' Battalion of the MNF by the BSF at Aizawl on 23rd June 1979 revealed the plot to assassinate Chief Minister T. Sailo and other important ministers.

To make situations worse, the MNF carried out atrocities on the *'Vai'* and murdered outsiders who had continued to stay in Mizoram following the assurance of their security by the constitutionally recognised Government. Sailo reported the grim situation in Mizoram to the Centre and accordingly the Centre declared the MNF and its allied organisations as unlawful under the Unlawful Activities (Prevention) Act of 1967. The Janata Government at the Centre under Morarji Desai placed Laldenga under arrest under sections 121, 121A and 120B of the IPC on 8th July, 1979. The Janata Party at the Centre toed the lines of the State and Sailo had an upper hand in the negotiation tables.[68]

Though Laldenga re-tuned his stand on the peace talks in the changed situation and changed leadership from Morarji Desai to Chaudhury Charan Singh at the Centre, after a series of meetings soon realised that there was no change in the stand of the Janata Government at the Centre and therefore, turned to the Congress to bail him out. The calculated move of toeing towards the Congress can be seen through the report in 'India Today' dated 16-31 July, 1979:

> Pu Laldenga has chosen Pu Lalthanhawla, a cultured and calculating politician who headed the Mizoram Congress which was linked with the Congress (I) as his advocate. Pu Lalthanhawla, who had served under Pu Laldenga, as Cabinet Secretary in the MNF till 1969, and as the later leader of the opposition in Mizoram Assembly, felt that the only way to bring back peace in Mizoram was to invite Pu Laldenga for negotiation and ask Brigadier T. Sailo to quit.

The change in the Central Government in 1980 brought newer hurdles for the pro-Janata Party Sailo Government in the Union Territory struggling to keep up with insurgency and counter-insurgency. The subtle message that the MNF and the Congress conveyed to the minds of the masses was that 'the Brigadier' was the chief stumbling block in the way to *remna leh muanna* ('peace and prosperity'). Out and out politics in Mizoram became a battlefield where the personality of the two titans clashed and pitched themselves against the external support of two contesting national parties: the Congress and the Janata Party. For instance, Laldenga's public message to the people of Mizoram on 14th December, 1979 blaming Sailo for creating fissures and cracks within the MNF was countered by Sailo's radio broadcasts on 4th January and 25th March 1980. Sailo in his message to the people of Mizoram gave details of the killings and violent dealings of the MNF. Through these broadcasts Sailo made it clear that the MNF were having double standards and that they were in actual working to achieve their objective within the framework of the Indian constitution contrary to the public projection made by the MNF Supremo Laldenga. Sailo also accused the MNF movement for all the backwardness of the Union Territory. He severely criticised the violent methods of the MNF and gave examples of States in the North-East that attained Statehood without violence. Sailo also made it clear that violence was delaying the goal of Statehood and blurring the vision of an *Ideal Zo Christian State*.

Laldenga also struck back and made his dissatisfaction with Sailo's government more pronounced when he said that 'the Sailo government must go. Sailo is a political tool in the hands of the Government of India in its political warfare against the Mizo people.' Laldenga dubbed Sailo as a stooge and a puppet tarnishing the image of the quintessential Zo/Mizo Hero.[69] Laldenga also repeated his allegations that the Sailo Government was violent and criticised its Special Forces tactics of counter-insurgency. He also alleged that some of the violent killings in Mizoram had been committed by Sailo's Special Forces, in the guise of the MNF rebels, in order to stall the peace efforts so that the Brigadier could continue with his chair. The year 1980 also saw a rise in the number of incidences of violence in Mizoram.

Things got tough for Sailo when on 30th June, 1980 the Chief Metropolitan Magistrate of Delhi dropped the criminal proceedings against Pu Laldenga "for waging a war against the Government of India".[70] The partnership between the MNF and the Congress (both at the Centre and in the Union Territory) paid well for Laldenga. However, being a legally elected leader Sailo was able to have his share of the Centre's attention. For instance, having experienced the double dealings and double standards of Laldenga during the earlier Peace Talk's, Sailo requested the Home Ministry to record the message of Laldenga asking his men to surrender and agree on the 'ceasefire' and broadcast if over All India Radio (AIR) from stations at Shillong and Aizawl. The suggestion was accepted and Laldenga's stand was made clear to the public that peace would be within the constitutional framework of India.

The Brigadier having deprived of the benevolence of the Janata Party at the Centre was left vulnerable to strong criticism from the Congress at the Centre and the Union Territory as well as the parallel-Government of the MNF (Mizoram Sawrkar). From late 1979 Laldenga sensed the possible return of Indira at the Centre and strategically began his pro-Congress stand and squarely blamed the Brigadier for the failure of peace talks and the terrible condition of the civilians in Mizoram. The allegations made by the MNF Supremo and the pressure tactics of the Congress from the Centre and within Mizoram made it almost impossible for Sailo to carry on with his office. The situation was almost a repetition of the pressure tactics and resignation of Ch. Chhunga government on 9th May 1977. Sailo was staunchly opposed to the suggestion made by the Centre (Congress) or the demands made by the MNF and the Mizoram Congress at the UT for the dismissal of the constitutionally elected PC Ministry. Sailo felt that the suggestion as well as the demand was an appeasement tactic to please the 'Rebel Leader'. With all these paraphernalia of challenges, the Ex-Army man continued to battle his existence and completed a full term in office on 4th May 1984, bringing to an end Brigadier T. Sailo's two terms as the non-Congress backed Chief Minister of Mizoram.

The Congress Party won the 1984 elections with the support of the MNF. Laldenga at this crucial stage reiterated the demands of the MNF such as special constitutional provisions at par with Jammu and Kashmir (Art. 370) providing for separate constitution and Flag and integration of the contiguous Zo/Mizo inhabited areas of Assam, Manipur, Burma and Bangladesh, election of the Governor, special safeguards for the Culture and border trade with Burma and Bangladesh etc.[71]

Through the power-sharing scheme the Mizoram Congress was able to absorb its former political rival and make the Mizo Union's presence invisible in Zo/Mizo politics. So much so that public memory, today hardly remembers its first Chief Minister (Union Territory stage) or the first Political Party in Mizoram.[72] The Congress thus initiated the first coalition through power sharing, a model which it later used once again very profitably in the post-statehood period for mellowing down the MNF. Interestingly the Mizoram Congress throughout the insurgency period never openly denounced the activities of the MNF or challenged Laldenga's leadership and his parallel government. Instead the Mizoram Congress under the young leader Lalthanhawla milked the Laldenga fan-following to its maximum advantage so as to clear the rubbles beneath its ground to make for a deep foundation of the party. The Mizoram Congress also exploited Article 356 to maintain the supremacy of the Centre in the State.

The Mizoram Pradesh Congress under the leadership of Lalthanhawla came to power on 5th May 1984 and remained in power till 20th August 1986. Laldenga's objective of ousting the Sailo government from power was achieved when the Congress won the Assembly elections and Lalthanhawla took over as the Chief Minister of the UT of Mizoram. Lalthanhawla was the blue eyed boy for Laldenga and having won the trust and confidence of the rebel leader Lalthanhawla was able to channel his way deep into Zo/Mizo politics. Both the MNF and the Congress had painted Sailo and his PC Party as the main villains for the failure of earlier Peace Talks especially the talks of 1982 when Sailo refused to step down in favour of Laldenga.

The Central government made its role as the final authority loud and clear in the Peace Process. For instance, Lalthanhawla who was initially reluctant to be a part of the interim government was persuaded by the then Home Minister of India Buta Singh to join as the Deputy Chief Minister. Another instance which clearly outlined the Centre's overwhelming presence was the 1988 incident where the Speaker of the House suspended the defecting group under the provisions of 'anti-defection law' (Rule 9 of the Mizoram Legislative Assembly Rules) and the Governor Hiteshwar Saikia (a Congress Veteran from Assam) challenged the Speaker and also rejected Laldenga's plea of testing his strength on the floor of the House. Instead the pro-Congress Governor dissolved the House and declared President's Rule.[73] The power sharing that followed in the interim period reflected that the Centre had the last say in the Peace Process. The genesis of party formation in Mizoram reaffirms that the party formation cannot be isolated from the process of identity formation.[74]

On the question of 'Authentic People's Representation' and the problematic Centre-State Relations the Government of India employed numerous tactics to check the secessionist activities of the Mizos from the year 1966. The elevation to the status of a Union Territory was 'one such rabbit' pulled out from the hat of the Centre Government. The Government of India decided that the main military phase of counter-insurgency operations against the MNF was over, and it was time for seeking resolution of the conflict through structural techniques aimed at changing the political framework, and distributive policies for providing better economic opportunities and rewards. The strategy of granting Union Territory status to the insurgency torn Mizo Hills had a lasting effect on the future course of events and politics in Mizoram in general. The new government needed a large number of civil services personnel such as secretaries, joint secretaries, deputy secretaries, and directors etc. to administer its various departments. This meant finding officers to man the numerous posts in these new establishments. The number of officers available from the Union Territory cadre of the Indian Administrative, Police and Forest Services for the senior positions in these various organisations and hierarchies, was inadequate and it became necessary to bring officers on deputation from other States, to set the new Mizoram Government going.[75]

At this point, a large number of Mizo officers working in other States and regions of India expressed their willingness to serve in Mizoram, and the newly elected political leaders in the Union Territory supported the idea. As a matter of policy, the Government of India had so far discouraged deputation of All India Services officers to their home States. But an exception was made in the case of Mizoram. What was done to tide over a temporary shortage of officers, as well as to oblige loyal Mizo politicians, turned out to be a blessing in disguise. Many of these officers were related to influential Mizo businessmen and politicians, including those in the MNF. Their arrival as senior officers of the government was a joyous event in the history of the community, and they became the nodal points of the most powerful social group in Mizoram, with a strong and abiding vested interest in their linkages with the rest of the country.[76]

Post 1972, the leaders were more interested in consolidating their political positions in the community than in attending to the developmental needs of their own people. The leaders' emotional expressions of the community's urgent needs made in public, or especially for outside audiences often stood in sharp contrast to gross financial irregularities. Until 1969; there were no audit systems to check them. Even later some glaring problems persisted. Yet, no criticism of these practices from the state authority (Centre and Assam) above them was regarded as legitimate.

The Assam language policy was conveniently exploited by the local stakeholders in the Mizo Hills to divert the attention of the local masses from the gross irregularities. Interestingly, when these same leaders interfered with the language rights of the minor tribes for educating their children in the Regional Council within the District Councils, it was not supposed to count as a violation of tribal rights.[77] But the leaders of the Mizo District Council, especially in the 1960s were, eager to blame the Assam and Central Governments for the relatively poor performance of their own representative institutions.[78]

The post peace politics in Mizoram has witnessed the protracted tug of war over the issue of the 'Authentic People's Representative Party' with both the prominent actors the MPCC and the MNF taking credit for the '*Remna leh Muanna*' ('peace and tranquillity').[79] The contested nature of the debate is best construed from the content of Rajiv Gandhi speech to the public in Aizawl during his Mizoram Tour right after the signing of the Peace Accord well summed up the sentiments and by and large it was a pat on the back for the Congress (both at the Centre as well as the State):

> 'now a new dawn will come over Mizoram- a new dawn that will bring in the re-union of families, the end of tension, the re-construction of villages and basically, the most important of all, the building of the economy of Mizoram." "Today we have the "Memorandum of Settlement" but we could not have had that, if it was not for certain sacrifices by Shri Lalthanhawla and other Congress leaders and congressmen in Mizoram. They have placed statesmanship and patriotism, above petty or party political interest. They have most of all, placed their faith in the Mizo people. It is the Country which needs such vision, such sensibility, and such sense of service'.[80]

The followers of the MPCC believe that the Congress in Mizoram has finally come of age in Zo/Mizo politics and its leader the shining example of a '*Tlawmgai Zo Pasaltha'* a new hero in the horizon of Zo/Mizo politics. Lalthanhawla is unequivocally credited to have singlehandedly ushered peace into the troubled hills along with the dynamic young visionary – Rajiv Gandhi. The MPCC made it loud and clear that in the absence of tactful and selfless leadership peace could not have been realised. For instance, Lalthanhawla volunteering to leave his elected office so that MNF supremo Laldenga could come to the negotiation tables is time and again emphasised for calling the MPCC the 'authentic people's party'. As opposed to this the MNF has time and again emphasised the great sacrifices made by the nationalist heroes to compel the Centre to come to the negotiation tables and chisel that honoured space that the *Zo hnahthlak* (Zo people) deserved within the ambit of the Indian Constitution. The MNF has gone public in taking the sole credit for the Peace and the sustenance of the peace and development in the state and have time and time again projected Laldenga as the 'father of the *Zo hnahthlak*'. The MNF felt that unlike the MPCC it has its roots strongly grounded in Mizoram and the aspirations of the Zo/Mizo people. Therefore, it is the 'authentic people's representative'. The MNF cynically snubbed the MPCC as 'Made in Delhi' and having its inclinations to the '*Vai*' cultures.

The MNF has also snubbed the Congress political leadership for trying to control the politics in Mizoram through 'money bags' and 'dole development'. The MNF has blamed the MPCC for acting as agents of the Centre or for being remote controlled by New Delhi.[81] Here it is interesting to note that the MNF which claims to be the 'authentic Zo nationalist representative' had won political battles by aligning with the BJP, also it had publicly showcased its 'reciprocal alikness' to the BJP on the issue of granting autonomy to the Chakma and the Indo-Bangladesh border issues and issues of cross-border infiltration. The BJP from 1998 onwards has been strongly supporting the *Bru* (*Reang*) as minority tribes who deserve autonomy within Mizoram and by the same logic partially supports the *Chakma*.[82] However, the BJP presents stiffness when it comes to granting more autonomy in the form of a graduation to UT status to the *Chakma*. The BJP both at the Centre and in Mizoram seem to be toeing a tight trapeze on the issue of infiltration of illegal immigrants in the region. This opposition to elevation of the CADC to a UT however, maybe due to the BJP's genuine concern for illegal infiltration in the North East or 'just opposition for the sake of opposition' for denying the Congress the credit for such a move which will permanently 'seal-off' the possibility of ever converting the traditional vote-bank of the Congress in Mizoram to its advantage.[83] Another obvious reason being that the BJP is cautious of hemming in its future possibility of any alliance with MNF for whom, the *Chakma* (*Chakma foreigner*) is a sensitive issue pricking the national ego of the *Zo hnahthlak*. In other words the mission of creating an exclusive space for the *Zo hnahthlak* or *'Zomi'* in the form of an *Ideal Zo Christian State* gets eclipsed by the presence of an ethnic enclave for the *Chakma* (*Chakma foreigner*). For instance, the BJP Mizoram Pradesh in its press release dated 29th July 1998 mentioned:

> *'Keini Mizoram BJP-te chuan Congress tihloh Party dangte hi chu, a hranpa taka thawpui theiloh kan nei lova, BJP hi Indian MNF ang an ni e, kan ti ang a, Nuclear Bomb pawh tipuak ngam, Sawrkar hnahthawk pension hun pawh kum 2-a pawhsei sak a, Lecturer-te hlawh pawh,*

siamthat saktu anih, keini Mizoram BJP hi Mizoram leh mipuite humhimtu nih hi a tum ber a ni.

Mizorama Foreigner-te thawn chhuak vek turin tan a la bawk, Rajya Sabha-a, Congress Committee hi Chakma UT a recommend pawh duh lovin, ruahsur hnuaiah BJP hotute chu kawngzawhin, ruahsur pawh pawisa lovin, a tawp rawt thleng tan latu a ni.'[84]

(The BJP in Mizoram is open to alliance with any political party excluding the Congress. The BJP is a nationalist party very close in its ideologies to the MNF. Infact the BJP at the Centre is the 'Indian MNF'. A party which dares to test the Nuclear Bomb, makes innovative changes like extension of the retirement age by 2 years for Government servants, revised salary for Lecturers etc. The BJP's interest in Mizoram is to preserve and promote the interest of the people of Mizoram.

The BJP is committed on its anti-foreigner stand unlike the Congress which had placed the recommendation for UT status for the Chakma in the Rajya Sabha. It was because of the BJP leadership that the recommendation was stopped. The BJP leaders' infact organised a rally opposing the recommendation. Not even the heavy showers could stop the BJP from exhibiting their displeasure against the Congress recommendation).

The public sphere[85] in Mizoram is thus oozing with protracted debates. Listening to these diverse voices that has filtered into the public sphere at one level helps to construe the contested nature of the debate over the authentic people's representation in Mizoram. At another level it helps to unravel the underlying tug of war between the centre and the state in the functioning of federal politics in India. A multifold recapitulation of the historical as well as political developments during the period 1960-2015 'helps one to understand the different strategies adopted by the Centre and the local stakeholders cutting across party affiliations for making democracy functional and make meaning of the constitutional provisions' by interpreting them to fit their vested logic. These can be understood as the 'circumvent and collations' weaving the thematic notions discussed in the paper.

'Being Secular' in Mizoram

Coming to the third aspect of the discussion in this chapter I would re-raise old questions which has haunted generations and communities elsewhere and pin them to the Zo context: what does being 'secular' or being 'non-secular' or 'asecular'[86] mean among the *Zo hnahthlak*? Does the notion of secular get cornered by the profound expression of Zo-Christian religiosity? The line wedging the 'Believers' from those clubbed as 'Non-

Believers' is neatly marked by those following the ways of Zo-Christianity, anyone deviating from that neat line is condemned as being a 'Non-Believer'. The discussions in the preceding sections arrives us to the understanding that the *Nexus of Patriarchy* plays the self-proclaimed role of cleansers of the Zo society and thus monitor the Zo community into a faith (Zo Christian) abiding, culture conscious, 'peoplehood'. Also as seen above in the discussions the leadership attunes itself to the directions and dictates of the Church and the *Nexus of Patriarchy*. For instance, the leadership grounds its popularity and legitimizes its authority (political, institutional, situational) by aligning itself to the volatile mood swings of the church and its agencies, thereby reaffirming the humorous popular aphorism: *'Mizoram-ah chuan Sawrkar a lalber a, Kohhran a thuber'* ('In Mizoram the Government is the highest authority, and the Church has the final say').

The constricting predominance of the Christian ethics in Mizoram can be understood by the fact that 'the government and the bureaucracy have not been able to touch the masses as the Church. Therefore inorder to gain the required connectedness to the 'people' the elites try to go with the tide and without any spirituality they enter the Church activities in order to gain popularity and mass appeal. So in short, they dictate terms in their interest through the church.'[87]

The influences of religion on politics and vice versa for instance can be gleaned through Laldenga's pressure tactics and invocation of the name of *Isua Khrista* (Christ) and his attempt to attract the masses. Laldenga challenged every other leadership that came up to lead the Zo/Mizo in the direction of political maturity. He first clashed with Ch. Chhunga and then later with T. Sailo both of whom were legally elected leaders of the Zo/Mizo people. Laldenga having a brief stint in the Indian Army wanted to create a following on the lines of 'one nation, one religion, one leader'. A quick glance at the process of entry and exit in the MNF as an organisation would help understand the overwhelming nature of Laldenga's personality and his hegemonic tendencies. Many insiders felt that Laldenga never liked the idea of having an alternative power centre or alternative leadership.[88]

The use of terror and violence became more pronounced during the clash of personality and leadership between T. Sailo and Laldenga during the second term of Sailo's office. The gruesome murders of *'Vai'* persons and liquidation of several important personalities of the MNF who had returned back to public life and the non-compromising stand of the MNF Supremo distanced the Church and its agencies from the MNF. The strategy and calculated moves made by Sailo in terms of using the card of

Development, Christian way of life and the cause of a Greater Mizoram and good life for the *Zo hnahthlak* attracted the inclination of the Church. Zairema's advice to Laldenga clarifies the wrong understanding that the Church or Christianity was responsible for triggering insurgency or separatism in Mizoram and North East in general.[89]

Laldenga having realised his growing distance from the Church in Mizoram and the negative image that had been projected through the MNF activities, changed his strategy once more. This time to appease the Church and keep them in good humour, the 'Mizoram Sawrkar' appointed Town Commanders[90] at Aizawl to launch a drive against Zu and use of narcotics. Laldenga exploited Christianity to serve his vested interest. For instance, he called for all the *Zo hnahthlak* to keep distance from the '*Vai*' who were 'idol worshippers' ('*Milim bia*') and determined to pollute the Zo Christians as the main stumbling block towards the creation of an Ideal Zo Christian State and unification of the Zo hnahthlak: 'Greater Mizoram'. This led to the operation of an insular ethnic consciousness harped on Zo Christianity. 'Such was the venomous content of the hate speeches made by Laldenga that any one who would listen would be charged and the first reaction would be to thrash the first '*Vai*' that one met on the streets', says Zaliana.[91]

Through the violent activities of the MNF, Mizoram earned its image 'of a disturbed Christian area demanding secession under the leadership of Laldenga' in the 'National News'. Laldenga once more changed his tune towards the Centre during the change in leadership from Morarji Desai to Chaudhury Charan Singh at the Centre. However, hopes were belied when the new Union Home Minister Y.B. Chavan was fixed on implementing the July 1976 Peace Accord. The renewed interest in the peace talk's offer was primarily because Laldenga hoped that the treason and criminal charges against him would be dropped. Laldenga after a series of meetings soon realised that there was no change in the stand of the Janata Government at the Centre. Laldenga then turned his attention to the Congress led by Indira Gandhi who had promised him that if she came back to power in January 1980 elections, she would honour her Government's commitments and let him leave the country if he wanted to. Laldenga felt that apart from her all the other leaders had proved 'untrustworthy' as the Janata Government had gone back on its commitments.[92] Interestingly Laldenga has branded the same Indira Gandhi during her leadership at the Centre in the pre-emergency period as "Hitler's wife" and often referred to her as '*Hmeithai*' ("the Widow").[93]

Laldenga sent a message to the people of Mizoram on 14th December, 1979 conveying his Christmas and New Year Greetings as if to say that the year of peace is getting closer with the 'New Year' (1980).[94] In his message Laldenga blamed Sailo for all the problems of the Zo/Mizo people including his personal detention during the 'Emergency'. Laldenga alleged that Sailo had advised him to surrender arms during a meeting with the Home Minister in 1977. Laldenga accused Sailo of attempting to create a rift in the MNF leadership and it was because of his handiwork that senior officers of the MNF like Biakchhunga had surrendered to the Government. Laldenga also alleged that the nomination of Biakchhunga as an MLA to the Mizoram Assembly by the Sailo Government was a reward for his assistance to the PC Party. He also pointed that his imprisonment on 8th July 1979 was the work of the conspiracy of the PC Party and the Janata Party (the Centre).

Mizoram serves interesting instances of enmeshing of popular ethic affiliations with that of religio-prophecies. For instance, the year 1980 was visioned as the predestined year when the *Zo hnahthlak* would be freed from subordination and would be unified into one single unit. Miss Parchi or Poparchi (35 years old) a Mizo/Kuki woman who claimed to have visions of God known as a flamboyant anti-Laldenga rebel. She preached a bizarre Gospel, predicting the birth of a mythical Mizo hero in 1980. Miss Parchi's *'Ramthuthlung Group'* had a Seventh Day Adventist background and preached that the Mizos would get their independence in 1980. The *Ramthuthlung cult* preached that as Mizoram would achieve independence in 1980 there was no need to continue with peace talks and the continuation of the armed struggle. She managed to influence important members of the MNF headquarters in Aizawl and preached anti-Laldenga gospel to the MNF members thus creating fissures in the MNF and rising dissatisfaction with Laldenga's leadership. She also managed to enter the inner circles of the MNF when she became a part of the MNF Organising Committee on Politics Affairs (COPAS) a scheme which aimed to bring all ethnic tribes of the same origin under one Government. A scheme Laldenga had kept close to his heart in the earlier days of his leadership.[95]

Throughout the insurgency, the flow of MNF returnees and surrender of arms alongside the 'new entry' (new recruits/ volunteers) into the MNF fold went on simultaneously. In other words, the entry into the MNF and exit from the MNF went side by side. An interesting phenomenon of corruption which emerged during the period was that of unemployed, educated and semi-educated Mizo youths including school-drop-outs making a bee-line to join the MNF for a short time. In anticipation of getting rehabilitation benefits and employment as MNF returnees', young unemployed people joined the MNF and whenever a surrender ceremony took place, some of the new entrants would line up as MNF veterans, who had under-gone severe hardships in the jungles of Chittagong Hill Tracts.

'Majority of the new recruits had joined the MNF for the thrill of it and for financial benefits and not for patriotic or political reasons'.[96]

The short term entry into the MNF was not just exploited by the youths to extract the benefits of amnesty but also by Ex-servicemen. Ironically, the Government of India was providing better facilities to the MNF returnees than to the Ex-servicemen who laid down a quality time of their life for the service of the 'Nation in the Making- India'. Naturally this created dissatisfaction among the Ex-servicemen and induced them to join the MNF for short term and return to public life in Mizoram. Many such MNF surrenderees got rehabilitated in the Police Department and other Government offices and continued to render services to the MNF as and when required mainly due to the fear of being liquidated by the MNF.[97]

Many of the over-ground MNF workers taking advantage of the liberalised amnesty and the changed political climate during the UT phase infiltrated and entrenched into the Government offices and exploited the constitutional/legal offices to expand the control of the MNF and defend their unconstitutional activities. For instance, many of the MNF returnees joined the different political parties and tried to make a pro-MNF wing from within those organisations. This was one of the prime reasons that led to the division of almost every political party into anti-MNF and pro-MNF wings during that period and eventually led to the questioning of the authority of the leadership of those political parties. For instance, the leadership of Brigadier T. Sailo was challenged by Thangridema the Speaker of the House during Sailo's first stint as the Chief Minister of the UT of Mizoram and as a result the PC Party was split into PC Party 'A' (T. Sailo) and PC Party 'B' (Thangridema).[98]

These interweaving political histories of political parties, the evolve of their leaderships, and their interactions with the Indian state and its constitutional provisions helps one to construe the uncomfortable fact that 'being secular', 'non-secular' or 'asecular' is profoundly integrated to the problems of 'choice' ('choice making'). Evidently no one particular political party or leadership can claim to be 'secular' and that each has its own share of being 'non-secular', and being 'asecular' in an operative scale. Also 'asecularism' seems to plunge deep into the aspirational baritone of the *Zo hnahthlak* and their conceptualisation of 'peoplehood' ('*mihringna*').

Some closing observations

Bringing my discussion to a closure I would reaffirm that performing religiosity, conducting oneself in a multi-religious, multi-ethnic setting is not as easy as said to be. The seemingly polarised ideas of the eclectic- the temporal, 'religion'-'politics', 'secular'-'non-secular' 'asecular' are in practice knotty convergences and thereby very difficult to disentangle. 'The everyday' of such concepts like religion, institutional democracy (political representations), secular politics alongside indigenous religiosity, everyday democracy, and peoplehood needs to be considered to engage in our studies of peoplehood and their imaginaries of the 'secular', the 'non-secular' and 'asecular'.

Notes & References

1. I use the term 'borrowed' to put across the point very strongly that the ideas 'religion' to be specific 'Christianity', politics in the form of institutional representational democracy were incorporated and injected into the Zo ways of life by way of colonization and proselytization. The notion of the 'secular' was a late incorporation into the everyday lexicon of the Zo people through the application of the Indian Constitutional provisions and its multifaceted interfaces with the Zo people. (ASC).
2. I use the term 'indigenous' to refer to the ideas of 'religion and religiosity' that was derived from the Zo cosmology of creation and ways of life that can be sourced to many of the folklores and tales among the Kuki-Chin-Mizo people. Similarly democracy (institutional) though a borrowed concept did manifest itself in a different operational conditions for instance though not aware of the more evolved form of 'democracy' (western), there are clear indications that the notional aspect of democracy which I call the 'everyday democracy' was performed among the Zo people for instance by way of the act of abandoning a hegemonic chief etc. (ASC).
3. By 'peoplehood' I mean the ways how a group perceives of itself as a common bounded entity much like the 'ethnie' but strongly grounded on feelings of 'compassion', 'consideration', 'sympathy-empathy'. Unlike the common nomenclature for referring to the pristine memory of having a rooted connection i.e., Zo hnahthlak, the notion of 'peoplehood' is neatly embedded on the imprints of '*mihringna*' (being human). However, those counted as '*mihring*' (humans) is subjected to temporal conditionings. In other words those counted within the ambit of 'peoplehood' is very calculated and a political (many a times theocratic) enterprise and not as linear as projected. (ASC).
4. I use this term to stress on the indigenization of the Christianity into the Mizo belief system and vice versa, i.e. Christianity as practices and preached in Mizoram. (stress intended to include all tribes professing Christianity in Mizoram: ASC). I owe this insight on the tactics of indigenization of Christianity & its usefulness in the Mizo society, identity etc., to my supervisor Dr. Bonita Aleaz, Professor, Department of Political Science, University of Calcutta. For a detailed reading on uniqueness of Mizo Christianity, see, Lalrinawmi Ralte. (1993). Chapter-VII, "Dance: An Example Of Crab Theology", Op.cit. pp. 193-209.
5. The code of *'Tlawmngaihna'* can be equated to the code of *'Pashtunwali'* practiced amongst the Pashtuns. Hero-worship being an inherent part of the traditional Mizo life continues to reflect in every day Zo/Mizo life even in contemporary times.

6. I have relied heavily on books and articles in Mizo language to support my arguments in this paper. For instance, Issac Zoliana's book in Mizo language titled '*Laldenga'* (2005) published by the author and printed at Gilzom Press, Aizawl; and also R. Zamawia. (2007). *Zofate Zinkawngah: Zalenna Mei a Mit Tur a Ni Lo* (Aizawl: Lengchhawn Press). Both writings in Mizo though heavily laced with chauvinistic jingoism have innumerable first-hand information on the MNF (Mizo National Front) movement and its leadership, and strongly countered the nationalist (Indian) perspective on the MNF movement and identity politics in Mizoram. Other books in Mizo include: C. Hermana. (1999). *Zoram Politics Thli Tleh Dan.* Vol. I. Aizawl: PRESCOM; F. Hmingthanga. (MCS Rtd.). (2003). *Mizoram Politic Thlirlet-Na (Mizo Hnam him Nan).* Aizawl: The Zo-Awm Press; L. Keivom. (1991). *Zoram Khawvel.* Aizawl: Lengchhawn Press; M. Lalmanzuala. (NA). *Zoram Kalsiam.* Aizawl: Sapthlengliana. Calcutta: Cambridge Laser Print Dakshinapan; Lalrawnliana (Col.). (1995). *Zoramin Zalenna A Sual.* Vol. I Aizawl: (NA); M.C. Lalrinthanga. (1993). *Mizoram Politik (1976-1986).* Aizawl: Lengchawn Press: A. Thanglura. (1983). *Zoram Politic Lumlet Dan*. Aizawl: Thakthing Bazar Press.
7. I am of the opinion that these 'Clannish Cult Churches' (3C) should not be confused with what we so often hear/read in Sociological/Theological studies as 'Popular Religious Movements' (PRM). Though much like PRM's the 3C's stress on healing, fighting evils and miracles but the similarity abruptly moves no further. The 3C's I observe harps closer to the pulse of the clan and clannish lineages. Also, their popularity tends to be around specified zonal areas maybe a part of a village and not the entire village, a closed group phenomenon. In that sense the 'popularity' is much limited. The official Christian Churches do not consider these 3Cs to be Christian in any sense and sneer their practices such as polygamy, communism of wives, institution of '*Chi thlak*' (practice of selecting a male or the leader of the cult to be the biological father or the 'sperm donor'. The objective of such a practice is to create a reservoir of 'pure progeny' that can be directly linked to the cult leader and future leaders could be selected from that reservoir) etc. (ASC).
8. The 'Lalzahavara- Nu Diheli' cult church evolved in the late 1970s and retained popularity through the 80s in Sangau village in Southern Mizoram. Lalzahavara declared himself as the god incarnate and the new Christ. Nu Diheli was his primary wife and the entire women in his cult were his wives. The men served as support systems to put the Zahavara cult into order. For details, Anup Shekhar Chakraborty. *Forthcoming*: 'Lalzahavara-Nu Diheli cult: The Sangau Experiential Clannish Cult Church'.
9. Anup Shekhar Chakraborty. (2009b). 'Where are 'Our women'? Locating Women through the History of Proselytization in Mizoram.' *Dharma Deepkia- South Asian Journal of Missiological Research- issue on Mission In Contexts Of Violence And Uncertainty*. Issue 30, Vol.13 No. 2 July-December.
10. David Hardiman. (2007). 'Healing, Medical Power and the Poor: Contests in Tribal India'. *Economic And Political Weekly*. April 21- April 27, pp.1404-1408. Also *See,* George Mark Moares. (1964). *A History of Christianity in India: From early times to St. Francis Xavier A.D 52- 1542,* Vol. I, Bombay: P.C Manaktala& Sons Private Ltd. pp. 246-264.

11. R.A. Lorrain. (1912). (Reprinted 1988). *Five Years in Unknown Jungles: For God and Empire.* London, Guwahati: Spectrum Publications. pp. 222-224.
12. Frederick. S. Downs. (1983). *Christianity in North East India.* Delhi: ISPCK.. pp. 47-48.
13. Anup Shekhar Chakraborty. (2009b). *Op.cit.*
14. Pu Zaliana. Senior Research Officer, Tribal Research Institute, Art & Culture Department, Government of Mizoram, McDonald Hill. *Personal Interview.* Zarkawt, Aizawl: 22nd, 23rd& 24th January 2008.
15. Pu Zaliana. *Personal Interview. Ibid.*
16. Pu Lallianchhunga, Lecturer, Department of Political Science, Mizoram University, .*Personal Interview,* Chaltlang Campus, Aizawl: 19th January 2008.
17. I have used the terms 'Being a Zo, Being a Christian' extensively in my PhD thesis "The Evolution of 'Zomi' Identity and Politics in Mizoram" (2005-2010) Department of Political Science, University of Calcutta, and also in my series of publications between 2007- 2013. I am not influenced by the similar sounding title of Joy Pacchua's book '*Being Mizo*' 2014. New Delhi: Oxford University Press.
18. The politics of leadership in Mizoram needs to be bulwarked against the silhouette of its complex imagery of a traditional hero, a leader, and the image of a Saviour, a redeemer as emitted through the pages of the Bible. In the traditional Mizo society, the *Pasaltha* was a man who showed great talent in hunting, courage warfare, prowess and vigour in sexual life (whether married or single). The *Pasaltha* was the knight in the shining armour, the chivalrous hero. Whatever he did was guided by the code of *Tlawmngaihna* which can be understood to refer to unconditioned service to people or community based on 'good will', sympathy, empathy, courage and honour.
19. The existing writings for instance, P.K. Bandyopadhyay. (1985). *Leadership Among The Mizos: An Emerging Dimension*. New Delhi: B.R. Publishing Corporation; Suhas Chatterjee. (1994). *Making of Mizoram: Role of Laldenga.* Delhi: M.D. Publications and my frequent interactions with ordinary people and the youths (both in Mizoram and those Zo/Mizo youths studying and living elsewhere in India) has impressed upon me that there is paucity of documentation of the 'life and times of Laldenga' and the 'politics of leadership in the region'. The only reliable resource that can be cited in this context being Suhas Chatterjee's (1994). *'Making of Mizoram: Role of Laldenga.'* The work though a well researched piece has its own short comings. For instance, it deals at length with the historical dimensions of Mizo politics and to an extent neglects the biographic detailing required especially if the title of the book is taken for granted; and also the book ends with the death of Laldenga in the 90s and the developments beyond remain yet to be catalogued. Thus the aspect of inquiry beyond the death of the enigma of Laldenga and the impact of his death on Mizo politics remains largely yet to be voiced.
20. For details *See*, Bimal J. Dev and Dilip Kumar Lahiri. (1983). *Lushai Customs and Ceremonies.* Delhi: Mittal Publications. Chapter 1, 'The Chief and the Village', pp.1-20.
21. Lorrain in his *Dictionary of the Lushai Language* defined *Hnamchawm* as 'the common people, all save those belonging to the ruling clan'. James Herbert

Lorrain. (Reprint 1975). *Dictionary of the Lushai Language*. Calcutta: The Asiatic Society. p.447. The *Hnamchawm* (Commoner) comprised the bulk of the Zo society. They were a heterogenous category comprising different clans and occupational types. They were the second tier in the three fold stratified Zo world. There was little that a chief could do once he lost the confidence of his villagers. Despite the risks that entailed abandonment that is the perils of the jungle having to be faced and the uncertainty and/or embarrassment that awaits a refugee etc., the loss of hope in leadership and the hope of a better prospect invariably prompted the villagers to out-migrate (*Pem Chuak*) to another (in-migrate, *Pem Lut*).

22. Anup Shekhar Chakraborty. (2014). "Vai Party Versus Zo/Mizo Party': The Contest Over the Issue of Authentic People's Representation in Mizoram' *Indian Journal of Political Science (IJPS),* Vol.LXXV. No.1, January-March, 2014. pp. 81-94.
23. Issac Zoliana. 2005. *Op.cit.*
24. On March 1st 1966, the Mizo National Front (MNF) declared Independence and set up its self-styled *'Mizoram Sawrkar'* with a President and a Council of Ministers, in charge of Home, Defence, Foreign, Finance and Public Information. The MNF frantically and secretly began preparing for taking over the military and civil administration of the Mizo District. All the towns of Mizoram viz. Aizawl, Lunglei, Champhai, Vairengte and Chhimluang were encircled by a 2000 strong Mizo National Volunteers Force to strike at 'zero-hour' One o'clock of March 1st 1966. They successfully struck at the appointed time. The engagement continued till March 3, 1966 when Aizawl fell to the hands of the MNF. Soon after this event, Mizoram became the centre of world attention.
25. Pi Vanramchhuangi ('Ruatfelanu'), Director HRLN Mizoram, Social Activist, *Personal Interview*, Chaltlang, Aizawl: 28th& 29th January 2008.
26. However, defections toppled him from office. Laldenga died in 1990 of lung cancer at the age of 63. The huge number of people that swarmed to participate in Laldenga's funeral in Aizawl in 1990 was a tribute to his charisma and the courage and statesmanship displayed in bringing back the insurgency ridden state to the fold of constitutionalism. The Congress government feared that discontentment with the Peace Accord might find expression in an emotional outburst at his funeral but the event passed off peacefully. *See*, Issac Zoliana. 2005. *Op.cit.*
27. The erstwhile 'uniformed guerrilla' ever ready for combat now gave way for a 'sophisticated suited statesman'. And it is the latter image of a suited (Black coated) Pu Denga that encapsulates the public memory in contemporary times. The effects of democratisation had its ripples even at the level of MNF Party's functioning. The change in the persona of Laldenga post-Statehood reflected to an extent the successes of India's democratic mechanism at channelling and taming the dissident voice.
28. Prasun Sonawalkar. (1989). 'Church playing vital role in Mizo polls'. *The Times of India*. Aizawl/Ahmedabad: 09 January.
29. To bring clarity to my arguments in this discussion I would reaffirm that the MNF insurgency days brings to the fore two strands of disjoined arguments to a point of convergence: *one*, the argument that the national actors (Congress as

well as Janata Party) had hidden agenda to dislodge rival centres of power at the states or Union Territories; *two*, the state actors themselves called upon the actors from the Centre to intervene in local statecraft or at least provided their safe entry into regional politics in order to meet their vested objectives.

30. I cite a personal experience where I and my Supervisor faced a query from a Senior Lecturer of a College in Kolkata who firmly believed that Christian Missionaries were instigating and supporting insurgencies in the North East. I take this opportunity to thank the Department of Political Science, University of Calcutta for providing with a platform to present a paper titled 'Understanding Politics in Mizoram through the lenses of Good Governance' in the UGC-DRS Programme (Phase 1) on "Democratic Governance in Indian States", University of Calcutta, on 14th February 2009 and have ample time to interact with college lecturers in and around Kolkata and get a taste of their take on politics in the North East.
31. *The Presbyterian Church Pamphlet* dated 12th March 1966. Aizawl: Synod Office.
32. The MNF Home Minister's Letter to the Presbyterian Church Leaders dated 16th March 1966. MNF Headquarters.
33. Zoram Baptist Church Appeal to the MNF dated 30th May 1966. Aizawl.
34. *Kohhran Thuchah* issued by the Church leaders of the Presbyterian and the Baptist dated 8the September, 1966. Aizawl.
35. Laldenga and the MNF returnees were accused of ushering prostitution or the 'KS' (*Kawng Sual*, those who have strayed to evil ways that is wrong turn) in the Christian State and introducing the 'Hotel culture', nightlife and bar culture, life styles which were strictly unagreeable to the Christian ways of life. Hotel Moonlight and the nightlife that this hotel provided during those days remains embedded in the public memory of the middle aged Zo people. The mere mention of the name 'Moonlight' invoked images of drinking, the 'KS', and the image of the Biblical spoilt cities Babylon, Sodom and Gomorrah.
36. Prasun Sonawalkar. (1989). 09 January. *Op. cit.*
37. *1987 MNF Election Manifesto*. MNF Headquarters, Aizawl.
38. Prasun Sonawalkar. (1989). 'House of Cards'. The Times of India News Service. Aizawl. *The Times of India*. Ahmedabad: 20 January.
39. For details *See*, Sumanta Sen. (1989). 'North-East moves towards Mainstream'. The Times of India News Service. Aizawl. *The Times of India*. Ahmedabad: 26 January.
40. *See*, Prasun Sonawalkar. (1989). 09 January. *Op. cit.*
41. *The Times of India*. (1989). 'MNF not to go back to insurgency'. The Times of India News Service, New Delhi: 24 February. Ahmedabad: 25 February.
42. Prasun Sonawalkar. (1989). 20th February. *Op. cit.*
43. Considered as the grand patriarch of Zo/Mizo politics Sailo was known for announcing his retirement from politics time and again in the post peace period, but each time plunge back to politics to give a last try. Though popular in public and considered to be a visionary, as well as a 'Statesman and a Diplomat', for his path breaking policies of development such as 'Bairabi Hydel Project' during his tenure as the chief minister of Mizoram (1978 -1984 with a short President's

Rule in between), Sailo was largely unable to convert his mass appeal and populist strategies such as the Zomi movement into electoral success. The mid-seventies crisis in Mizoram was his high-tide and most successful stint in Zo/Mizo politics when he was projected as a veritable 'Saviour' 'the political messiah' of the helpless Zo/Mizo.

44. H. M. Bareh. (2001). *Encyclopaedia of North-East India, Mizoram*. Vol. V. New Delhi: Mittal Publications. p. 21.
45. Prasun Sonawalkar. (1989). 09 January. *Op. cit.*
46. Issac Zoliana. (2005). *Op.cit.*
47. For instance, the leadership provided by Nehru and Indira to the Congress at Delhi to an extent continued to spray hope for a better dealing with the local sentiments and demands. The Gandhi factor continues to enthral the Zo/Mizo people because of the fact that Gandhi revered the teachings of the Bible and this acted as a binding factor between Gandhi and the Zo/Mizo people.
48. Kamarupee. (1991). Assassination and After in North-East. *Economic & Political Weekly*. June 1-8, p.1383.
49. Praun Sonawalkar. (1989). 09 January. *Op. cit.*
50. *Election Manifesto of the Mizoram Congress (I)*. January 1987. MPCC Headquarters: Aizawl.
51. Zozam News Service. (2010). 'Hawla Thubuai Kawng Chhuk Chho'. *Zozam*. Aizawl: 3-9 March. pp.21-27.
52. Zodinsanga. (2013). 'Mizo Marksmanship: The ruling Congress fights charges both religious and temporal in Mizoram'. *Outlook The Magazine*. 2 December. (http://www.outlookindia.com/magazine/story/mizo-marksmanship/288627 (last accessed on 20.04.2017).
53. For instance as late as 1989 Laldenga himself had publicly referred to the Congress (I) as 'the Party of the '*Vai*'' and accused it 'of plotting defection to topple his Ministry'. *See*, The Assam Tribune. (1989). 'Congress (I) Plots Defection In Mizoram: Laldenga'. Aizawl: 17 January. Guwahati: 18 January. For more discussions on the *Vai* party and Zo/Mizo party *Cf.*, H. Ramdinthara. (2010). "Made In Delhi" ditak chu to zawk nge? *The Zozam Times*. Aizawl: 9 March.
54. For instance, the leadership provided by Nehru and Indira to the Congress at Delhi to an extent continued to spray hope for a better dealing with the local sentiments and demands. The Gandhi factor continues to enthral the Zo/Mizo people because of the fact that Gandhi revered the teachings of the Bible and this acted as a binding factor between Gandhi and the Zo/Mizo people.
55. *See*, *Then Thumna, Bung-18, District Council Term 2-Na (1957-1962), in* R. Zamawia. (2007). *Zofate Zinkawngah: Zalenna Mei a Mit Tur a Ni Lo*. Aizawl: Lengchhawn Press. pp.148-70.
56. *See*, Chapter 5 'Men and Mice' pp 50-58, *in* S. Guru Dev. (1996). *Anatomy of Revolt: In the North East India.* New Delhi: Lancer Books.
57. There is no consensus on the exact date and day when the MNF matured into a political party from the root body the Mizo National Famine Front. While two of the original eight members who formed the MNF are of the opinion that the

MNF was floated on 28th October, 1961; the other three C. Hermana, H. Zirliana and A. Rohnuna faintly remember that it was a Saturday night. A Rohnuna also mentions that the meeting went way past mid-night. Another member who could not attend the secret meeting that night Lalnundawta's testimony also supports the view that it was a Saturday night. *See*, R. Zamawia. (2007). *Op.cit.* 169-170.

58. The MNF during the Mizoram Assembly in 1978 distributed and played tape-recorded speech of Laldenga through which Laldenga denounced the People's Conference of Brig. Sailo and called upon the people to boycott the election. Though it created some difficulty for the People's Conference, it did not have much impact on the Mizo people, as such. *See*, H.K. Sareen. (1980). *Insurgency In The North-East India: A Study of the Sino-American Role.* New Delhi: Sterling Publishers Pvt. Ltd.p.71.

59. Laldenga through his newspaper tabled before the people his visions of an independent Zoram which would be an Ideal Zo Christian State for all the *Zo hnahthlak*. The 'Mizo Aw' was print nationalism at its best and the intelligentsia and the young educated were swayed by such nationalistic arguments and helped the imagination of Mizo/Zo nation.

60. F. Hmingthanga. (MCS Rtd.). (2003). *Mizoram Politic Thlirlet-Na (Mizo Hnam him Nan)*. Aizawl: The Zo-Awm Press.

61. A.C. Ray. (1982). *Mizoram Dynamics of Change.* Calcutta: Pearl Publishers/ ICSSR.p.236.

62. *See*, '*State And Local Politics*', Chapter 4, pp.123 *in* Paul. R. Brass. (1991). *Ethnicity and Nationalism: Theory and Composition.* New Delhi: Sage Publication.

63. Brigadier T. Sailo was the son of Vanchheuva the Chief of Thuampui village in Lunglei district.

64. Ch. Chhunga faced a psychological blow when his 15 year old son, Chalthanzuala left his home at Aizawl and joined the MNF rebels on 15th June 1974. This came as a personal loss for the leader who was known as being a staunch anti-MNF and supporter of India. The public image that Ch. Chhunga has built over the years was brought to question and his leadership was questioned. The Congress though being a partner of the Mizo Union exploited the issue and pointed fingers at Ch. Chhunga's leadership and his party's commitment to the anti-MNF stand. Ch. Chhunga succumbed to the strategies of the Mizoram Congress and finally on May 9th 1977 Ch. Chhunga resigned. The psychological pressure from within and without was too heavy to bear, though Ch. Chhunga said that his 'Ministry was resigning on the expiry of its five years term in the Assembly'. The resignation of Ch. Chhunga was followed by imposition of President's Rule (Article 356) a strategy which was later repeated even in 1988 when the Laldenga Government was toppled by the Mizoram Congress. A. C. Ray. (1982). *Op.cit.* p.236.

65. Lalsangliana, the eldest son of Brigadier T. Sailo studying at St. Edmund's College, Shillong along with eight other Mizo youths joined the MNF on 18th July 1966 and moved to Sylhet in East Pakistan for training as Special Forces meant for liquidation of political enemies etc. Lalsangliana became the Staff Officer of Laldenga and was later dismissed from the MNA along with Biakchhunga, Vanthanga and others in 1979.

66. Pu Zaliana. *Personal Interview. Op.cit.*
67. It is indeed ironic, but nevertheless, true that the very P.C. Government was accused of committing serious human rights violation after it launched a bitter and bloody anti-MNF operation using the State's police force designated as 'Special Force'. Several MNF personnel and people sympathetic towards the MNF were killed; and in the process, many innocent lives were taken. *See*, Brig. Verghese & C. L. Thanzawna. (1997). *A History of the Mizos.* Vol. II. New Delhi: Vikas Publishing House. pp.231-232.
68. Verghese & Thanzawna. (1997). *Op.cit.*
69. Pu Zaliana. *Personal Interview. Op.cit.*
70. Verghese & Thanzawna. (1997). *Op.cit.* p. 241.
71. Issac Zoliana. (2005). *Op.cit.*
72. A personal account would help to substantiate this statement. When my younger sister Asha Chakraborty participated for the Lelte Miss Mizoram contest in 1996 she introduced herself as representing 'Saron Veng which happens to be the locality of the first Chief Minister of Mizoram Pu Ch. Chhunga', the media and public was taken aback and took time to recall the forgotten enigma in Mizo politics Pu Ch. Chhunga. (ASC)
73. P. Lalnithanga. (IAS Rtd.). (2005). *Emergence of Mizoram.* Aizawl: Lengchhawn Press/Mizoram Publication Board.
74. Anup Shekhar Chakraborty. (2015a). *Politics of Autonomy & Ethnic Cocooning in Mizoram.* New Delhi: Authorspress.
75. P. Lalnithanga. (IAS Rtd.). 2005. *Op. cit.*
76. Based on innumerable discussions which sometimes became really charged and heated on the issue of the 'Vai' and the 'Gorkha' with my father, Mr. A.S Chakraborty, (Rtd. S.P (Security) Mizoram). Who has served in the Mizoram Police for over 30 years; also substantiated by the informal talks with Mizo as well as Gorkha police officials in Mizoram.
77. R.N. Prasad. (1987). *Government and Politics in Mizoram 1947-1986.* New Delhi: Northern Book Centre; R.N. Prasad & A. K. Agarwal. (1991). *Political and Economic Development of Mizoram.* New Delhi: Mittal Publications.
78. M.C. Lalrinthanga. (1993). *Op. cit.*
79. For other instances of direct and indirect mud-slinging between the MNF and the Congress *Cf.*, *The Assam Tribune*. (1989). 'Congress (I) Plots Defection In Mizoram: Laldenga'. Aizawl: 17 January. Guwahati: 18 January; *The Assam Tribune*. (1989). 'Mizoram Campaign At its Crescendo'. Aizawl: 18 January. Guwahati: 19 January; *The Assam Tribune*. (1989). 'Petition Against Mizoram Government Filed'. Aizawl: 06 March. Guwahati: 07 March; *The Assam Tribune*. (1989). 'Lalthanhawla Ministry Faces Opposition Campaign'. Aizawl: 24 March. Guwahati: 25 March; *The Assam Tribune*. (1989). 'Church Role In Mizo Polls Questioned'. Aizawl: 01 March. Guwahati: 02 March; *The Assam Tribune*. (1989). 'Mizoram Denies Charges of Rigging Assembly Polls'. Aizawl: 04 March. Guwahati: 05 March; *The Assam Tribune*. (1989). 'Mizoram Government To Probe Into Losses of Mizofed'. Aizawl: 28 March. Guwahati: 29 March.
80. Verghese & Thanzawna. (1997). *Op.cit* p.268.

81. For other instances of direct and indirect mud-slinging between the MNF and the Congress *Cf.*, *The Assam Tribune*. (1989). 'Congress (I) Plots Defection In Mizoram: Laldenga'. Aizawl: 17 January. Guwahati: 18 January; *The Assam Tribune*. (1989). 'Mizoram Campaign At its Crescendo'. Aizawl: 18 January. Guwahati: 19 January; *The Assam Tribune*. (1989). 'Petition Against Mizoram Government Filed'. Aizawl: 06 March. Guwahati: 07 March; *The Assam Tribune*. (1989). 'Lalthanhawla Ministry Faces Opposition Campaign'. Aizawl: 24 March. Guwahati: 25 March; *The Assam Tribune*. 1989. 'Church Role In Mizo Polls Questioned'. Aizawl: 01 March. Guwahati: 02 March; *The Assam Tribune*. (1989). 'Mizoram Denies Charges of Rigging Assembly Polls'. Aizawl: 04 March. Guwahati: 05 March; *The Assam Tribune*.(1989). 'Mizoram Government To Probe Into Losses of Mizofed'. Aizawl: 28 March. Guwahati: 29 March.
82. *Ibid.*
83. BJP State Headquarters. 1998. *Press Release* No. BJP/MZ/17/98/15. (1998). Aizawl: Mizoram. 29 July.
84. *Ibid.*
85. Craig Calhoun. (ed.). (1992). *Habermas And The Public Sphere*. Cambridge, MA: MIT Press; Jürgen. Habermas. (1962). (1991).*The Structural Transformation of the Public Sphere: An Inquiry into a category of Bourgeois Society* (Trans. Thomas Burger with Frederick Lawrence). Cambridge, MA: MIT Press; Michael. Pusey.(1987). *Jürgen Habermas: Key Sociologists*. London: Routledge.
86. Charles Taylor. (2007). *A Secular Age*. Cambridge, Mass.,: Harvard University Press; Craig Calhoun. (2008). 'A Secular Age'. *European Journal of Sociology*. Cambridge Journals Online. 49 (03): 455–461; Barry A. Kosmin and Ariela Keysar. (ed.). (2007). *Secularism & Secularity: Contemporary International Perspectives*. Hartford, CT: Institute for the Study of Secularism in Society and Culture (ISSSC); Max Weber. (2001). *The Protestant Ethic and the Spirit of Capitalism*. London, Routledge Classics.
87. Pi Vanramchhuangi. *Personal Interview. Op. cit.*
88. Belonging to the South (a Pawi tribe) Laldenga felt that the northern attitude had to be corrected. Likewise, he felt uncomfortable in the presence of other sophisticated much educated leaders like Ch. Chhunga and Brigadier T. Sailo who were also originally from the south and almost his contemporaries age-wise. He felt threatened by the contesting claimants to leadership. Lalthanhawla being young and subordinate (Lalthanhawla had served in Laldenga's MNF for a brief stint) did not threaten Laldenga. More over Lalthanhawla unlike Ch. Chhunga and T. Sailo never directly confronted the leadership of Laldenga. Lalthanhawla was more interested with making a foothold in the Zo/Mizo soil for a party (Congress) which for a very long time was seen as a *'Vai'* Party. Lalthanhawla from the very beginning kept himself as the agent of the Centre and acted accordingly. Where as the other three regional parties namely the Mizo Union (Ch. Chhunga), P.C Party (T. Sailo) and the MNF (Laldenga) contested the role of the Centre and changed their stand or attitude towards the Centre depending upon the kind of response that they managed to get from the Centre (national parties: Congress and the Janata Party/Janata Dal).
89. Rev. Zairema in a letter to Laldenga asking the latter to put an end to the strife wrote: We admire the courage of your conviction. However, we would like to

remind you that India has herself never been one nation. The Telegus are as different from the Punjabis as the Bengalis from the Mizos. Yet, we together are determined to build one mighty nation. In this process, each of us has a right as well as a responsibility. *See*, K.C. Baral *in* R.N. Prasad. (ed.) (1994). *Autonomous Movements in Mizoram*. New Delhi: Vikas Publishing House Ltd.

90. The Town Commander of the MNF at Aizawl was the literal ruler of Aizawl and the most powerful symbol of the parallel government of the MNF styled as the 'Mizoram Sawrkar'. Even though he was a 'Wanted person' no one in authority (legally recognised) seemed to have the courage to arrest him. He would be seen visiting the UT Ministers and having dinner with them and often would ask those in office to release vehicles for him, give licences and contracts to persons of his choice. He was also held as the 'Robin hood' by many Zo/Mizo who were often victimised by the Security Forces in their action against the MNF. Petty local shopkeepers in special benefited from the frequent notices put up by the Town Commander which most often would prohibit the purchase of items available in Mizo shops from that of non-Mizo shops or work only under Mizo contractors and not under non-Mizo contractors; diktats on inter-marriages between Mizos and non-Mizos, inter-dining, participation in non-Mizo festivities and wearing Indian dress/clothings (sarees, dhotis, caps, salwars etc.).
91. Pu Zaliana. *Personal Interview*. *Op. cit*.
92. Verghese & Thanzawna. (1997). *Op.cit*. p.234.
93. The latter name reflects the patriarchal mind set of Laldenga which undermines a widow or a *'Hmeithai'* as something not worth respect according to the Zo Patriarchy.
94. Verghese & Thanzawna. (1997). *Op. cit*. p. 198.
95. *Personal Interviews*. A.S. Chakraborty and L.B. Chhetri. Kolkata. 20th June 2017.
96. Verghese & Thanzawna. (1997). *Op. cit*. p. 141.
97. P. Lalnithanga. (IAS Rtd.). (2005). *Op. cit*.
98. A.C. Ray.(1982). *Op. cit*. p. 243.

4

'Belonging', 'Claims of Belonging' and the 'Tolerance' debates in an Ideal Zo Christian State

Understanding the Contests: Post-Peace Accord manifest Ethnic Murmurings

The discussions in this chapter would glean into the issues of 'Tolerance and intolerance' in the state of Mizoram by taking the issues of two tribal communities namely the Chakma (Takam) and the Reang/Bru (Tuikuk). The calm ushered by the Peace Accord 1986 in Mizoram has been put to test severely by the musings and rumblings of minorities like *Chakma, Reang, Hmar, Lai, Mara* and others. The intra/inter ethnic rumblings (demands for privileges of Sixth Schedule and Autonomous district councils, Union Territory etc.) in Mizoram post-Statehood have put to scanner the 'claims of being the most "Peaceful State" in India; needless to stress that the public sphere is buzzing with the critical debates on 'tolerance'.

Tucked in the remote western (north-western, south-western) belt of Mizoram between the Chittagong Hill Tracts (CHT) now in Bangladesh and fringed by the Indian state of Tripura in the north, the *Chakma* and the Reang remain the permanent 'problem people' for the *Zo hnahthlak*. Speaking a language[1] incoherent to the Zo and following ways of life not attuned to the blueprints of Zo Christianity, the *Chakma* like the *Reang* (*Bru*) have been scorned as *'Pathian siam theihloh!* (Those one who failed God!).[2] Also, *the Zo hnahthlak* i.e., northerners pointedly blame the *Chakma* and the *Reang* (*Bru*) for lowering the developmental scale be it literacy over all education,[3] HDI or making state of Mizoram 'backward'[4] in general or bringing shame to the *Ideal Zo Christian state*.

The Zo tribes and their sub clans who form the majority in Mizoram attempt to dominate all the socio-politico-eco-cultural arenas of society in Mizoram. This process of maintaining and sustaining the majoritarian 'Zo voice' over and above the marginal tribes undergoes unique strategies of inclusions and exclusions. For instance, the Zo/Mizo tribes from the north have craftily attempted to take charge of the territories of the *Chakma* and the Reang by unleashing a wave of proselytization and politics of name change and border fencing.

1. The Chakma Story

The *Chakma* tribes traditionally hold the riparian territories of the Karnaphuli, the Chittagong Hill Tracts and the Arakans. Like the many tribes living in the directional construct the 'North East of India', the *Chakma* are clubbed into the frame of a 'cross-border'[5] tribe. The Colonial encounter in the Indian state of Mizoram (the region cusped between Chittagong Hill Tracts and the Chin Hills) created differences in identity among the *Northerners* and the *Southerners* (*Mara*,[6] *Lai*[7] and *Chakma*) through their administrative lines across the traditional homeland of the *Zo hnahthlak* (Zo people).[8] The long term impact of which, was the creation of a mental divide between South (*'Chhimlam mi'*) and North (*Lusei-Hmar, Zo/Mizo*) in Mizoram. The group of tribes in the present day Aizawl circle commonly referred to as the '*Lusei-Mizo* group' believe they are the real/authentic/ pure 'Mizo' and therefore the 'original settlers'/ the first to arrive/ the 'sons of soil' and expect other peripheral and southern tribes and western tribes to accept and subsume themselves into the *generic* Mizo identity. They also expect the marginal tribes to speak the *Duhlian* (Mizo) dialect which has been elevated to the position of the lingua franca of the state of Mizoram. The process of identity-formation over the years Mizo-ised the ethno-cultural proximates belonging to the larger or more amorphous *Kuki-Chin* groups in India and Burma, with a majority of the fifteen to seventeen local tribes assuming a more distinctive Mizo identity by virtue of adopting Christianity, a Lushai dialect (*Duhlian)*, with Roman script. The *Chakma* people in contemporary Mizoram have been mustering their claims to belonging and being the 'sons of soil' and thereby voicing their aspiratorial 'claims' to cartographically chart their emic self-defined identity in a map called Chakmaland (Union Territory). The claims to 'belonging', and the over arching narrative of 'not belonging' (socially, culturally, historically, politically etc.) to Mizoram unleashes the complex notions of Citizenship or recognition as people through the unique experience of a 'Regulated

Citizenship' filtered through a process of *inclusions and exclusions*[9] as directed or scripted by the *Nexus of Patriarchy* and its visions of an *Ideal Zo Christian State*.[10]

Though officially treated as 'tribes' of Mizoram, the *Chakma*, till today are not considered as 'belonging' to Mizoram by the *Zo hnahthlak* and classed and tolerated as 'over staying guests'. The *Chakma* feel neglected and deprived of economic benefits due to their being non-Christians. The issues of the distinctness of the *Chakma* from that of the Zo/Mizo have been milked by the dominant stakeholders from the state as well as outside to either assimilate or eliminate the minority *Chakma* tribes.[11] The *Chakma* Autonomous District Council (CADC) with its headquarters now at Chawngte (earlier known as Kamalanagar) continues to be the public irritant and the source of intolerant ways in the Zo/Mizo politics. The existence of Bengali medium high school, Buddhist culture and pidgin Bengali language along with distinct cultural markers makes the *Chakma* a permanent pariah in a state that openly declares itself to be an *Ideal Zo Christian State*. Where to tuck away the *Chakma*? What to do with the *Chakma*? How to mould 'them' into 'ourselves' or fence them 'off' from their counterparts in CHT[12] continues to be the concern of the *Nexus of Patriarchy* in Zo/Mizo politics.

The current Medical dystopia and public outburst[13] (June 2017- Oct 2017) of the Zo "Youth" led by the MZP[14], MSU[15], the CYMA[16] etc., in Mizoram against the *Chakma* needs to be understood against the fore mentioned backdrop of traditional animosity, threat perception and claims to 'being the first settlers' (and therefore 'sons of soil') in the territory now named Mizoram. Along with the historical issues, one needs to glove-in the 'current discriminations' on the basis of ethnicity and language in Mizoram as reflected from the various official Recruitment Rules (RRs), notified by the government of Mizoram, which prevent the linguistic minorities from availing jobs.[17]

Also, the issue of 'State Quota' has always been a very emotional issue and the past has seen many such ethnic clashes and outbursts due to the 'reservation' issues. We can take the case of tension of the early 90s centred on the issue of 'Quota' for Medical and Engineering. In the 90s few quotas were given to the children of prominent *'Vai'* officials posted in Mizoram. Upset that the children of outsiders were admitted to medical colleges at the expense of natives, 'student protestors clashed with the police in Aizawl and attacked shops and vehicles of 'outsiders'. Following which a curfew was imposed in the capital'. One of these prominent figures was Kiran Bedi's daughter 'Tara'.[18] Looked at from the arguments posed by the MZP the act of giving quotas to *'Vai'* who had worked in Mizoram for not even two years was not acceptable. The public cry forced the Congress government to wake-up and re-think 'their mistake'. The MZP organised rallies and dharnas against Kiran Bedi and chanted the slogan *'Kiran Bedi go back'*. The situation was so tense that Kiran Bedi had to flee Aizawl in the dead of the night.[19] The MZP had cut down the 'super-cop' to her human stature. The movement in course of time took the form of identifying all *'Vai'* without legal documents living in Mizoram. By the end of 1993 the movement opened the proverbial Pandora's Box in the identity politics in Mizoram and the MZP dabbled with multiple issues from checking the list of legal *'Vai'* in Mizoram to that of permit and license; to reviewing who should be given the benefit of affirmative action through reservation; head count of the original Gorkhas; checking the *'Burma mi'*; relocating the Assam Rifles from the heart of the City to a less prominent place in the fringes of Aizawl.

Seen from this genealogical account of 'the Quota' and outburst against the outsiders, we can agreeably note that the current imbroglio substantiates in fine measure to the politics of reservation only for the *Zo hnahthlak* and the associated tolerance debates as operative in Mizoram. This time the *Chakma* have been picked aside precisely because the *Chakma* have 'come of age' in the sense that the first and second generation *Chakma* have been able to reap the benefits of education (English, Mizo) in that state (or maybe outside the state) and made a claim to that coveted 'Quota'[20] in the 'much revered and exclusive realms of Medical studies'.[21]

The youths from the two students unions (MZP and MSU) in Mizoram came together to protest against the allocation of Mizoram Quota to the 'four Chakma students'[22] who cleared the NEET 2017. This was the first time that Chakma students had cleared the entrance examinations and made their claims to the provisions of state Quota in Medical studies. The 'Zo public opinion' mustered their protest against the decision of the state government to 'allot seats to the Chakma' and banners and placards fluttered across the state in special at Aizawl. The writing on the wall brought the Congress led state government to its toes. The Churches and the vigilant groups in the self acclaimed Christian state made it loud and clear that they considered the Chakma: "Toppers but not 'indigenous'[23]" and therefore 'No Quota for Chakma'.

Under Mizoram's Higher and Technical Education Department's selection rules for medical entrance examinations, candidates are divided into three categories: indigenous Mizo tribes, non-indigenous permanent residents of Mizoram, and students of parents working as Union government employees in Mizoram. "Till 2014, the Chakma were part of the first category, until the MZP and other Mizo groups objected," explained an official of the department. "This forced the government to amend the rules." According to the new rules framed in 2015, category one was meant only for "Zo-ethnic people" of the state – and the Chakmas were shifted to the second category, said the official, who did not want to be identified. However, the Chakmas moved court and managed to get a stay on the new rules, forcing the government to withdraw them.[24]

Post 2016 the government proposed, 95% of all seats would be reserved for the first category, and the Chakmas would no longer be part of that category. Previously, there was no numerical cap on reservations – the first category just got more preference than the second and so on. The Chakmas approached the Gauhati High Court again and, the court stayed the proposed rules. After the disruption on July 19 2017, counselling was held on July 20 2017 – amidst tight security. The counselling in 2017 continued amidst protesters shouting outside the venue. The four Chakma students, Darshan Chakma, Nibir Chakma, Mini Chakma and Nibhir Tongchangya, were allotted seats in Gauhati Medical College, Dr Sampurnanand Medical College in Jodhpur, Burdwan Medical College in West Bengal, and Jawaharlal Nehru Memorial Medical College in Raipur, respectively. The students even paid their admission fees but following the ethnic tensions that teased out of the event following the clash between the protesting student activists with the police, the state Government changed its stand. The Higher and Technical Education Department cancelled the admission later that evening, stating that the counselling exercise that took place earlier that day was not valid, and that fresh counselling would take place soon. Pu R Romawia, minister for higher and technical education in Mizoram, issued a press release to that effect, affirming that the government had decided that, for the current year's counselling process, and the first category would be reserved for the "sons of the Zo-ethnic people". When asked if the decision contravened the high court's ruling, Romawia told: "This is a very sensitive matter; I don't wish to comment on it."[25]

The Chakma students and youths have vehemently protested and expressed their concerns at various places in Mizoram as well as elsewhere across India through various mediums and have jumped the scale from the real to the virtual spaces against the practiced 'Institutionalized discriminations' inflicted by the Government and people of Mizoram.

1.1. 'Politics of Camouflaging' and the Chakma: Limits and Dead-ends

The '*Politics of Camouflaging*' that was a useful tool for the *Chakma* to counter the attitude of the northern tribes between 2000-2013 has now finally ceased to be effective in 2016-2017 in the context of reservation of seats or 'Mizoram State Quota' in Medical colleges across India. Recently due to the increased activities of local evangelists/missionaries from the north, many among the *Chakma* have converted to Christianity. Several Christian rites and rituals for instance, prayer by the head of the family before a meal, going to Sunday Schools, singing and dancing in the church, using Mizo words such as '*piangthar*' (born again, convert) to describe their 'new religion informed identity' etc. All these religio-cultural appropriations have entered into the everyday lived practices of the *Chakma* convert. The Christian Chakmas as the 'new believers' refrain from participating in indigenous festivals like 'Bizu', drinking alcohol, or consuming food offered in the local puja. The Christian Chakmas show a tendency to appropriate Mizo cultural markers. The non-converts on the other hand stick to their animistic/Sanskritized ways of life. The strategies of the *Nexus of Patriarchy* in mobilising community resources and networking among the northern communities have been emulated at the *Chakma* circles.

Here it is pertinent to note that the *Chakma* emulating the northerners have built up institutes to protect their rights, raise their concerns and make the Zo more tolerant towards the *Chakma* through the Young Chakma Association (YCA) on the lines of the Young Mizo Association (YMA); the Mizoram Chakma Welfare Committee (MCWC), Mizoram Chakma Students Union (MSCU), Chakma Mahila Samitti (CMS) and Mizoram Chakma Development Forum (MCDF). On a whole the major concern of these organisations had been to the integrate all the *Chakma* dominated areas of Mizoram into a single administrative unit under the Sixth Schedule provisions of the Indian Constitution, educate themselves and mobilise their identity consciousness around their backwardness as a minority tribe within Mizoram. Through their institutions, the *Chakma* in Mizoram have time and time again fed the Central government with demands for speedy development, relay of current and past informations relating to the discriminations faced by them under the Zo/Mizo hegemony. The *Chakma* have been stressing that the Aizawl centric inclinations of development and the inaction of successive governments be it the Congress or the MNF at Aizawl have failed to improve their living conditions. The *Chakma* also felt that being denied the opportunity to learn Mizo at school level has been a major discriminatory policy deliberately carried over by the Zo/Mizo government from Aizawl to check the entry of the *Chakma* into government services. The *Chakma* also accuse the state government of Mizoram of following 'an exclusive knowledge system' and of failing to provide the *Chakma*, with equal educational opportunities and reservations in government jobs etc.[26]

The Activist Citizenry among the *Chakma* compelled the state government of Mizoram to change its apathy and become tolerant towards the *Chakma*. Undoubtedly the *Chakma* are divided on the issue of the Zo/Mizo identity[27] and tolerating it. There exists a section among the *Chakma* which supports the idea of being recognised as authentic citizens of Mizoram while accepting and tolerating the Zo/Mizo hegemony with certain reservations. For instance, being recognised as *'Zo/Mizo Chakma'*; having their distinct ethnic enclave in the form of a territorially unified Chakma Autonomous District Council. Contrarily a section of the *Chakma* continues to maintain a stiff resistance to the Zo/Mizo hegemony; and insists on nothing short of a Union Territory status for the *Chakma*. Amidst all these projected attitudes and debates, the *Nexus of Patriarchy* and the northerners in general continue to exhibit their inability to accept or tolerate the *Chakma* in totality. This further substantiates the line of argument that 'assimilation like emulation is never a final solution rather just a stop gap/ piece meal solution in ethnic contests.' The 'politics of camouflaging' which cushions the notions of 'tolerance' at an operative scale, in that sense meets its 'dead-ends' at times and contesting communities surreptitiously negotiate their 'way out' to disentangle the braided ethnic contentions over resources and allocations and in doing so revisit the circles of 'tolerance'.

2. The Reang Story: Locating the Bru (Reang/'Tuikuk') in Zo/Mizo Society

The origin of Reang is said to be Maian Tlang, a hill near Rangamati of Bangladesh. Some opine that they originally belong to the Shan state of Burma where they migrated from Chittagong and then into Tripura during 14th century. The Reang folklore of the two brothers *Bruha and Braiha* speaks of the west-ward migration of the Reangs. The party led by Braiha in course of the migration went ahead and the party led by Bruha failed to catch up with the elder brother. As a result the party led by Bruha stayed back in the Zo hills and came to be known as Bru; while the party led by Braiha went ahead into Chittagong Hill Tracts and from there on to the present day Tripura and became the original settlers of that region.[28]

The Reang/Bru/Tuikuk are largely restricted to Mamit and Kolasib districts. Like the Chakma the Reang/Bru/Tuikuk are branded 'Problem tribes/people' by the *Zo hnahthlak*. Popular social imagery of the Reang/Bru/Tuikuk among the Zo people is that of a 'non-human', a primitive entity. In 1995, following a clash between Mizos and Brus, the Young Mizo Association and Mizo Students' Association demanded that Brus be removed from the state's electoral rolls, contending that the tribe was not indigenous to Mizoram. This led to an armed movement led by the militant outfit that styled itself as the Bru National Liberation Front (BNLF), and a political outfit styled the Bru National Union (BNU). These reactionary militant movements among the Brus wanted more political autonomy for Mizoram's Brus, and demanded a Bru Autonomous District Council. In October 1997, militants of the Bru National Liberation Front allegedly shot down a Mizo forest guard at the Dampa Tiger Reserve located in Mamit district. The incident evoked a hostile reaction, and the Brus were at the receiving end of a violent backlash by the Mizos, forcing the Brus to flee the state in large numbers to neighbouring Tripura. Of late there has been an in-migration of the Reangs from Tripura to Mizoram due to the turmoil in that state. The recent census report shows a remarkable rise in Reang population in Mizoram within a very short period.

The Reangs or Brus as they call themselves have been strongly resisting the subtle process that has been initiated by the northern majority tribes through their generic identity 'Mizo'. The large number of missionaries being sent to the Reangs areas to bring them to the fold of the book (Bible and the Law) is reflective of the mission of assimilation within the Mizo Identity. The state is sponsoring studies to come out with reliable work to support their Mizo/Zo linkages so as to tone down the emergent ethnic consciousness built around the 'Koch-bork folklores' of the Coch and Bodo tribes of Assam and Coochbehar. The *Zo hnahthlak* are struggling how to tame the wild Tuikuk? Where to hide them? 'What to do with them?'

2.1. *Pem Chuak* (Move out): The flight to Tripura

The Reang demand for an Autonomous District Council, which had triggered their large-scale exodus from Mizoram in 1997, has been revived by Bru National Liberation Front (BNLF) militants, who are fighting for the tribe's autonomy in that state. A decision to this effect was taken by BNLF leaders at a recent secret meeting in a forest hideout near the Assam-Tripura border. Sources in the intelligence wing of the state police said the BNLF had slowed down its activities in Mizoram and North Tripura, hoping for a solution to the twin issues of repatriation of Reang refugees stranded in Tripura camps and autonomy for their tribesmen in Mizoram. However, the dilatory tactics adopted by the Mizoram government and its consistent refusal to consider either of the demands even after 10 rounds of peace talks, have induced rethinking in the BNLF ranks. BNLF chief Surjyamoni Reang targeted the Government of Mizoram of master-minding the massacre of the Brus by the NLFT and the Indigenous Nationalist Party of Tripura (INPT). "If the Chakmas, Pawis and Lakhers in Mizoram can have district councils based on the Sixth Schedule, why not Reangs, who are the second largest community in the state?" asked Surjyamoni. He asserted that from now on the BNLF would carry forward the Reangs' agitation for an ADC in Mizoram. They said BNLF would soon start its movement for an ADC for the Reangs in Mizoram. He, however, did not indicate how the agitation would be launched and whether it would be an armed movement or a democratic agitation carried out by over-ground political groups like the Reang Democratic Party (RDP).Reangs said his tribesmen, despite being the second largest tribal group in the state, were the most persecuted community in Mizoram. Faced with "discrimination and exploitation", they had started demanding an autonomous council to protect their identity, culture and socio-economic interest. The movement had gathered momentum in 1997 in southwest Mizoram. The RDP had launched an agitation for the council, which would comprise four Reang-dominated Assembly constituencies in southwest Mizoram. In a retaliatory action, Mizo tribesmen had attacked the Reangs, forcing more than 30,000 people to flee the state. These refugees have been stranded in six camps of North Tripura's Kanchanpur subdivision for nearly seven years now.[29]

The displaced Brus took refuge in a town called Kanchanpur in northern Tripura, on the Mizoram-Tripura border. Now, they are spread across seven refugee camps on the Jamui hills, which separate Tripura from Mizoram and Bangladesh. The number of Bru refugees living in these camps is estimated to be around 35,000. The Bru Displaced People's Forum, however, claims the number to be much higher. The Brus/Reangs living in the camp have in the past alleged that the Tripura government was making life as difficult as possible for them in order to make them leave. Residents of these camps are not entitled to employment opportunities under any government scheme. As talks of repatriation began, violence struck again. In November 2009, Bru militants reportedly killed a Mizo teenager, triggering another spate of brutal retaliatory attacks on the Brus who had stayed behind, and another round of exodus to Tripura.

In 2014, the Tripura High Court had called the situation in the camps "ridiculous". According to reports, each adult in the camp in 2014 was eligible for an allowance of Rs 5 per day and 600 grams of rice. Minors get Rs 2.5 and 250 grams of rice. According to leaders of the Bru Displaced People's Forum, people in the camps still have little access to potable water and medical services.

2.2. Fisted ethnic stands

The various bodies of the Bru/Reangs insists that Brus who return are not safe in Mizo-dominated villages, and that they should be provided with cluster villages, a demand that the Mizoram government has termed as unreasonable. "What will we do if there's no land for our *jhum* farming?"

asked Sawibunga. Jhum refers to a method of slash-and-burn farming traditionally practised by the Brus. The demand for five hectares of land per family was not negotiable, he added.

The Brus have in their demand list that the Mizoram government should provide at least one government job per family and cash assistance of Rs 1.5 lakhs for each repatriated family. The most contentious demand, however, is "the facilitation of the creation of an autonomous district", something that the Mizoram government has refused to even consider.

The Brus in their application to the Supreme Court have alleged that around 1,000 families living in camps in Tripura have not been identified by the Mizoram government as eligible to return to Mizoram. The Brus/ Reangs have cited community hurt on this selective stand of the Zo hnahthlak on issue of a right to return to the homeland. The Brus/Reangs have criticised the Zo Civil Society and the Churches of restricting the path to '*Pem lut.*' The state government of Mizoram and the vigilant stakeholders like the MZP, YMA have accused the Bru/Reang leadership of deliberately sabotaging the repatriation process by repeatedly changing their demands.

The BNU, which was demanding an autonomous tribal district, claimed that 1,391 Bru houses in 41 villages were burnt down and several people were raped and killed. Mizoram police put the number of homes torched at 325 in 16 villages, and did not confirm rape or murder. A large number of Bru families fled to North Tripura. Thousands of families, with some 30,000 members, were given shelter in six relief camps in Kanchanpur and Panisagar subdivisions.

Depending on one's vantage point, displacement and deterritorialisation may shape the social construction of 'nationness', naturalness, history, identity and enmity. The construction of a national past is a construction of history of a particular kind; it is one that claims moral attachments to specific territories, motherlands or homelands, and posits time-honoured links between people, polity and territory.[30] How such collective histories come to challenge one another, or to engage in struggles over history and truth, can become a particularly challenging question among minorities and displaced people (*Reang* and *Chakma*). According to the 'Minorities at Risk Project, *Assessment for Mizos in India*, 2000':

> Disagreements between the Mizos and the Reang (also referred to as Bru), another tribal group that resides in Mizoram, erupted in violence in 1998 and resulted in the exodus of thousands of Reang into neighboring Tripura state. The Reang remain in refugee camps in Tripura and a rebel organization, the Bru National Liberation Front, is demanding the creation of a separate Reang state or autonomy within

Mizoram. The BNFL, fighting for separate autonomous district council and treatment at par with the 'Kashmiri Pundits' in western Mizoram, signed an MoU with the Central and the State governments in April 2005 leading to the surrender of about 1,040 BNLF militants.[31]

The Home Secretary, Government of Mizoram, met the BNLF leaders to pacify them from taking up the issue in the Supreme Court and the non-implementation of repatriation by the Mizoram Government.[32] However, the dilatory tactics adopted by the Mizoram government and its consistent refusal to consider either of the demands even after 10 rounds of peace talks, have induced rethinking in the BNLF ranks. BNLF chief Surjyamoni Reang targeting the Government of Mizoram says 'If the Chakmas, Pawis and Lakhers in Mizoram can have district councils based on the Sixth Schedule, why not Reangs, who are the second largest community in the state?'. The *Reang* agitation for an ADC has gathered momentum from 1997 in west Mizoram.[33] The *Reang* or *Bru*[34] as they call themselves have been strongly resisting the subtle process that has been initiated by the northern majority tribes through their generic identity 'Mizo'. The large number of missionaries being sent to the *Reang* areas to bring them to the fold of the book (Bible and the Law) is reflective of the mission of assimilation within the Mizo Identity.[35] The state is sponsoring studies to come out with reliable work to support their Zo/Mizo linkages so as to tone down the emergent ethnic consciousness built around the '*Koch-borok folklores*' of the Koch and Bodo tribes of Assam and Coochbehar.

Ethnicity, Religion and the questions on 'being Secular'

The issue of Bru/Reangs 'coming Home' has startled the Zo hnahthlak in Mizoram. Public debates and the sermons from the pulpit across the state has questioned the issue of the Bru/Reang's right to return (*Pem Lut* (Move in)). Communitarian actions and political interventions are interpreted through ecclesiastical lens and the civil societies and vigilant groups in the state of Mizoram look with suspicion the action of the Bru/Reang 'coming Home', the return of the ousted problem people is seen as a move to destabilize the Ideal Zo Christian State. The electoral dispute that engulfed Mizoram throughout November 2018 and the fisted public mood against the state Election Commission CEO S. B Shashank needs to be gleaned against a larger backdrop of fisted ethno-religious mood swings in Mizoram. Visiting this ethno-religious mood-swings unravels the tensions in ethnicity, religion and the uneasy questions on 'being Secular' in Mizoram.

Protest rallies demanding the ouster of the State's Chief Electoral Officer S.B. Shashank for allegedly misusing his official position to transfer a Mizo

IAS officer whom Shashank had been reported as 'responsible to restricting the return of the Bru/Reang and being a sympathizer of the *Zo hnahthlak*.' According to Mr. Shashank's report to the ECI, the action against Mr. Chuaungo had its genesis in the "unprecedented" theft and destruction of 5,400 electoral roll revision forms on August 23-24 from Mamit, the district where the majority of the displaced Brus are from. Apart from interfering with the electoral rolls revision in Mamit, Mr. Chuaungo meddled in the "process of security management of conduct of election."[36]

No. CYMA 74/2018-2019/1 of 3.11.2018
CENTRAL YOUNG MIZO ASSOCIATION
MIZORAM : AIZAWL

CENTRAL YMA THUCHHUAK

Central YMA Executive Committee Emergency Meeting Dt. 3.11.2018-a neih chuan,kan hma lawk 28.11.2018-a MLA inthlanna lo awm turah, inthlanna felfai leh muanawm a awm theih nan a daltu nia lang S.B. Shashank, IAS, Dt. 5.11.2018 tlai ni tlak hma ngei a Mizoram chhuahsan tura NGO Co-Ordination ten an lo rel chu tha a ti a, a hlawhtlin theih nan Hnam chhan hnatlang nei thei tuin Mizo mipuite leh YMA member zawng zawngte lo inring lawk turin a beisei a ni.

Sd/- LALHMACHHUANA
General Secretary,
Central YMA

Memo No. CYMA 74/2018-2019/1 — Dated Aizawl the 3rd November, 2018

Copy to :-

1. The Station Director, AIR/DDK, Aizawl Station - Chanchinthar (News Item-a) min lo puanzar sak turin.
2. The News Editor, LPS/ZONET - Chanchinthar (News Item-a) min lo puanzar sak turin.
3. The Editor, ____________ Chanchinbu - A chanchinbu zahawm taka News Item-a min lo chhuah sak turin.
4. File.

3/11/18
(LALHMACHHUANA)
General Secretary,
Central YMA

Source: Notice of the CYMA serving S. B. Shashank the 'Quit Notice', November 2018.

Source: WhatsApp Image in circulation 'Protesters at Aizawl' (ariel view) November 2018, Mizoram.

The protest rallies across the state attempted to halt the entire election process and the elections scheduled in December 2018. The protest movement took the form of a viral wave in the form of 'Save Mizoram Movement' both in real and the virtual space. Banners and posters displayed by the protesters asked the Election Commission of India to take a call on Mr. Shashank. "You will be responsible if Mizoram's record of holding the most peaceful elections in India is turned into a nightmare," one of such posters read.

The vigilant groups of the *Zo hnahthlak* craftily converted the issue of a transfer of a junior imcumbent by a higher incumbent as an insider versus outsider issue. The social media and medium of Whatsaap were used to replay the tensions between 'sons of soil' and the need to be fisted and protect Mizo/Zo culture and identity from polluting infiltrators through the hashtag movement #shashankout #supportchuaungo.

Source: WhatsApp Image in circulation November 2018, Mizoram.

On November 2nd 2018 Mr. Shaskank was issued 'Quit Mizoram Notice' and asked to leave Mizoram for having Lalnunmawia Chuaungo, a 1987-batch Mizo IAS officer of Gujarat cadre on deputation, transferred out for interfering with electoral rolls pertaining to the displaced minority Bru community. The deadline for Mr. Shashank to "quit Mizoram" expired on November 5 evening.

The regional political parties rallied behind the Church and the vigilant groups as they found it safe to go by the diktats of the Church based bodies. The Mizoram Pradesh Congress accused Mr. Shashank of being a Bharatiya Janata Party stooge and sought his removal. The BJP, trying to gain a foothold in Mizoram the only northeastern State where it or any of its regional allies are not in power also demanded Mr. Shashank's removal in a bid to trash the allegation.

In a letter to Prime Minister Narendra Modi and the Chief Election Commissioner on November 3, Mizoram Chief Minister Lal Thanhawla sought the reinstatement of Mr. Chuaungo as the Principal Home Secretary. The ECI had, following Mr. Shashank's complaint on October 29 placed Mr. Chuaungo under the disposal of the Ministry of Home Affairs (MHA). The Letter sent by the Congress leader described the elections commissions

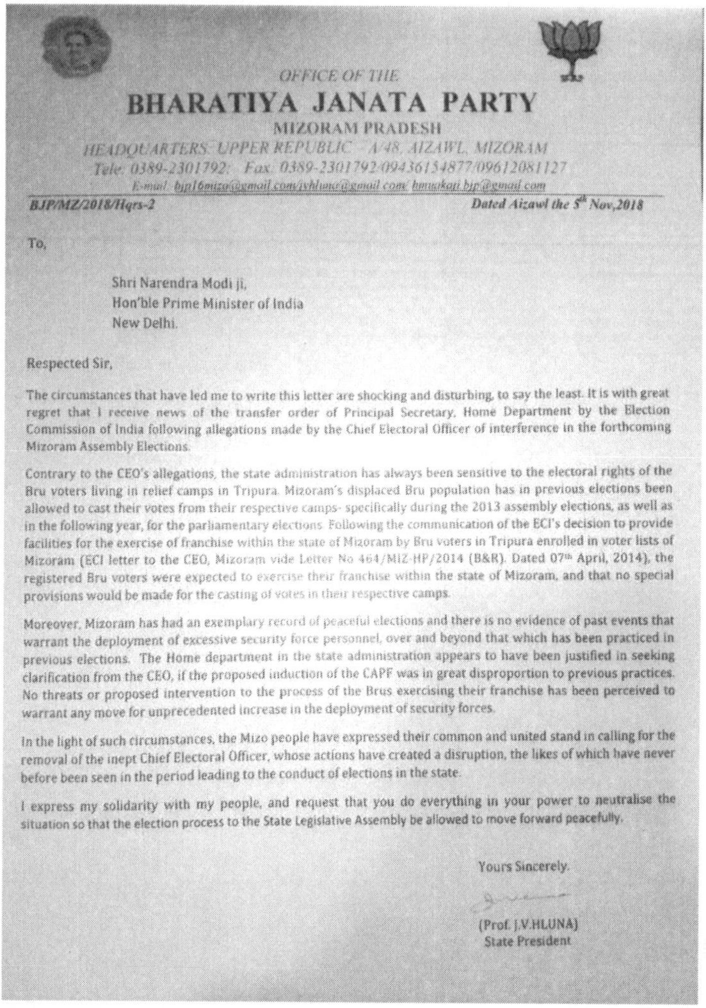

OFFICE OF THE

BHARATIYA JANATA PARTY

MIZORAM PRADESH

HEADQUARTERS: UPPER REPUBLIC – A/48, AIZAWL, MIZORAM

Tele: 0389-2301792; Fax: 0389-2301792/09436154877/09612081127

E-mail: bjp16mizo@gmail.com/jvhluna@gmail.com/ hmuakati.bjp@gmail.com

BJP/MZ/2018/Hqrs-2 **Dated Aizawl the 5th Nov,2018**

To,

Shri Narendra Modi ji,
Hon'ble Prime Minister of India
New Delhi.

Respected Sir,

The circumstances that have led me to write this letter are shocking and disturbing, to say the least. It is with great regret that I receive news of the transfer order of Principal Secretary, Home Department by the Election Commission of India following allegations made by the Chief Electoral Officer of interference in the forthcoming Mizoram Assembly Elections.

Contrary to the CEO's allegations, the state administration has always been sensitive to the electoral rights of the Bru voters living in relief camps in Tripura. Mizoram's displaced Bru population has in previous elections been allowed to cast their votes from their respective camps- specifically during the 2013 assembly elections, as well as in the following year, for the parliamentary elections. Following the communication of the ECI's decision to provide facilities for the exercise of franchise within the state of Mizoram by Bru voters in Tripura enrolled in voter lists of Mizoram (ECI letter to the CEO, Mizoram vide Letter No 464/MIZ-HP/2014 (B&R). Dated 07th April, 2014), the registered Bru voters were expected to exercise their franchise within the state of Mizoram, and that no special provisions would be made for the casting of votes in their respective camps.

Moreover, Mizoram has had an exemplary record of peaceful elections and there is no evidence of past events that warrant the deployment of excessive security force personnel, over and beyond that which has been practiced in previous elections. The Home department in the state administration appears to have been justified in seeking clarification from the CEO, if the proposed induction of the CAPF was in great disproportion to previous practices. No threats or proposed intervention to the process of the Brus exercising their franchise has been perceived to warrant any move for unprecedented increase in the deployment of security forces.

In the light of such circumstances, the Mizo people have expressed their common and united stand in calling for the removal of the inept Chief Electoral Officer, whose actions have created a disruption, the likes of which have never before been seen in the period leading to the conduct of elections in the state.

I express my solidarity with my people, and request that you do everything in your power to neutralise the situation so that the election process to the State Legislative Assembly be allowed to move forward peacefully.

Yours Sincerely,

(Prof. J.V.HLUNA)
State President

Source: WhatsApp image in circulation BJP President Mizoram J.V Hluna's Letter to Narendra Modi November 2018.

Officer Mr. Shashamk as "inexperienced and incompetent", and mentioned that the civil society in Mizoram "does not take this (inept handling of electoral process) lightly" and that the government fully supports "their long-standing demand that the Brus now living in Tripura transit camps should come and cast their votes inside Mizoram like every other Mizo from outside the State do at the time of elections".

The Bru/Reang from the late 1990s have been mooting their religio-cultural differences (Vaishnavaite-animist) from that of the predominantly

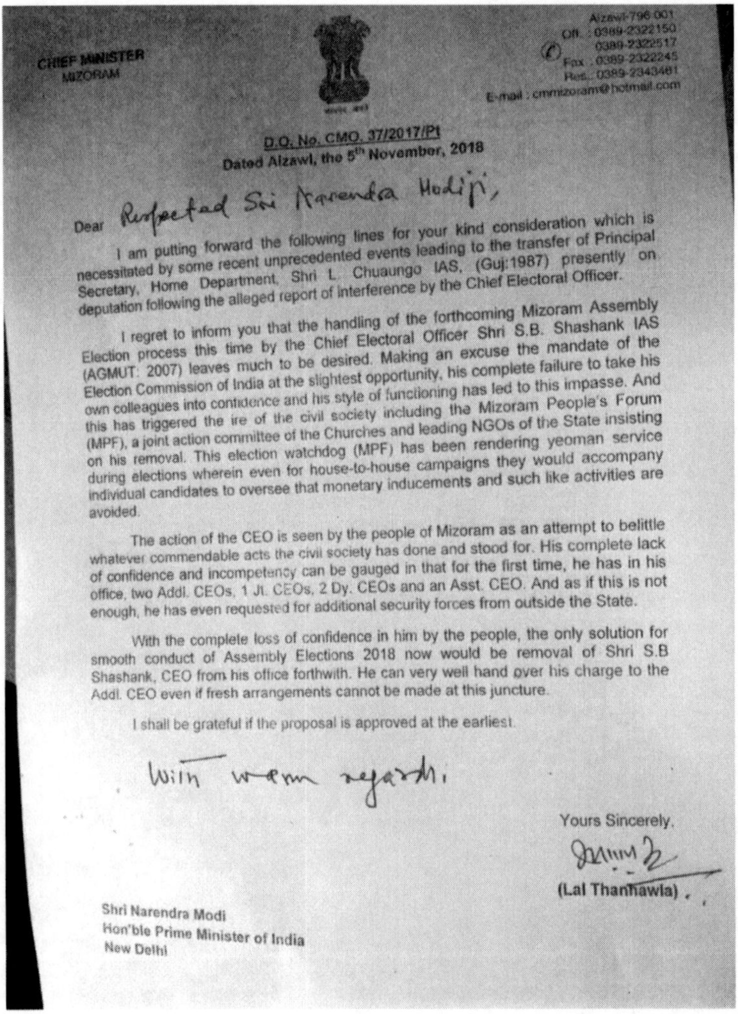

CHIEF MINISTER
MIZORAM

Aizawl-796 001
Off. : 0389-2322150
0389-2322517
Fax : 0389-2322245
Res. : 0389-2343481
E-mail : cmmizoram@hotmail.com

D.O. No. CMO. 37/2017/Pt
Dated Aizawl, the 5th November, 2018

Dear Respected Sri Narendra Modiji,

I am putting forward the following lines for your kind consideration which is necessitated by some recent unprecedented events leading to the transfer of Principal Secretary, Home Department, Shri L. Chuaungo IAS, (Guj:1987) presently on deputation following the alleged report of interference by the Chief Electoral Officer.

I regret to inform you that the handling of the forthcoming Mizoram Assembly Election process this time by the Chief Electoral Officer Shri S.B. Shashank IAS (AGMUT: 2007) leaves much to be desired. Making an excuse the mandate of the Election Commission of India at the slightest opportunity, his complete failure to take his own colleagues into confidence and his style of functioning has led to this impasse. And this has triggered the ire of the civil society including the Mizoram People's Forum (MPF), a joint action committee of the Churches and leading NGOs of the State insisting on his removal. This election watchdog (MPF) has been rendering yeoman service during elections wherein even for house-to-house campaigns they would accompany individual candidates to oversee that monetary inducements and such like activities are avoided.

The action of the CEO is seen by the people of Mizoram as an attempt to belittle whatever commendable acts the civil society has done and stood for. His complete lack of confidence and incompetency can be gauged in that for the first time, he has in his office, two Addl. CEOs, 1 Jt. CEOs, 2 Dy. CEOs and an Asst. CEO. And as if this is not enough, he has even requested for additional security forces from outside the State.

With the complete loss of confidence in him by the people, the only solution for smooth conduct of Assembly Elections 2018 now would be removal of Shri S.B Shashank, CEO from his office forthwith. He can very well hand over his charge to the Addl. CEO even if fresh arrangements cannot be made at this juncture.

I shall be grateful if the proposal is approved at the earliest.

With warm regards.

Yours Sincerely,

(Lal Thanhawla)

Shri Narendra Modi
Hon'ble Prime Minister of India
New Delhi

Source: WhatsApp image in circulation Lalthanhawla's Letter to Narendra Modi November 2018.

Christian Zo hnahthlak and their experience of being ousted overnight into the borders of Tripura to substantiate their collective fears and insecurities of living among the *Zo hnahthlak*. The collective fear was used as a ground for permitting the Bru/Reangs to vote either from refugee camps in Tripura and Assam, or in poll booths on the Tripura-Mizoram border. The *Zo hnahthlak* from Mizoram in turn suspected this as a ploy to increase the 'Tuikuk (Bru/Rean) vote banks' and affect the demography of the state election.

Some Closing Observations

Most of my respondents from the north and dominant Mizo group felt 'the *Reang* (*Bru*) are 'nobody tribes', they are like gypsies'.[37] Zaliana says with full zeal that '*Tuikuk* (*Reang* (*Bru*)) and *'Takam'* (*Chakma*) should pray and revere the Mizos as gods because they have been so benevolent to them. They (*Reang* and *Chakma*) do not use the money sent to them for development seriously and the elites siphon the funds for their own interest.' *'Tuikuk Pathian siamtheilo' 'kha siam kan tum'* ('we are trying to make humans out of those people who failed God'). 'No report of atrocities against Mizo by *Tuikuk*. The NHRC has been filled with false allegations. Saikapthianga (Mizo MLA from that area) and his family have been really benevolent on them. On the contrary, it is the *Reang* (*Bru*) who have committed crime and violence. For instance, they raped and murdered the Mizo missionary Rohmingthangi who was working among them (*Chakma* and *Tuikuk*). It has never been vice versa. Mizos do not kill or commit atrocities on the minorities. Do we have any reports on custodial deaths? Or reports on crimes? Not one' says, Zaliana.[38] The *Reang* (*Bru*) have been creating trouble in Mizoram and demanding ADC status. The *Reang* (*Bru*) are a cross border migratory tribe with no fixed territory. If their demands are fulfilled than every other ethnic minority will demand it. The *Reang* (*Bru*) are 'a problem tribe' and should go back to Tripura.[39]

There was no agreement on the issue of emergent ADC status by the minority ethnic communities such as *Bru* (*Reang*) in Mizoram. Few of my respondents felt that granting Autonomous district to sub-tribes was not feasible 'It will spoil the peace and development in Mizoram. Can the *Reang* (*Bru*) and the *Hmar* justify their claims? The present Mizoram is a total Sailo area that is not at all a territory of these small groups. These smaller groups have lost their land to the other tribes in and around Manipur, Tripura, Nagaland, Assam (Haflong) and other areas in Myanmar and Bangladesh. The present territory of Mizoram especially the northern part was a total 'lusei-sailo' area, excluding Sakawrdai area which was the village of a Hmar chief. So how do they (the *Reang* (*Bru*) and the *Hmar*) justify their demand for an ADC without bases in history?'[40] Few of my respondents even linked the 'Zo Reunification demand' with that of the frustrations of not being able to achieve an ADC status thus: 'the leaders of the movements know that they lack historical proof to support their demands of an ADC status. It is but natural that they are demanding the cause of Zo unification'.

The Accords meant for evening-out the rough edges of the demands for ADCs or 'Ethnic Enclaves' are seen primarily as instruments through which contending parties seek to make their respective interests visible. Accords instead of putting an end to the battle become the nuclei through the whole battle of arguments and counter-arguments resurface in any given society. In short the accords become embedded with contestations and become subject to different/multiple interpretation depending upon time and space.

The case of the Autonomous District Councils in Mizoram reflects the complex web of 'Governance-Autonomy, Federalism, Ethnicity and Development; and that of 'Identity. The constant flux in the mood of the identity formation can be seen through the case of the *Mara,* the *Lai* and the *Chakma*. This aspect of 'acquired' identity has its contemporary manifestation in the highly clichéd and contested *generic* as well as *phonetic* identity. The discussions also brings out the complex within tribe relations which are moulded by strictures of patriarchal control and are exerted very intensely over issues of identity formation, centre-state relations and issues of governance; and such relations continue to be moulded in the strict notions of Zo/Mizo understanding of identity and development.

Local autonomy has not solved the problem of ethnic conflict. The case of the *Mara*, the *Lai* and the *Chakma* throws up a number of issues on autonomy, ethnicity and governance. More often than not, autonomy is considered a panacea for ethnic conflicts. Autonomy unites people (as with the *Mara*, the *Lai*, the *Chakma* or the *Chhim lam* (southern) tribes) as well as divides (the *Mara-Lai-Chakma* division) or marginalises (Zo/Mizo versus Mara and Lai; Mara-Lai versus Chakma; Mizo/Zo versus Chakma etc.) sub-communities. The Mizoram experience re-confirms that 'Autonomy' becomes a part of the problem and not the solution. The minorities such as the *Chakma* or the *Bru* (*Reang*) or any other 'marginal/peripheral' group feel discriminated [41] against and seek further autonomy in the form of Autonomous District or Union Territory or Statehood depending on the time and space factor.

Likewise another interesting feature of the Autonomy Movements in Mizoram is that they are viewed in terms of 'Ethnic enclaves' for cocooning a certain group. There is an inevitable conflict between autonomy and over dependence on the 'dole-development' from the Centre. My study also indicates and offers enough clues in the direction that successful processing of ethnic demands can encourage new demands from those who were not able to speak out before. This emulation effect can be seen as a signal of social mobility and benefits amassed by the middle-class out of the ethnic movements. This encourages the other ethnic groups to channel their claims around newly created ethnic labels. The initiation of the power sharing model in the post-statehood period for mellowing down the MNF; the exploitation of Article 356 to maintain the supremacy of the Centre in the

State; the provisions under Article 371G (Constitutional amendment, 1986) in respect of the religious or social practices of the Mizos, customary laws and procedures and such other provisions, all indicated a smooth exchange of power relations between the centre and the state. This process can be seen as the filtering of democracy to the roots to tap new sources of strength from the deeper strata of society thereby contributing to the 'successes of India's Democracy'.[42]

Likewise, the issues of ethnicity, religion, electoral participation converged into uneasy areas of being secular. Being Christian and being non-believer continued to regulate the notion of being recognized as people in the state of Mizoram. Institutional protectionism through ADCs hardly proved effective for marginal tribes who did not fall in line with the blueprint of an *Ideal Zo Christian State* as directed and regulated from the northerners' collegiums the *Zo hnahthlak*.

The case of the Chakma and that of the Bru/Reang shows differences and commonalities in issues relating to minorities within minorities in the state of Mizoram. Also, these two cases provide interesting perspectives teasing uneasy questions of secularism as operative among proselytized communities in South Asia. The intolerance of the *Zo hnahthlak* to any possible articulation (even in the form of a positive critique) in deviation to the norm prescribed by the Nexus of the Church and the patriarchies from the north seem to dismantle the notions of being secular and tolerant in plural societies. The case of Mizoram shows that the *Zo hnahthlak* regulate their conduct in tune with the blue-print of the Church and its agencies, the churches are not simply mere places of worship rather they serve multiple purpose from serving as places of worship, to congregation, networking, social services and community and individual healing etc. Verrier Elwin had aptly noted that among the Mizos 'Christianity means medical care, education and English language, and a richer material life…'[43]

Notes and References

1. Anup Shekhar Chakraborty. (2011). 'Educational Policies and Social Exclusion: A Case Study of Chakma Tribes in Mizoram.' *Social Action- issue on New Education Policy and Social Exclusion (A Quarterly Review of Social Trends).*Vol. 61 No. 3, July-Sept., 274-85.
2. Mizo Saying to express the non-changing, stubborn nature of the Tuikuk and Chakma tribes.
3. Anup Shekhar Chakraborty. (2016). 'Exclusive Knowledge System: Exclusionary Educational Policies of Government of Mizoram and the Chakma', Chapter 3 (pp.33-80) *in* Anup Shekhar Chakraborty and Padam Nepal. (ed.). (2016). *Politics of Exclusions and Inclusions in India: Construing Commonalities and Complexities.* New Delhi: Authorspress.

4. Interestingly 'Backwardness' is one of the markers through which the *Chakma* have been rallying their identity against the Northerners in the state of Mizoram. The Census of India 2001, found the *Chakma* community to be the "most illiterate" community in the state of Mizoram, a state having the second highest literacy rate in India. *See* for details, Government of India. (2001). *Census of India (2001)*. Registrar General and Census Commissioner, New Delhi.
5. This 'clubbing' into a 'cross-border' tribe is not emic to the said tribe or group precisely because 'border' as inherited from the 'Raj' (British India) and thereafter as negotiated by successive governments in post-independence times has been unable to hold to the social imaginaries and undo the inter-generational memories of traditional 'game-land, areas and riparian territories that the said group held close as their 'own', inherited from their fore-fathers, and somewhere down history through the craft of cunning statecraft and external aggression was forcibly taken over by the 'rival forces'. The 'border' in that sense made little or no meaning to the said tribes and they found surreptitious ways to negotiate the border. (ASC).
6. Chawngkhuma Chawngthu. (2005). *Mara Khawtlang Nun*. Aizawl: Mualchin Publication & Paper Works. Also See, Stephen Fuchs. (1973). (1977). *The Aboriginal Tribes of India*. London/Madras: The Macmillan Press Ltd. pp. 203, 215-16.
7. The Lai/Pawi are the immediate neighbours of the Mara/Lakher and inhabitant the area 'Lai Autonomous District'. The *Pawi/Lai* story also speaks of similar experiences of the process of partition in the sub-continent. Though the *Lai* (*Pawi* or *Chin*) have close affinities to the Lushai group, their relations historically have never been cordial.
8. Before 1898, the head of the Lushai District was called a Political Officer. At first there were two political officers- one for the South Lushai Hills and another for the North Lushai Hills. After the amalgamation of the two districts the designation of the head of the district was changed to Superintendent. Shakespear was the first Superintendent of the Lushai District. The Superintendent enjoyed tremendous powers for instance he regulated the successor to the chieftainship, appointed guardians to the minor chiefs, partitioned the existing villages, formed new villages, appointed new chiefs, determined the boundaries of the villages and areas to be occupied by the chiefs etc. For details *See*, V. Venkata Rao. (1978). Chapter 18, 'The Sociology of Mizo Politics'. pp. 215-232 *in* S.M. Dubey. (ed.). (1978). *North East India: A Sociological Study.* New Delhi: Concept Publishing Company.
9. Anup Shekhar Chakraborty. (2009a). 'Regulating Citizenship: Politics of 'Check-In' and 'Check-Out''. *Refugee Watch Online (A Co-Publication of Refugee Watch)*, 18 February. Also *See*, 'Introduction' (2012) *in* Padam Nepal and Anup Shekhar Chakraborty (ed.). (2012). *Politics of Culture, Identity and Protest in North-east India*, Vol. 1 & 2. New Delhi: Authorspress.
10. Anup Shekhar Chakraborty. (2007). 'Politics of Silencings: Echoes of the Margins from Mizoram'. *Indian Journal of Political Science (IJPS)*.Meerut, Chaudhury Charan Singh University. Vol. LXVIII, No. 4, Oct.-Dec.
11. Anup Shekhar Chakraborty. (2011). *Op.cit.*

12. Newslink. (2006). 'Chakmas want border fencing stopped'. Aizawl: 5 April; Sentinel. (2006). 'Indo-Bangla border fencing in Mizoram: Chakmas demand implementation of rehabilitation packages'. Guwahati: 11 April; Sentinel. (2008). 'Chakmas demand suspension of border fencing'. Aizawl: 16 January. Guwahati: 17 January.
13. Rahul Karmakar. (2017). 'Chakma students protest discrimination by Mizoram govt'. *Hindustan Times*, Guwahati: 07 Aug.
14. The MZP (Mizo Zirlai Pawl) is the largest students' representative in Mizoram and also the most active agency of the *Nexus of Patriarchy* in the state of Mizoram. It acts as a mechanism of systemic control through which the politics of 'Exclusions' and 'inclusions' is put to function. The MZP was originally formed as the Lushai Student's Union in 1935 in Shillong. By 1942 the inter-tribe, intra-clan contest over nomenclature led to the adoption of a more acceptable nomenclature 'Mizo Zirlai Pawl'. The change in nomenclature signalled among many things the breaking of the 'Sailo-Lusei hegemony' that had since the days of the 'Raj' predominated the politics and society among the Zo people. By the 60s it had absorbed many traits and ways of the Assam Students' Union and in 1970 shifted its base to Aizawl. Thereafter, the MZP aligned itself with the powerful churches and switched allegiances to different political parties in power and significantly marked its presence in Zo/Mizo politics. It came into public prominence for its role as a partner in collection of donations for the MNF (Mizo National Front) movement from 70s through the 1980s.
15. The MSU is a faction organisation of the MZP. They have emerged as the 'other' students association. The gradual rise of the MSU taking pertinent issues of Mizoram and 'problematizing' them during the 2010-2017 shows that the 'students' are fractioned on various lines and that their aspirations are not quenched by the solitary MZP.
16. Originally established on 15 June 1935 as the *Young Lushai Association(YLA)*, it was later renamed the 'Young Mizo Association' on 7 October 1947. It was initiated by the Welsh Christian missionaries who understood the need of cultural conservation of the Mizo tribe, who were under pressure of political and social modernisations. Every Mizo is a member of the YMA and life revolves around this 'philanthropic' institution. The YMA is administered by a central committee (Central YMA (CYMA)), headquartered at Aizawl, under which there are 5 sub-headquarters, 47 groups and 772 branches. However, the picture perfect public face of the institution has a hidden side masked in the 'mask of Hegemony' and all pervasive control of everyday life both public and private among the *Zo hnahthlak*.
17. Chakraborty. (2011). *Op.cit*.
18. The '*Vai*' students of Pacchunga College (Aizawl) of that period called her 'Tara Gubbara' suggesting that she was on the larger scale of the weighing machine. Based on conversations with '*Vai*' college students of that period, Pachhunga College was affiliated to NEHU, Meghalaya and conducted the class XII examinations.
19. Kiran Bedi's daughter was one such beneficiary to get admission in a medical college in Delhi by arranging a domicile certificate from the State government of Mizoram, which mentioned that she completed her 'Plus two examination' in

Mizoram. This resulted in a state wide protest by the students body the MZP and vested groups. The issue gained prominence when politicians provoked student community by pointing out that an outsider like Kiran Bedi was using 'Mizo quota' for her daughter. Within 2 days, the student group of 50 began to swell into rioting mobs of 2000 students demanding Kiran Bedi to surrender her daughter's medical seat. The Chief Minister was forced nullify Bedi's daughter's domicile certificate and notified the medical college to cancel her admission. Kiran Bedi rushed to the law minister (Dr. Thansanga) requesting him to pursuade the state machinery to intervene and take control of the situation, but in vain. The minister said that the issue has now turned into 'Mizo vs Non-Mizo' and adviced her to leave Mizoram before the mob would even try to kill her!! As the mob surrounded her house, and the state Govt being blind to the situation, Kiran Bedi had no choice but to vacate. She & her family took the exit route out of Mizoram that night and safely reached Delhi. Based on information gathered from college students who actively staged protests during that period. Names withheld on request. (ASC).

20. Mizoram like few of the states in North East India does not have its own 'Medical Colleges'. An arrangement has been struck whereby 38 seats (as in January 2017) in various government-run medical colleges across the country have been earmarked for students from Mizoram. These seats are allotted on the basis of their performance in the National Eligibility Entrance Test (NEET) and counselling exercise organised by the Mizoram Higher and Technical Education Department. (ASC).

21. Based on my study '*Good Health', 'Well Being' And Social Imaginaries In Health Migrations: North Bengal And North East India Construed*' (2016, GOWB Sponsored NIAS Research), I found that 'the doctor is the next most coveted job/ profession/ occupation among the Zo people in Mizoram, next only to the 'Pastor''. (ASC).

22. Four Chakma students were among the top 38 list of Medical studies aspirants. They were placed fourth, ninth, 17th and 23rd however the presence of Chakma names in the Medical toppers list made the Zo restive. The counselling, which was to be held on July 19 2017 at Aizawl, had to be cancelled after protests at the venue by Mizo Zirlai Pawl, the MSU and other vigilant groups. The Mizo Zirlai Pawl contended in a series of press releases that the Chakma students ought not to be included in the same category as other indigenous Mizo students.

23. The indigeneity of the Chakma tribe is a contentious subject in the North East of India and they have been subject to an array of tagging such as "Chakma foreigners", "illegal migrants from Bangladesh", "breeders", "backward" etc. They have been accused of infringing on the rights of the indigenous people of the state, multiplying at a rate "not possible by way of normal human reproduction" and a threat to security of India and the concerned state in the North East.

24. Rahul Karmakar. (2016) 'Students group hails HC orders on Mizoram Courses'. *Hindustan Times*. Jaipur: 25 June.

25. Rahul Karmakar. (2017) *Op.cit.*; Sumir Karmakar. (2017). 'Chakma student denied Medical seat'. *The Telegraph*. Guwahati: 10 August.

26. Anup Shekhar Chakraborty. (2016). *Op.cit.*

27. Anup Shekhar Chakraborty. (2011). *Op.cit.*
28. Tribal Research Institute (TRI). (1986). *A Brief History of Riangs In Mizoram.* Aizawl: United Press/Everly Press. pp.1-22.
29. Special Correspondent. (2004). 'Fresh storm brews over Reang refugees'. The Telegraph, Kolkata /Agartala: 10 July.
30. Hannah Arendt. (1951). (1973). *The Origins of Totalitarianism.* New York/ London: Harcourt Brace Jovanovich; Ernest Renan. (1990) 'What Is a Nation?' *in* Homi Bhabha (ed.) *Nation and Narration*. New York: Routledge. pp 8-22; Benedict Anderson. (1983). (1991). *Imagined Communities: Reflections on the Origin and Spread of Nationalism.* London: Verso.
31. 'Minorities at Risk Project, *Assessment for Mizos in India'*, 31 December 2000. Online. UNHCR Refworld, available at: http://www.unhcr.org/refworld/ docid/ 469f3a911f.html (accessed on 13 October 2008).
32. *Newslink*. (2007) 'Home Secretary meets unhappy Brus'. Aizawl: 21 November.
33. Special Correspondent. (2004). 'Fresh storm brews over Reang Refugees'. *The Telegraph*. Kolkata/Agartala: 10 July.
34. The origin of Reang is said to be Maian Tlang, a hill near Rangamati of Bangladesh. Some opine that they originally belong to the Shan state of Burma where they migrated from Chittagong and then into Tripura during 14th century. The Reang folklore of the two brothers *Bruha and Braiha* speaks of the west-ward migration of the Reangs. The party led by Braiha in course of the migration went ahead and the party led by Bruha failed to catch up with the elder brother. As a result the party led by Bruha stayed back in the Zo hills and came to be known as Bru; while the party led by Braiha went ahead into Chittagong Hill Tracts and from there on to the present day Tripura and became the original settlers of that region. *Cf.*, TRI, (1986). *A Brief History of Riangs In Mizoram.* Aizawl: United Press/Everly Press. pp.1-22.
35. The BJP is exploring the possibility of using the Reang (Bru) issue to enter into a Christian majority state politics. Supporting the displaced Bru is in effect an attempt to break the glass ceiling.
36. Rahul Karmakar. (2018). Mizoram NGOs want Chief Electoral Officer removed. *The Hindu*. Guwahati: 06 November, accessed on 12/12/2018.
37. *Personal Interviews*: Prof. Lianzela & Professor Thangchungnunga (Department of Economics, Mizoram University). Tanhril, Aizawl: 24th January 2008; Pu Lallianchhunga (Lecturer, Department of Political Science, Mizoram University). Chaltlang Campus, Aizawl: 19th January 2008; Prof. Lalrinthanga (Public Administration, Mizoram University). Chaltlang Campus, Aizawl: 19th January 2008.
38. Pu Zaliana. *Personal Interview. Op.cit;*
39. *Personal Interviews*: Prof. Lianzela & Prof. Thangchungnunga. *Op.ci*; Professor Lalrinthanga. *Op.cit*.
40. *Personal Interviews*: Pu Zaliana. *Op. cit.;* Pu Lianhmingthanga. (Senior Research Officer, 'Tribal Research Institute', Art & Culture Department, Government of Mizoram, McDonald Hill). Zarkawt, Aizawl: 21st and 22nd January 2008; Pu Lalrinkima. (Lecturer, Department of Political Science, Lunglei Government

College). Lunglei: 1st February 2008; Prof. Lalrinthanga. *Op. cit.*; Prof. F. Lalremsiama. (Department of History, Johnson's College). Khatla, Aizawl: 26th January 2008.

41. Poor exploitation of natural resources and inadequate economic infrastructure, combined with the lack of trained manpower, forces the state to become the largest employment agency. The obverse side of a high literacy rate is educated unemployed, which the government cannot now absorb. All these culminate in a spiral of dissatisfaction.
42. This is obviously an inspiration from Atul Kohli's edited work titled '*The Success of India's Democracy*'. (2001) Cambridge: Oxford University Press.
43. Elwin Verrier. (1960). *A Philosophy of NEFA*. Shillong: Gov. of Assam. p. 110.

5

Mizo Women, the Nexus of Patriarchy and 'Being Secular'

'Where are 'Our Women'?' is a contested question in the Zo/Mizo Christian World, which has embarked on the mammoth project of building an '*Ideal Zo Christian State*'. The debate on the positionality of Women in Mizo Society is a long drawn one. While some eulogise the pre-colonial position of women and blame the colonial/ post-colonial contacts with the British and the 'Vai' as a cause for the decline of the status of women in the Mizo society; Others hold that gender bias was and is inherent in the Mizo social system itself and that the British rule sustained the patriarchal hegemony, which even today continues to linger under the garb of modernity and socio-economic-political development in Mizoram. For the larger audience across India the public visibility of Mizo women in the market places, public offices, and other 'sites and spaces that matter' is construed as signposts of 'empowerment' and social privilege, despite the conspicuous absence from the realms of Politics and higher positions in the Churches. The position of women in Mizoram presents a paradoxical case of 'being everywhere yet being nowhere'; their visibility is in fact regulated by the dictates of the Zo Churches and the *Nexus of Patriarchy*. The discussions in the chapter would construe the anxieties of the *Nexus of Patriarchy* as reflected through the proposal (19th October 2018) of the YMA (Young Mizo Association) for boycott and denial of ST status to Mizo women marrying Non-tribals. Such insular tactics reflecting patriarchal insecurities and verging towards unsecular diktats have become more pronounced in recent times across the North East. The discussions in this chapter would attempt to make meaning out of the ongoing 'politics of regulations' and intolerance operative in Mizoram.

I

Gleaning Socio-Cultural-Politico-Economic Realities of the Zo Hills

In a predominantly Christian state where a large section of the population claims to be devout Christian, the Church naturally encapsulates every aspect of Zo/Mizo life. The Church's influence on the Zo/Mizo tribes is really deep and interestingly the church itself has undergone a process of being Mizoised through *ruaithre* (community feasting) and *'zai leh lam'* (song and dances).[1] In short, there is a strong *localization of the Gospel* in Mizoram. An abstract of a news item in Times of India dated January 9th, 1989 conveniently explains the predominance of the Church in Zo/Mizo politics:

> In a state where 85 percent of the population is Christian, the Church is playing a vital role in the 21st January elections to the State Assembly and has even indirectly supported the Congress in a significant message to the people of the state, ten denominations of the Church, active in the state, have laid down guidelines for the voters and candidates, to be followed during the election. The message, issued shortly after the imposition of President's Rule on September 7th last year (1988), however, does not name any party or individual. During the last (1987) elections, the MNF was voted to power, as the Church had given a call to vote for that party which would bring peace to the State... "In the course of the campaign, we (*the Church*) deem it best that no public feast be held under the name of any party. The different parties, instead of campaigning from house to house, may launch their campaigns through public meetings. Party politics with its potential to create antagonism loosened the solidarity of the Mizo community and is also a stumbling block for the Churches."[2]

All political leaders cutting across party affiliations have project themselves as pious, god fearing citizens and publicly at least maintain their subservience to the Church. The desire to create an *Ideal Zo Christian State* has been strongly portrayed and at times has led to the voyeuristic intervention of the church and its agencies in both the private and public arena. The dual operation of Proselytisation and Colonialism introduced marked structural and functional changes in the everyday life of Zo/Mizo society.[3]

The church is omnipresent in Mizoram, its activities providing the crux of social life. But, while collectivism gives people a sense of social security and an umbrella in times of distress, it also fosters attitudes of conformity.[4] In Zo/Mizo context, the dictates of the *Nexus of the Patriarchy* regarding the dress code, behaviour, disapproval of marriage outside the community, expressions of concern and fear over assimilation and hybrid-identities and so on, have further sustained the politics of panoptics and challenged the same.[5] In most cases women become the 'last frontiers of nationalism', especially when the patriarchy declares 'that "Our" Women need to be protected from "Others"'; the onus of 'Mothering and Birthing a Nation' falls on their shoulders.[6]

Christianity brought about strong Western influence on dress and music; and also began to exert its influence on cultural norms. It disapproved of what it termed 'pagan customs' of drinking rice beer and traditional music and dancing. These features of tribal life almost disappeared and it was only after statehood that efforts were made to revive them. Proselytisation triumphantly transplanted the 'head-hunters' to 'soul-hunters' to the point where religion and culture are now entangled and undistinguishable.[7] The arena of culture serves as a battle ground for debates on prohibition with two camps clearly demarcated; those favouring the cause[8] and those against prohibition. Hardly surprising then that the Zo/Mizo are just as furiously perplexed over the question of their identity as they are aggressively proud of it.[9]

Zo/Mizo Women claiming their positional order in Zo/Mizo Cosmology

One of the pertinent questions that pose the proselytized Zo/Mizo society is that of locating the position of women amidst the all encompassing *Nexus of Patriarchy*. 'Where are 'Our Women'?' is a contested question in the Zo/Mizo Christian World. The debate on the positionality of Women in Mizo Society is a long drawn one. While some eulogise the pre-colonial position of women and blame the colonial/post-colonial contacts with the British and the 'Vai'[10] as a cause for the decline of the status of women in the Mizo society; Others hold that gender bias was and is inherent in the Mizo social system itself and that the British rule sustained the patriarchal hegemony, which even today continues to linger under the garb of modernity and socio-economic-political development in Mizoram. Women in the Mizo society like in most societies held a secondary place; men headed the family and controlled the socio-religious-political affairs.

The post-colonial Zo/Mizo politics propelled by the *Politics of the Pan Optics* relied heavily on the youth and students' organizations like the Young

Mizo Association (YMA), the Khristian Thalai Pawl (KTP) and also the Mizo Zirlai Pawl (MZP) for '*systemic or structural control*'.

It is an undeniable fact that the realms of women and men are always clearly demarcated in any society and stereotypically, the role of the healer is "reserved" for Zo/Mizo women while Zo/Mizo men justify violence in the name of *protection*. Thus, women are directly not party to the actions of the men and may even disagree with them but, given their operating spaces they often follow the decision of their men. The high moralistic standards applied to women also, make them the best targets to "hurt your enemy where it hurts the most". Further, women may be entrusted with the responsibility of caring for the captured as a subtle means of evoking their sympathies and creating a more human face. The message conveyed through these contradictory actions demonstrates the willingness of the Mizo's to let the 'Vai' exist within restricted spaces, under the condition of total acceptance of decisions made by the Zo/Mizo community.

The 'Vai' over the years have moulded their survival strategies which includes 'adopting Zo/Mizo names', 'converting to Christianity' and marrying local tribal women'. These survival strategies or *politics of camouflaging* helps the Vai to bargain their existence in the Zo world. This politics of camouflaging can be adopted for a plethora of reasons from that of personal security to that of private business or for being accepted as a '*Denizen*'.

Language (spoken words) and symbols (dress code and colours) were often used as weapons to show Zo/Mizo women their spatial position and inferior status in the social hierarchy. For instance, men in the Zo/Mizo society consider 'puanfen' (skirts) to be the symbol of femininity i.e. inferior and make it a point never to wash 'skirts', whatever the situation be, this is true for male domestic helpers as well. Men in the Mizo society, usually try to dictate terms to their women, as to what they wear, whom to marry etc.[11] Women in the Mizo society has been ascribed the role of an 'out-let' (thereby reduced to the position of the sexual organs) to creation but not the status of a procreator, for such a revered position is reserved only for the male-the vigour, the powerful Pasaltha (Brave Mizo Hero). It was for this reason also that the men in the Mizo society consciously and unconsciously treated women as a sexual being whose urges need to be repressed and directed.

Mizo Women and Organizational Initiatives

Zo/Mizo Women in contemporary times have jumped the glass ceiling and leaped over to the position of determining their agency through institutional initiatives and also through the twin activities of Western Education and the Evangelical activities. In course of time Zo/Mizo women have challenged the patriarchal hegemony through the formation of women's organizations like the MHIP- *'Mizo Hmeichhe Insuihkhawm Pawl'*,[12] MHT- *'Mizo Hmeichhe Tangrual'*, and PHP- *'Puitu Hmeichhe Pawl'* etc, for safeguarding the interests of the Mizo.

The focus of the MHIP has been fleeting between reformation, empowerment and protection of the weakest links in Mizo society. For instance, immediately after the signing of the Peace Accord and the formation of the State of Mizoram, the MHIP declared 1987 as *'Hmeichhe Kum'* (Women's Year) and aspired to bring about changes in the Patriarchies in operation. Realizing the stiffed response of the Patriarchies through the late 90's the MHIP switched its focused first on 'Women's Empowerment.' The MHIP declared the period 1997-2001 as 'Women's Year' in Mizoram for creation of awareness on issues such as 'the low status of women in the society' and 'to review the Mizo customary law'. In this regard, the MHIP had toured the length and breadths of the state covering remote and interior villages and conducting workshops, seminars and group discussions.

The formation of these women's organisation represents *the second instance of rebellion against tradition* in the Zo/Mizo society and also symbolizes the *emergence of women* from the spatial existence of the *private* to the *public*, and the creation of an external medium for women's voices to be echoed at the public level through *'Politics of Whispering Bamboo'*.[13] These movements organized by women for themselves mark important multi-layered processes. First, the emergence of women from the spatial existence at 'the private' to 'the public' that is the flow of women's voices from the private *'Politics of Whisperings'* to the public *'Politics of Whispering Bamboo'*. Second, it reflects the attempt of women to be part of the socio-political mechanisms functioning in the society and thereby, become stakeholders in the state-building process itself. Third, it is an attempt to regulate the hegemony of the 'Nexus of Patriarchy' and act as the conscience of the Zo society itself. Fourth, it is an attempt by women to create a space for their own voices and protect their rights as citizens and human persons.[14]

Zo/Mizo women through these organizations attempt to consolidate their 'positional order in Zo/Mizo society' and resurrect themselves from the 'common disadvantages' scripted by Patriarchy. These organisations at different times and in different degrees have fought for women's rights ranging from reforms and revisions of the Customary Rights, Property Rights to Rights of Inheritance etc. These organisations also reflect the mustering of women's voices on the lines of 'common victimhood' and 'common disadvantages' in the Zo/Mizo society. Women in the Zo/ Mizo society through the construction of their own spatial zones have provided a breathing space for venting the voices of the marginals. They have been successful in bargaining their own roles within the larger ambit of state building and thus helped proliferate the benefits of Democracy to the margins. These initiatives of claiming the positional order in the Zo/Mizo cosmology signifies their attempt to muster their voices in unison and leap towards a higher positional order than that earmarked by the Patriarchy. These institutional initiatives of mustering empowerment has introduced greater economic enterprise and elevated women to the position of styling and commercializing culture and Zo Identity to the needs and demands of contemporary globalised settings. For instance, more and more Zo/Mizo women are taking to using modern sophisticated technologies to weave 'their cultures', 'their identities', into fabrics and handlooms. The traditional Mizo/Zo 'Puan' that women wear is today injected with cross cultural influences of patterns and colours. Similarly, more and more rural women are taking keen interest in horticulture, and agriculture and moving towards greater self reliance through Self-Help Groups and organizational consolidation. Also Zo/Mizo women have taken to higher studies and entered into male bastions such as the Bureaucracy, Medical Sciences, and also the Church. Zo/Mizo women thus have entered as strong active actors in developments in Mizoram. Though politically still a 'back-bencher', Zo/ Mizo women have discovered and chiselled their spatial positions and actively challenged the traditional ordering of things. The emergence of the women's organisations can be seen as an effort at balancing the skewed socio-politico- economic situation specific to the Zo/Mizo situation and hence, an effort towards empowerment of women through democratic mechanisms and a move towards the realization of Human Development and sensitizing the Patriarchy.

Mizo Women Organizational Initiatives: Limits, Dead-ends and way forward

The mustering of empowerment through organizational initiatives of Mizo Women has come to meet its limits and dead-ends post 2006 with the compilation of *Customary Laws.*[15] It was only in 1980 that *The Committee on Mizo Customary Laws* (CMCL) was formed, and the Mizo Customary Laws Compiling Committee was formed in 1982. The committee on Mizo Customary law took 20 years to complete the task and to come up with the latest version of *Mizo Hnam dan* or Mizo Customary Laws (2006).

The Customary Board Committee was formed with the objective to revise/reform the Mizo customary laws and attune it with the current needs of time. Interestingly those assigned the task remained at loggerheads on multiple issues. From the very beginning there was non-consensus on terms such as 're-draft', 'compile', 'codification' etc. The 'Committee' seemed to be debating among themselves whether the committee was responsible for making changes and reform the laws or compile and codify the customary laws. The members could not come into an agreement on whether customary laws could at all be changed. While some members felt that they are to 'make changes' while a good many felt otherwise.[16]

Amidst these polar confusions the MHIP lobbied for the reforms of Mizo Customary Laws relating to: 1) Property Rights- inheritance rights for widow; 2) Remarriage issues- On the death of a wife the Mizo man could re-marry without conditions or could have sexual intercourse. The Customary Laws did not attach any taboo to men taking new wives or lovers in such circumstances. But the reverse was not applicable to a Widow women, when her husband died the widow may have no sexual intercourse with anyone at least for three months and even then not until she had performed *thlahual*. Until this is done she should remain in her husband's home. Only after completing these formalities could the Mizo women re-marry; 3) Increase of *Sawn man* - According to the Mizo Customary Laws, an illegitimate child is never a man's problem; the custom is that if a woman is pregnant with illegitimate child *Sawn*, she is entitled to receive Rs 40/- which is called '*Sawn man*' from the *Sawn's* father. If the *Sawn's* father refused to pay the price, he cannot claim the father's position. But, there are no laws of punishment if he refuses to pay. If he pays the price, the father gets the custody of the child, after the child reaches 3 or 4 years old. If a woman has any sexual intercourse with another man while pregnant it would be considered infidelity and would have to repay the fine of rupees forty to the *Sawn's* father. On the other hand, the customary laws do not extend any punishment to the man who had sexual intercourse with a pregnant woman. A woman with a *Sawn* is considered an outcast by the society; suffering severe image damage which destroys her future prospects. Men are never blamed nor made to suffer and they hardly take any responsibility.

Most male members of *the Committee on Mizo Customary Laws* argued that the committee's purpose was to 'revise' some of the old laws i.e., to remove laws which were redundant in the context of contemporary Mizo society. Though they agreed that the customary laws were favourably inclined to men and selectively put women at a disadvantage, they considered corrective changes as 'outside the preview of the customary laws' and kept it as something pristine and non-changing. The hegemonic opinion was that 'Customary Laws would cease to be Customary if they were reformed or interpreted to suit the mood swings of contemporary Mizo situations.' However, this extended selectively only to women's rights and that there have been several reforms in the customary laws such as the discontinuation of *Tlangchil.* The *Tlangchil* was a practice where the members of the community could take actions against a person who violates the rules and regulations of the Zo community. The *Tlangchil* was close to 'mob- justice' and regulated through notions of an 'eye-for an eye'.[17]

The critics of the Customary Laws drive forward the point that the Customary Laws are marked by severe limitations when it comes to punishment. Penalty in the form of a fine or monetary Compensation rather than on social –justice[18] is a common feature of the Lushai-Kuki-Chin people. Thus every act in the Mizo society is compensatable in economic terms as almost every object, article or body is said 'to have a price' ('*Man a nei*')[19] and naturally 'fine is the only remedy for any sort of crime' which is a unique feature of the Chin- Kuki tribes to which the Mizos or the Zos belong. If a man, for instance, wishes to evade the responsibility of a child born out of wedlock, he simply pays an adequate fine called 'Sawn man' of rupees forty to the girl's father or brother and avoid the responsibility of the fatherhood. The provisions of *Sawn man* under 'Notification No. JUD. 10/58/114 of 3rd Oct. 1958' further states that incase the same man, fathers a second child to the women there is no need to pay *Sawn man*, the fine is applicable only on every alternate child. These legal provisions based on the Mizo Customary Laws reflect the discriminatory nature of Mizo justice functioning against women.[20]

Change in the Mizo society has been considered to be a change for convenience rather than progress and naturally it has been caught in the dilemma of tradition and modernity. For instance, changes in the laws of Inheritance[21], which can be considered to be reflective of modern democracy culminating in the new found 'Economic independence' of women, has not resulted in changing the power relations in the Mizo society. The Mizo Hnam Dan[22] i.e. traditional/customary laws continue to dictate the terms of Marriage price[23], dowry and divorce. Even though Mizo women enjoyed considerable freedom[24] in Nula-rim (courting), marriage, sex, and divorce, they somewhat played a muted role when it came to the matters of property, decision-making, and politics. These freedoms granted to Mizo women are not backed by evangelical motives but are accepted merely for the fact that they are advantageous to men.[25] The discriminatory processes acting against women at various levels snip their chance to play an active role in politics and other determining position. For instance, a state, which boasts of nearly 87 per cent female literacy and where women out-number men in as many as 26 out of the 40 constituencies, only one woman has so far been elected to the State Assembly ever since it attained statehood.[26] Women face challenges even in the field of the Mission and find it difficult to break the glass ceiling even in the field of being ordained.

Violence against women in the form of rape, sexual harassment/abuse, domestic violence, and other psychological and physical violence have been on the rise as evident from the increase in the number of crimes committed against women year by year.[27] Although this can be seen as a positive phenomenon that the habit of lodging complaints to authority has been on the rise, it is more often than not in common experience that most of the violence committed against women neither are reported to the authority nor are registered. The Human Rights & Law Network (HR&LN), Mizoram, in its study on the specific issues like sexual abuse, rape and many other forms of sexual harassment among minor girls, ranging from the ages of 5 (five) years till high school and college years observed that many of these cases never reached the police.[28] The reason could be generalized under three points: firstly, women who are raped are often looked down upon by the society, and thus rape is never openly discussed. Secondly, women are not aware about the various rights and provisions available under the Indian law; and thirdly, as a Christian State, the idea of forgiveness is of common practice. Instead of lodging complaints and reporting the incidents to the authority, people make compromises or conciliations between them based on the Christian principle of 'forgive and forget'. Thus, the victims would feel more at ease forgiving them. Even with regard to domestic violence, it was found that victims of violence hardly complained or reported the matter to the authority. The victims simply seemed to have kept secret the incidents just to avoid wide publicity in view of their future in a very close-knit society as the Mizo people.[29]

'Justice' under Customary Laws among the Zo/Mizo exemplifies gender inequality in the case of divorce. Since there is no scope for legal safeguards for women under the traditional system of marriage, a woman has no claim over properties in case of divorce. She is allowed to take back whatever she has brought in at the time of marriage. Any accumulated wealth that might have been jointly acquired with the husband after marriage belongs to the husband in case of divorce. Moreover, a man can simply oust a woman from the house without assigning any reason thereof and just uttering '*Ka Ma Che*' or '*Ka Mak Che*' ('I divorce you'). Since children of divorced parents normally stay with the mother, supporting children even after divorce also tends to rest on the mother's shoulders.[30]

The Psychology of Compensation, which is the moving force behind the Mizo/Zo sense of justice and also the inherent contradictions[31] in the expected sexual behaviour of the Zo People, continues to undermine the very existence of women and the marginalized. The psychological impact of all these discriminatory processes functioning through diverse mediums at different levels in everyday life, results in 'Emotional Dependence'.[32] As a result even though women are educated and play an important role in the Mizo economics they seldom become active actors at the political arena. The hegemony of the *'Nexus of Patriarchy'* systematically displaces women and the marginals form the space of power and authority. The inherent sexism and forced subordination results in the birth of this exclusively skewed phenomenon of displacement of women and marginals from the realms of politics – power and authority.

The MHIP has been seeking state intervention demanding the adoption of Indian Christian Marriage Act (1872), 'The Christian Marriage Bill (1994)', 'The Christian Adoption and Maintenance Bill (1994)', 'The Indian Succession (Amendment) Bill (1994)' and Protection of Women from Domestic Violence Act (2005) etc. These demands of the MHIP have been strongly opposed by the *Zoram Kohhran Hruaitu Committee* (ZKHC), a conglomeration of different churches. The opposition comes from their understanding that these laws are meant for the Christian population in India and therefore unsuitable for Mizo Christians. The *Nexus of Patriarchy* has been apprehensive about these demands and put forth the argument that these interventions would undermine the Mizo Customary Laws and also dilute the local customs and ways of life of the Zo People. These interventions would also mean the filtration of alien customs and ways of life into the Zo/Mizo culture and therefore polluting. The State (Government of Mizoram) has evaded these demands citing that it cannot go against the *Kohhran* (Church) further affirming that the '*Kohhran* (Church) being '*thuber*' (final word)', the State (Government in Mizoram) could not uphold the proposals. Vanramchhuangi mentioned that 'the Government feared that it would be ousted by the Churches especially the Synod if it dared to bring institutional changes like a 'marriage registration' though it felt perfectly comfortable to openly undermine the Supreme Court of India's stand on 'marriage registration'.[33]

Kimi (name changed) felt that 'the Church feared that it would be stripped of their authority on matters of Marriage and Family, two prominent realms where the Church and its elders have the final word'.[34] While Zuali (name changed) felt that 'the adoption of Indian Christian Marriage Acts would mean the institutionalization of offices higher in authority than the ordained Pastors of the Churches. Under the current system the Church has the final authority when it comes to 'Marriage' and registration of marriage. Ordained pastors and sometimes church elders act as the marriage officer.'[35]

'The power balance between the Church and the Sawrkar (Government/ State) that currently is favourably tilted towards the Church would be disbalanced, and this is unacceptable for the *Kohhran* (Church)', says Kima.[36]

Amidst all these resistances the MHIP was able to lobby the Government to pass *Mizo Divorce Ordinance Act* (2008). The Ordinance (2008) though largely toothless gave 'rights to shelter or separate residence if the husband is cruel', and petition for a divorce. The mustering of empowerment of Mizo women has made the *Nexus of Patriarchy* largely uncomfortable. The *Nexus of Patriarchy* has remained resolved on issues relating to regulation of Mizo Women in select spaces of their choice. 'Control and Regulation' of 'Women' therefore, becomes the primary concern of the Patriarchy and its agencies. Most profoundly this regimentation and control is experienced in the realms of choices of marriage and being 'good Zo/ Mizo women' or being branded as *Kawngsual* (lost their way, or a prostitute).

The incident of Bairabi[37] can be issue in focus for understanding the 'politics of regulation and control' as operative in Mizoram. Two Mizo women were asked to leave their village for marrying non-Mizos in Bairabi[38], 130km from Aizawl. Bairabi is the only town connected by railways in Mizoram and has always been a trading centre and naturally close contacts with outsiders exists. Mapuii and Zorampari, both in their 30s were on October 18 2011 asked to leave their village as soon as possible for marrying non-Mizos by Bairabi YMA Coordination Committee. All their belongings were thrown out of the houses by members of the committee on Tuesday morning. In this connection, Kolasib Deputy Commissioner, Niharika Rai and police requested the committee to revoke their notice but they (committee) turned down the request. Bairabi falls under Kolasib district. The village had already passed a resolution on women who marry non-Mizos way back in 2001. As per their resolution, if any Mizo woman marries a non-Mizo she should leave the village and live with her husband. President of Bairabi Young Mizo Association (YMA) C Lalbiakenga and Secretary Lalbiakzama informed NNN (Northeast News Network) that they (Mapuii and Zorampari) were asked to leave as per the resolution passed in 2001. They were not ostracized. According to villagers, Mapuii had married a businessman from Rajasthan in 2005 while Zorampari also married to a non-Mizo. Both of them had children with their husbands. The first notice was given to in them in September to leave the village within that month but as they ignored the notice the committee had given the notice on October 11 and the action was taken thereafter. The incident had forced Kolasib Addl. DC Zairemmawia and SDPO, Francis L Ralte to rush to Bairabi and hold a meeting with the committee members.

The controversial demand of the YMA in 2018 that demanded an enactment of a law to deny ST status to any Mizo woman who marries a non-tribal was inkeeping with the mood to regulate and control womens choices and decisions in issues relating to marriage and family. The *Zo hnahthlak* has always been scornful of inter-community marriages especially with the 'Vai'. A popular statement discouraging such marriages with the *Vai* says *'Ali a fapa chu Ali a ni'* ('the son of Ali is Ali' meaning that the child born out of inter-community marriages will have his fathers name and of mixed blood therefore an 'outsider'). The mother being a local does little to help the children born out of such marriages. But as is the spirit of the Zo/Mizo society every problem has a solution or 'compensation'. The most easy solution is to make the children adopt a series of strategies to overcome their 'otherness' including taking name echoing their Zo linkages for instance, most children born out of such wedlock are christened with names beginning with a prefix 'Zo'; changing fathers name or adopting the mother's father's name as the biological father in school and other certificates (so as not to hamper the possibilities of the child to enjoy the benefits of reservation in future). Adopting the religion of the mother being the most ready and obvious solution. All these strategies are geared to make the children enjoy the benefits of the state in terms of affirmative actions, scholarships, quotas for studying in higher education etc. *'to make life secured'*.

Even though the *Vai* is brushed aside to the economic space, the *Vai* continues to camouflage his identity behind the veil of the local women. For instance, the permit for the trade or shop or any local business including contracts will be in the name of a local person mostly women. The *Vai* in Zo/Mizo economics is not a free player. The women continue to be partners in the game and also the agencies of the Patriarchy have to be constantly paid donations failure to do so will lead to both *'Vai'* businessman and local women being branded as the 'partners-in-crime' functioning against the vision of an *'Ideal Zo Christian State'*. Vanramchhuangi in one of her articles in local daily *Vanglaini*, 9 April, 2005 titled *'Vai suppliers Vrs MZP'* mentions the unhealthy flow of finances between the two groups which amounts to extortion and corruption in Mizoram:

> *Mizo Zirlai Pawl-ten Vai Supplier hnenah pawisa an khawn thin tih hi phungleng atangin ka hre fova, an lo khawn thin tak tak a nih chuan Zirlai pawltre che tutee maw (Vai hnena Supply hna pe theitu) ang vel an nih dawn chu ka ti deuh a ni. Ram leilung faten an thawh vel theih reng; hnam dang hnena hna pek ching hi chuan hna pek te hnenah pawisa an khawn thin a nih loh taka leh vai bawng sakei she tit a ila vai bawng sakeiin a she phah ka ring chiam lo!* (The MZP extorts

money from *Vai* suppliers and give then contracts for assignments which could have been given to people from within the state. The activities of the MZP betray the cause of the 'sons of the soil' and the Zo Khristian State).

The agencies of the *'Nexus of Patriarchy'* seasonally organise mechanism to check the inflow of 'outsiders' in order to regulate the spaces of the 'others'. The most popular mechanism to regulate the flow of people is through '*Vai* Bandhs'.

Taking the Womens issues in question the discussion in this chapter fills the several gaps in grasping the operation of religion, politics and ethnicity in Mizoram, and at the same time uncovers the realms of what is cordoned as the ecclesiastical and non-changing pristine with that of the realms of 'this worldly' affairs that can be changed, and circumvent according to the convenience of the Church and its agencies. The case of the Zo/Mizo womens position unravels the constricting spheres of the regulated public and private spaces as outlined by the *Nexus of Patriarchy* and the final words of the Churches. Thus everyday lives of people especially women is largely channeled by ecclesiastical cosmology of Zo Christianity.

Notes and References

1. The role of religion in Mizo politics and society is strongly being critiqued by the intelligentsia, media and the youths. For a detailed discussion on the various strands of contestations and critiques See, The Assam Tribune. (1989). 'Church Role In Mizo Polls Questioned'. Aizawl: 01 March. Guwahati: 02 March; The Assam Tribune. (1989). 'Counting In Mizoram On January 23'. Aizawl: 08 January. Guwahati: 09 January; Lalruatfela Nu. (2007). 'Sorkarhnahthawk work culture chhiatchhanKohhran leh NGO-II'.Evening Post.Aizawl: 7 March; Lalruatfela Nu. (2007). 'Sual do kawnga enforcement-teaiakohhran leh NGO chakzawkchhan'. Evening Post.Aizawl: 28 March; LalhnunaSailo. (2008). 'Synod thuchhuahkhaantihturdiktak a ni'. Vanglaini.Aizawl: 25 January; Liankila. (2006). 'Kristianna leh Politics'. KristianTlangau. Mizoram Presbyterian Church Synod.Aizawl: February. pp.14-16.
2. Prasun Sonawalkar. (1989). 'Church playing vital role in Mizo polls'. The Times of India News Service. Aizawl. *The Times of India*. Ahmedabad: 09 January.
3. Frederick. S. Downs. (1983). *Christianity in North East India*. Delhi: ISPCK: pp. 14-15; E.J. Thomas. (1993). *Mizo bamboo Hills Murmur Change (Mizo Society Before And After Independence)*. New Delhi: Intellectual Publishing House.
4. Le Bon, G. (1895). (1977). *The Crowd: A Study of the Popular Mind*. New York: Penguin; Lévi-Strauss, C. (1966). *The Savage Mind*. Chicago: University of Chicago Press; McGuigan, J. (1997). Cultural Methodologies. London: Sage; Mead, G. H. (1934). Op.cit.; Olson, M. (1965). The Logic of Collective Action. Cambridge Mass: Harvard University Press.
5. Anup Shekhar Chakraborty. (2008a). 'Emergence of Women from 'Private' to 'Public': A Narrative of Power Politics from Mizoram' *Journal of International*

Women's Studies (JIWS), Bridgewater. Vol. No. 9, 3 May; Anup Shekhar Chakraborty. (2008b). 'Mustering Empowerment experiences from Mizoram: A Leap from 'Private' to 'Public' Living Spaces.' *Global South SEPHIS e-magazine*. Vol. 4 No. 4, July.

6. Anup Shekhar Chakraborty. (2009b). 'Where are 'Our women'? Locating Women through the History of Proselytization in Mizoram.' *Dharma Deepkia- South Asian Journal of Missiological Research issue on Mission In Contexts Of Violence And Uncertainty.* Issue 30, Vol.13 No. 2 July-December.
7. Anup Shekhar Chakraborty. (2007). 'Politics of Silencings: Echoes of the Margins from Mizoram' *Indian Journal of Political Science (IJPS)*. Vol. LXVIII, No. 4, Oct.-Dec.
8. The supporters of Total Prohibition also cite the economic advantages for the state. For details See, Mizoram Express. (2009). 'Mizoram reaps Rs. 186 lakh revenue from liquor related fine'. Aizawl: 27 December.
9. Zote, Mona. (2006). 'Heaven in Hell: A Paradox'. (Section IV: The Conflict of Identities) in Geeti Sen (ed.). (2006). Where the Sun Rises When Shadows Fall: The North-East. New Delhi: Oxford University Press/ India International Centre.
10. The term 'Vai' is a Mizo word used to describe the people of India who have Aryan features. The term is derogatory and signals anger, scorn, and racist overtones. B.B Goswami looks at the construction of the Vai from the perspective of 'out-group' – 'in-group' psychology. For the Mizos the term Vai as an out-group has three broad meanings. In one sense all non-Mizos including the British people are Vai. In another sense, all the people living in the plains of India are Vai. In the third sense the plains people of Burma are also considered to be Vai but in contrast to the Indian, the notion is more positive and traditional. For detailed reading on the Vai and 'in-group- out-group' problem in Mizoram, see B.B Goswami, "out-group from the point of view of In-group: A Study of Mizos", *in* S.M. Dubey. (1978). *North East India: A Sociological Study*. pp. 99-110.
11. For instance wearing of trousers (men's clothing) is scorned, so is the wearing of salwar kameez ('Vai kawr', Indian dress). Likewise marrying a 'Vai' leads to social ostracization and stigmatization of the children ('Vai fa').
12. MHIP was formed on 6th July, 1974 at State Social Advisory Board office. The motive behind the formation of MHIP was that, when Mizoram was accorded Union Territory status, it was necessary to form a large organization in order to carry out various development schemes. MHIP was formed with the intention to include all women in Mizoram, when it was first formed, it was named "Mizoram Hmeichhe Insuihkhawm Pawl" (United Organisation of Mizoram Women), which was later changed into "Mizo Hmeichhe Insuihkhawm Pawl" (United Organisation of Mizo Women) on 20th Aug, 1998. The change in nomenclature and the focus on 'Mizo' in place of the territorial name 'Mizoram' infused apprehension from fringe tribal communities and drove unease whether it encompassed all women irrespective of tribal divides in Mizoram or just the particular Mizo Women. The MHIP continues to be the largest women's organization in Mizoram and all other women's organization such as Mizo Hmeichhe Tangrual Pawl (MHTP) (Mizo Women's Organisation), Mara Chano Py (M.CH.P) (Mara Women's Organisation) from southern Mizoram are all affiliated to the larger umbrella of the MHIP.

13. Anup Shekhar Chakraborty. (2008b). *Op.cit.*
14. *Ibid.*
15. N.E Parry compiled the Customary Laws in his book 'A monograph on Lushai custom and ceremonies' published in the year 1927. The authenticity of Parry's codified Lushai Customary Laws is densely contested for the reason that the colonial gaze could have injected prejudice and western ideas of jurisprudence, Christian ideas of morality, sin and punishment etc. In that sense the production of a codified 'Lushai Customary Laws' by a White person of privilege could have already transcended the notion of an "authentic", "true" interpretation of social order and customs of the Mizo society. In short, between the 'spoken word', the translation and codification in the form of a written text, much could have been affected by the colonial gaze, and missionary sanitization and the final 'filtered' product remotely distinct from the 'original'. Mizoram is the first state to have written customary laws among the states of North East India (ASC).
16. Pastor L.H. Lalliansanga. (2009). *Personal Interview.* Beckbagan, Kolkata: 30th September; Pastor Lalnuntluanga. (2009). *Personal Interview.* Beckbagan, Kolkata: 31st September; Pastor B. Lalnunzira. (2009). (Lecturer, Bishop's College). *Personal Interview.* Beckbagan, Kolkata: 30th September; Pi Bawichhingpuii (2008). (Director, 'Tribal Research Institute', Art & Culture Department, Government of Mizoram, McDonald Hill). *Personal Interview.* Zarkawt, Aizawl: 23rd January; Pi Ramthianghlimi. (2009). (Student, Bachelor of Theology). *Personal Interview.* Beckbagan, Kolkata: 31st September; Rev. K. Lalthlanpuia. (2009). *Personal Interview.* Beckbagan, Kolkata: 31st September; Rev. Zaithanmawia. (2009). *Personal Interview.* Beckbagan, Kolkata: 30th September.
17. Bimal J. Dev and Dilip Kumar Lahiri. (1983). *Lushai Customs and Ceremonies.* New Delhi: Mittal Publication. p.17; B. Lalthangliana. (2017). *Culture and Folklore of Mizoram.* Aizawl: Publication Division, Ministry of Information and Broadcasting Mizoram.
18. Stevenson, H.N.C., F.R.A.I. (1943, Falam). (First Indian reprint 1986) *The Economics of the Central Chin Tribes.* Aizawl, Mizoram: Tribal Research Institute: Everly Press; Chatterjee, Suhas. (1995). An Analysis of Mizo Jurisprudence. Proceedings, NEIHA, 16th session Silchar, Shillong: Modern Offset.
19. Ray. (1982). *Op.cit.* pp. 73-74.
20. *Mizo Hnam Dan.* (1996). Mizo Hnam Dan. Mc. Awia/Arbee Publication & Printing. Venghlui: Aizawl. Bung 5. 'Inngaih Thu Leh Sawnpai Thu'. pp. 44-48.
21. Women have the right to inheritance under the Lushai District Act, No.1, 1956 (Inheritance of Property). A daughter or a wife can inherit property only if the deceased has no heir on the male side. Women, however, are entitled to their own property i.e. the dowry, called 'thuam', which she gets during her marriage from her parents. A written 'will' formally executed may now confer woman the right to inherit the family property.
22. The traditional laws or the 'Mizo Hnam Dan' are a novel attempt of combining the British laws and the traditional Kuki-Chin-Lushai customary laws. These were complied by B.C Carey and famously known as the Chin Hills Regulations

of 1896. Under the chiefs derived their authority from the British Superintendent

23. The Indian Christian Marriage act in not applicable in Mizoram and the customary law has fixed the bride price at rupees 420/- reducing women to a cheap purchasable commodity

24. This freedom however does not suggest that the terms of justice for men and women are equal nor does it enable women to enjoy an advantaged position in the Mizo social system. It basically provides freedom of choice as determined by the patriarchy. This has to be understood in the light of the Engelsian debate. I owe this insight to Dr. Samita Sen, Reader, then associated with the Department of History, University of Calcutta. (At the CODESRIA/SEPHIS Extended Workshop, Dakar, 2006).

25. E.J. Thomas. (1993). *Mizo bamboo Hills Murmur Change (Mizo Society Before And After Independence).* New Delhi: Intellectual Publishing House. p. 16.

26. S.N. Singh. (1994). *Mizoram- Historical, Geographical, Social, Economic, Political & Administrative*. New Delhi: Mittal Publications. pp 173-174; Government of Mizoram. (2002). *Statistical Handbook of Mizoram*, 2002. Aizawl: Directorate of Economics & Statistics. Table No. 6.1, pp.82-83.

27. Government of Mizoram. (2002, 2003, 2004, 2005. 2006, 2007, 2008). *Statistical Handbook of Mizoram.* Aizawl: Directorate of Economics & Statistics.

28. H.K. Laldinpuii Fente. & C.Lalhmanmawia. (2006).*Violence Against Women and Related Issues in Mizoram*. Aizawl: Human Rights & Law Network, Mizoram/National Commission For Women, New Delhi.

29. H.K. Laldinpuii Fente & C.Lalhmanmawia. (2006). *Ibid.*

30. *Mizo Hnam Dan*. (1996). *Op.cit*. Bung 4. 'Inthen'. pp. 31-43.

31. Ralte. (1993). *Op.cit*. pp. 25-29, 43-49.

32. Daly. (1973). *Op.cit.* pp. 54-55.

33. Pi Vanramchhuangi ('Ruatfelanu') (Director HRLN Mizoram, Social Activist). *Personal Interview*. Chaltlang, Aizawl: 28th & 29th January 2008.

34. Kimi. (name changed). *Personal Interview*. Chaltlang, Aizawl: 30th January 2008.

35. Zuali. (name changed). *Personal Interview*. Kulikawn, Aizawl: 21th January 2008.

36. Kima. (name changed). *Personal Interview*. Vaivakawn, Aizawl: 20th January 2008.

37. Mizo women asked to leave village for marrying non-Mizo Aizawl.: The Morung Express. NNN. October 20, 2011. (accessed on 20.11.2018).

38. *Ibid.*

Index

K

L

M

N

O